Jean Rhys

Wide Sargasso Sea

EDITED BY CARL PLASA

Consultant editor: Nicolas Tredell

Published by
PALGRAVE MACMILLAN
Houndmills, Basingstoke, Hampshire RG21 6XS and
175 Fifth Avenue, New York, N. Y. 10010
Companies and representatives throughout the world

PALGRAVE MACMILLAN is the global academic imprint of the Palgrave Macmillan division of St. Martin's Press, LLC and of Palgrave Macmillan Ltd. Macmillan® is a registered trademark in the United States, United Kingdom and other countries. Palgrave is a registered trademark in the European Union and other countries.

First published 2001 by Icon Books Ltd

ISBN 1–84046–268–X

This book is printed on paper suitable for recycling and made from fully managed and sustained forest sources.

A catalogue record for this book is available from the British Library.

Transferred to digital printing 2003

Printed and bound in Great Britain by
Antony Rowe Ltd, Chippenham and Eastbourne

Contents

INTRODUCTION   7

This begins with an overview of Jean Rhys's life and work, and goes on to provide brief outlines of the main critical and theoretical concerns informing the five chapters to come. It concludes with the suggestion that the play of narrative voices in *Wide Sargasso Sea* itself prefigures the many-sided critical debates that have grown up in the wake of the novel's publication.

CHAPTER ONE   14

'A Considerable Tour de Force by Any Standard': Reviews and Early Criticism

This chapter is divided into two sections. The first charts the immediate critical impact of *Wide Sargasso Sea* in Britain and America, with reviews by Francis Hope, an anonymous author in *The Times Literary Supplement* and Walter Allen, all of which privilege issues of literary style and the exploitation of women by men. The second section focuses on three of the most significant early Caribbean critical assessments of Rhys's novel (produced during the late 1960s and early 1970s), for which questions of race and colonialism are, by contrast, paramount. Extracts from Wally Look Lai and Kenneth Ramchand are given here, as well as a short polemical piece by Edward Kamau Brathwaite, challenging Look Lai's appropriation of the text for a nascent Caribbean literary canon.

CHAPTER TWO   38

'The Creole is of Course the Important One': Rewriting *Jane Eyre*

This chapter examines critical analyses of the intertextual dialogue between *Wide Sargasso Sea* and Charlotte Brontë's *Jane Eyre* as they evolved between the mid 1970s and late 1980s. Particular emphasis is placed on feminist and postcolonial approaches, as well as the theoretical debates about the politics of narrative which Rhys's novel has stimulated. The work of four critics is covered, with extracts from Dennis Porter, Elizabeth R. Baer, Gayatri Chakravorty Spivak and Benita Parry.

CHAPTER THREE   65

'Like Goes to Like': Race and the Politics of Identification

This chapter includes extracts from articles written by Helen Tiffin, Lee Erwin and Maria Olaussen between the late 1970s and early 1990s. Each of these critics offers a different assessment of *Wide Sargasso Sea*'s racial politics, with particular reference to the controversial patterns of white/black identification by which the novel is traversed. Tiffin's early celebration of these patterns is modified by Erwin, who sees them as a source of ambivalence in Rhys's text. In a more sceptical reading, Olaussen shows how the black women with whom the novel's white Creole heroine identifies herself are figured in terms of racial stereotypes that render Rhys's project politically retrograde.

CHAPTER FOUR   96

'There is Always the Other Side': African Caribbean Perspectives

This chapter spans the period from the mid 1980s to mid 1990s and explores the ways in which critics have addressed the specifically African Caribbean dimensions of Rhys's novel. The first three extracts come from Teresa F. O'Connor, Alan Richardson and Regina Barreca and are united by a concern with Rhys's fictional representation of the black ritual practice of obeah. The fourth piece, taking up the second half of the chapter, is from Judie Newman. Here the critical focus switches from obeah to the liminal figure of the zombie, which Newman persuasively reads as a powerful trope for forms of colonial, sexual and literary domination.

CHAPTER FIVE   121

'Not Even Much Record': The Place of History

This chapter shows how three critics, writing between the early and late 1990s, have sought to historicize *Wide Sargasso Sea*. It begins with a brief extract from Maggie Humm, which reads Rhys's novel against the grain of the images of blackness circulating in Britain during the 1950s and

1960s, the time of *Wide Sargasso Sea*'s composition. This extract is followed by two much longer readings from Peter Hulme and Laura E. Ciolkowski, both of which locate the text firmly within the Caribbean of the 1830s and 1840s. For Hulme, *Wide Sargasso Sea* reworks incidents from its author's own colonial family history, while, for Ciolkowski, it provides a subtle commentary on nineteenth-century discourses of race and sexuality and the intersections between them.

NOTES   151

SELECT BIBLIOGRAPHY   160

ACKNOWLEDGEMENTS   165

INDEX   166

A NOTE ON REFERENCES AND QUOTATIONS

Throughout this Guide, the 1997 Penguin edition of *Wide Sargasso Sea* (edited by Angela Smith and abbreviated as *WSS*) and the 1998 Oxford World's Classics edition of *Jane Eyre* (edited by Margaret Smith and abbreviated as *JE*) have been used for all references and quotations.

INTRODUCTION

■ I think of calling it 'The first Mrs Rochester' with profound apologies to Charlotte Brontë and a deep curtsey too.
But I suppose that won't do (I'm supposing you've studied Jane Eyre like a good girl).
It really haunts me that I can't finish it though. ☐

Jean Rhys[1]

First published in Britain on 27 October 1966, *Wide Sargasso Sea* is Jean Rhys's most celebrated work. Set just after the abolition of British colonial slavery in 1833–4, the novel retells the story of Charlotte Brontë's *Jane Eyre* (1847) from the perspective of Bertha Mason – renamed by Rhys as Antoinette – the white Creole heiress who becomes Rochester's supposedly mad first wife. Much fêted in its own day, *Wide Sargasso Sea* has retained its status, over the last thirty-five years, as the pre-eminent text within the Rhys canon, giving rise to a formidable critical literature. This Readers' Guide traces the novel's critical history as it has evolved from the earliest reviews to the theoretically informed analyses of the present, placing particular emphasis on intertextual, feminist and postcolonial approaches. The varied critical materials that the Guide brings into play provide a comprehensive framework, enabling students to engage with Rhys's text for themselves.

Rhys was originally born Ella Gwendoline Rees Williams in Roseau, Dominica, on 24 August 1890, the daughter of a Welsh doctor and a white Creole mother of Scottish and Irish ancestry. She came to England in 1907, where she lived until the end of the First World War. In 1919, she moved to Europe, marrying Jean Lenglet, a Dutch–French song-writer, journalist and (as it turned out) secret agent, who was the first of three husbands.[2] Most of Rhys's time in Europe during the 1920s was spent either in Paris or Vienna, and it was in Paris that she met the novelist and critic Ford Madox Ford (1873–1939), a significant figure in the development of the Modernist aesthetic which was at its height during the post-war years. As well as becoming Ford's mistress, Rhys became his literary protégée, publishing her first short story, 'Vienne', in Ford's *transatlantic review* in 1924. This example of 'quintessential modernist writing with a feminized perspective'[3] was followed by *The Left Bank and Other Stories* (1927), a collection of 'sketches and studies of present-day Bohemian Paris',[4] which came complete with Ford's own twenty-seven-page Preface. After the appearance of *The Left Bank*, Rhys returned to England, publishing four novels within the space of just over a decade: *Quartet* (1928); *After Leaving Mr Mackenzie* (1930); *Voyage in the Dark* (1934); and *Good Morning, Midnight* (1939).

Rhys's movement from Dominica to England and Europe, colonial margin to metropolitan centre, has been described by fellow Caribbean expatriate, V. S. Naipaul, as both a relocation and a dislocation, effecting a cultural and psychological 'break in [Rhys's] life'.[5] Such a sense of fracture also characterizes the life of Rhys's writing, as the initially impressive productivity that marks its opening phase was not sustained. The short-story collection and early novels received a fairly muted critical response, had gone out of print altogether by the beginning of the Second World War and were succeeded by a long period of silence and obscurity, leading many to conclude that Rhys was simply dead. Happily, this was not the case and she was gradually rediscovered, as the result of inquiries made by first Selma Vaz Dias in 1949 and then, in 1957, Francis Wyndham, long an admirer of Rhys's work. Wyndham had learned from an article written by Vaz Dias that Rhys, now living a reclusive existence in Cornwall, was 'busy writing a novel on a most exciting subject'[6] and was eager to commission the text for André Deutsch, the publisher for which he was working. The novel in question was *Wide Sargasso Sea*, its 'exciting subject' the unwritten narrative of colonial neurosis and sexual predation hidden in the gaps and evasions of *Jane Eyre*. In sharp contrast to the fictions of the 1920s and 1930s, *Wide Sargasso Sea* was an instant hit, both critically and with the reading public. This highly favourable reception was given concrete institutional form in 1967, when the novel won a Royal Society of Literature Prize and a W.H. Smith Annual Literary Award. As well as thus accruing to itself considerable critical prestige, *Wide Sargasso Sea* conferred belated recognition upon Rhys's previous work, prompting the steady reissue, in Britain and America, of all four novels between 1967 and 1973. In addition, it led to a series of late publications. These included *Tigers Are Better-Looking* (1968), which incorporates nine selections from *The Left Bank*; *My Day: Three Pieces by Jean Rhys* (1975); and *Sleep It Off Lady* (1976). The fragmentary *Smile Please: An Unfinished Autobiography* appeared posthumously, following Rhys's death on 14 May 1979, aged eighty-eight.

While Rhys signed the contract for *Wide Sargasso Sea* on 1 June 1957, anticipating that it would take just 'six to nine months' to deliver the novel to her publishers in final draft, the process of composition was painfully delayed over more than nine years. One reason for Rhys's initial, if sorely misplaced, confidence in expediting the project was that, as she

told Diana Athill, 'a large part of it [was] already written'[7] and had probably been in existence, indeed, from as early on as 1939.[8] Rhys is more
expansive about the mysterious ur-text to *Wide Sargasso Sea*, as well as
other lost and sundry narratives, in a letter to Wyndham of 22 July 1962:

■ One thing I have never told you. I wrote this book before! – Different
setting – same idea. (It was called 'Le revenant' then). The MSS was
lost when I was moving from somewhere to somewhere else and I
wonder whether I haven't been trying to get back to what I did. (An
impossible effort). Perhaps that has added to all the other difficulties.
It was a sad affair, for a lot of stories disappeared too – and an
unfinished novel 'Wedding in the Carib Quarter'.
I tried to rewrite 'Le Revenant' but could not – another title would
have been found – however I discovered two chapters (in another suit-
case) and have used them in this book. You will see perhaps.
As for 'Wedding in the Carib Quarter' it disappeared *completely*. I
found some notes on it the other day, and they made no sense at all
any more. A pity.
I was a bit sad. But 'Le Revenant' came to life *or back* again (in a
way) when I met Selma and was talking to her.
The first one was easier to do and perhaps more banal, but I was
very excited about it and desperate when it got lost. All this was long
ago. I was writing quickly then – far better circumstances.[9] □

Unlike her estimation of the time required to write *Wide Sargasso Sea*, the
novel's original title – which means 'One who returns from the dead; a
ghost' (OED) – proves to be uncannily well judged. As it comes 'to life *or
back* again', 'Le Revenant' itself precisely conforms to the logic of revenancy,
while also reawakening the spectre of 'Charlotte's lunatic',[10] whom Rhys
had first encountered while reading *Jane Eyre* shortly after her arrival in
England. At the same time, the title sets up a broad resonance with the
strange syncopation of Rhys's literary biography as a whole, which saw
her vanish into nowhere before undergoing a 'slow and uneven [...]
resurrection'[11] at the hands of Vaz Dias and Wyndham. 'Le Revenant'
returns to haunt its author, just as its eventual transformation into *Wide
Sargasso Sea* provides the spectacular conduit for Rhys's own ghost-like
return to the literary scene she had left 'long ago'. The ways in which
Rhys's critics have negotiated the complexities of that return are the subject of this Guide.
Chapter One is divided into two sections. The first provides a snapshot
of the immediate critical reaction to *Wide Sargasso Sea* as it unfolds in
Britain and America. It features three reviews by Francis Hope, an
anonymous author writing for *The Times Literary Supplement* and the
prominent English critic, Walter Allen. These early pieces are mainly

preoccupied with the novel's stylistic properties (seen by Hope as the sign of Rhys's Modernist inheritance), and its treatment of the power relations between men and women. In its second section, the chapter shifts the focus towards the critical debate on *Wide Sargasso Sea* which began to develop among Caribbean critics between the late 1960s and early 1970s, including extracts from seminal readings by Wally Look Lai, Kenneth Ramchand and Edward Kamau Brathwaite. For these critics, issues of literary style and sexual conflict emerge as less important than the questions of slavery, race and colonialism with which Rhys's text is saturated. Yet even as Look Lai et al. challenge the critical emphases of their English counterparts, the stances they adopt are themselves sometimes in tension with one another. This is highlighted, for example, in the extract from Brathwaite, which takes issue with Look Lai. For Brathwaite, the essential problem with Look Lai's analysis of *Wide Sargasso Sea* – and its ending, in particular – is that it is overly optimistic, significantly downplaying the historically determined frictions which define and regulate white/black relations in the Caribbean.

As this introduction itself suggests, it is difficult – and perhaps not even desirable – to uncouple *Wide Sargasso Sea* from *Jane Eyre*, and it is the intertextual dialogue between Rhys's novel and Brontë's which forms the central concern of Chapter Two. The four extracts featured here are taken from critical work produced between the mid-1970s and late 1980s, and duly reflect, in different ways, the influence of the feminist and postcolonial paradigms that established and refined themselves during this period. In the first extract, Dennis Porter reverses the chronological relation between the two texts, reading *Wide Sargasso Sea* first and *Jane Eyre* second in order to show how the meanings of Brontë's text are subtly reconfigured by the critique of colonial power and white male sexuality contained in Rhys's text. For Elizabeth R. Baer, the emphasis is firmly feminist, falling on the points of alliance between Rhys's fictional heroine and Brontë's – Antoinette and Jane – as objects of patriarchal oppression. In Gayatri Chakravorty Spivak's groundbreaking analysis of Rhys's novel, attention is directed, by contrast, to questions of cultural and racial difference. Writing from a postcolonial angle, Spivak points out the irony involved in Rhys's revision of Brontë, arguing that *Wide Sargasso Sea* silences the black female subject in the same way that *Jane Eyre* denies a voice to the white Creole woman. The chapter closes with an extract from Benita Parry that unpicks the contradictions in Spivak's reading and makes the converse case for *Wide Sargasso Sea* as a novel in which a black female voice is effectively accommodated.

Despite the differences between them, Spivak and Parry are implicitly in agreement that *Wide Sargasso Sea* is a text which poses important questions about the politics of narrative and the ways in which the telling of one story is invariably predicated on the blockage of another. For the

critics examined in Chapter Three, by contrast, the shared concern is
with what might be called the politics of identification in Rhys's text. The
chapter begins by briefly backtracking to an article written by Helen
Tiffin in the late 1970s. In this piece, Tiffin outlines the analogies which
Wide Sargasso Sea habitually sets up between the racial and sexual oppression of the white Creole woman, on the one hand, and the plight of the
colonized black slave, on the other. What is particularly striking about
Tiffin's article is its failure to question the legitimacy of such analogies:
can Antoinette's sufferings be genuinely equated with the historical
trauma of Caribbean slavery and the Middle Passage? Tiffin's assumption
that such an equation is valid places her in marked opposition to Lee
Erwin and Maria Olaussen, whose respective readings of Rhys's novel
are given at greater length as the chapter moves forward into the more
racially self-conscious critical terrain of the late 1980s and early 1990s.
At the same time, Erwin and Olaussen are significantly at variance in
their assessment of *Wide Sargasso Sea*'s racial politics. In Erwin's deconstructive view, Rhys's text exploits the motif of white/black identification
while simultaneously putting it into question. For Olaussen, however,
Wide Sargasso Sea not only uses such a motif uncritically but also represents blackness itself – especially the black female – according to stereotypes that are troublingly familiar: black woman as mammy; black
woman as whore.

Like its white Creole heroine, *Wide Sargasso Sea* inhabits an interstitial
or hybridized space, shaped as it is by the influence, or confluence, of two
radically different cultural traditions – English and African Caribbean.
The novel's English cultural inheritance is most obviously signalled in
terms of its status as a rewriting of *Jane Eyre*, while its African Caribbean
legacy is perhaps less immediately apparent, to Western readers at least,
though equally important. This aspect of the text is evidenced in its
engagement with the black spiritual practice of obeah and the liminal
figure of the zombie, and addressed by the critical material selected in
Chapter Four. This chapter, which covers the period from the mid-1980s
to the mid-1990s, begins with three relatively short and markedly different discussions of obeah. In the first of these, Teresa F. O'Connor
explores the connections between Rhys's novel and obeah's historical
role as a strategy of resistance used by black slaves against white masters.
In the second, Alan Richardson compares and contrasts Rhys's figuring
of obeah with the ways in which it is conventionally depicted in early
Romantic literature, critically leapfrogging *Jane Eyre* to a prior literary-
historical moment. The third extract is a feminist meditation on *Wide
Sargasso Sea* from Regina Barreca, who turns to the inscription of obeah
in Rhys's novel as a way of thinking about women's writing in general
and its potential for patriarchal subversion, in particular. The chapter's
fourth and fullest piece, from Judie Newman, switches the critical frame

of reference from obeah to the zombie figure itself. In a fascinating analysis, Newman suggests that Rhys's interest in the zombie is partly stimulated by its popular cinematic representation, especially Val Lewton's *I Walked with a Zombie* (1943). She goes on from this to argue that the zombie functions in Rhys's novel as a remarkably pliable trope for colonial, sexual and literary domination alike.

The Guide concludes, in Chapter Five, by offering three critical accounts of the relation between *Wide Sargasso Sea* and history, all of which appeared between the early and late 1990s. In a brief first extract, Maggie Humm situates the novel in the context of the Britain of the 1950s and 1960s, the place and period in which it was largely written. In an original – if sometimes questionable – reading, Humm argues that Rhys's text challenges the negative images of blackness in public circulation during this time, while also helping Rhys to resolve her private ambivalence towards the figure of the black mother/nurse. The next two extracts are from Peter Hulme and Laura E. Ciolkowski and return the text squarely to the nineteenth-century Caribbean context in which it is for the most part set. Drawing on Freud's notion of the family romance as a point of theoretical departure, Hulme offers a scintillating and at the same time scholarly reading of the relations between fiction and history in Rhys's text. These relations are not at all clear-cut. As Hulme demonstrates, *Wide Sargasso Sea* does not so much provide a faithful reflection of historical realities as cunningly rewrite them, particularly the less salubrious episodes in the colonial archive of Rhys's own family. In the final extract, Ciolkowski examines *Wide Sargasso Sea* as a text which inquires into and critiques the role played by sexuality as a signifier of racial difference, devoting most of her attention to the processes involved in the construction of Englishness. Rochester's sense of himself as an Englishman, she argues, is not only bound up with a violent denial of his own desires, but at the same time threatened by the dangerous libidinal excesses with which he associates his white Creole wife.

One of the most noticeable ways in which *Wide Sargasso Sea* departs from *Jane Eyre* is in terms of form. As an autobiography – the story Jane Eyre tells about herself – Brontë's novel is a monologic text. Rhys's, by contrast, is closer to a polylogue, woven together from a plurality of narrative voices that are always in varying degrees of dispute with one another. (It is not for nothing that the first two words in *Wide Sargasso Sea* are 'They say' [*WSS*, p. 5], a phrase which discreetly gestures towards the multiple utterance to come.) First and foremost, there are the narrative voices of Antoinette and Rochester, each offering a violently different interpretation of the disastrous events that chain them together. These are supplemented and intercut with several others, variously belonging, for example, to the black servant, Christophine, the mixed-race Daniel Cosway/Boyd and the working-class Grace Poole. Such a polyphonic structure echoes the narrative experiments of the Modernist novelists who were Rhys's initial contemporaries. At the same time, it prefigures the multi-accentual debate that *Wide Sargasso Sea* has inspired among its critics. This Guide, it is hoped, will constitute a useful and engaging addition to the critical exchanges that have taken place to date.

CHAPTER ONE

'A Considerable Tour de Force by Any Standard': Reviews and Early Criticism

■ Critics at three corners of the triangular trade lay claim to Jean Rhys. In England scholars read her as 'British woman writer', painter of grim urban settings and social subtypes, catching time, place, mood, and the values that upheld a fading imperial world: England after Victoria, before Hitler. To American critics her work speaks mostly of woman-as-victim, although they recognize her insight into British society. In the Caribbean Rhys is the exponent of the 'terrified consciousness' [...] of the ruling class. For all three groups, Rhys presents problems of classification which disguise problems of interpretation and acceptance. ◻

Jean D'Costa[1]

In a recent overview of Jean Rhys criticism since *Wide Sargasso Sea*, Elaine Savory notes that the act of reading Rhys – or any other writer, for that matter – can never be innocent, neutral or objective. 'Rhys criticism is always informed', she notes, 'by the cultural location and politics of the critic, even in those cases where political commentary is explicitly avoided or minimised'.[2] This statement provides a useful perspective from which to approach the material included in this chapter, which is divided into two sections. The first section covers three major reviews of *Wide Sargasso Sea* produced by English critics, while the second considers three of the most significant early Caribbean assessments of Rhys's text. Between these two sets of critical responses there are some striking contrasts. The English reviewers concern themselves mainly with the novel's aesthetic qualities – its style and language – while also reinforcing the shibboleth of Rhys as high priestess of female doom. For their Caribbean counterparts, on the other hand, the focus tends to be much more on questions of colonial history and racial conflict. Such differences of critical emphasis would seem to confirm Savory's contention that the production of textual meaning is invariably shaped by the cultural location within which it takes place.

Reviews

Wide Sargasso Sea met with immediate critical acclaim, eliciting, as Hunter Davies puts it, 'rave reviews everywhere'.[3] Amongst other things, the reviews pronounced Rhys's text – as a rewriting of Charlotte Brontë's *Jane Eyre* – to be 'an inspired piece of literary research', while at the same time calling it 'a superb creation in its own right'.[4] They also praised its author for her ability to combine the 'gift of penetrating psychological motivation' with a style 'lucid yet pictorial'.[5]

One of the earliest reviews of *Wide Sargasso Sea* is Francis Hope's 'The First Mrs Rochester'. This originally appeared in the *New Statesman* for 28 October 1966 and is reprinted below.

■ When we run out of new stories, we revise old ones. Poets are widely experienced in this field, particularly when the revision brings forward a (neglected) minor character [...]. Novels on such themes are rarer, though by no means unknown. The heroine of Jean Rhys's novel is one of the most arresting minor characters in fiction: the mad West Indian wife in *Jane Eyre*. This short, moody, claustrophobic book is the story of the young Creole girl in Jamaica who became, briefly and disastrously, the first Mrs Rochester. Told mainly in the first person, it covers her childhood in a family ruined by the liberation of the slaves, her honeymoon in the Windward Islands, and her final confinement in a strange cold house in England.

Since only this last, brief section really overlaps with the world of Thornfield Hall, [*Wide Sargasso Sea*] is far from being the literary exercise which summary might suggest – a sort of Gothic summerhouse on Miss Brontë's grounds. The puzzled young husband is as different from Charlotte Brontë's Mr Rochester as one could expect even from her own premises: for a Victorian readership it was morally wrong of Rochester to cut himself off from his former self, but not psychologically implausible. As for the heroine, she is so firmly established as one of nature's victims, a confused and resentful patient in a world which apparently makes no effort to make sense, that one doesn't need to foreknow her frightful end to feel for her. There are resonances, but no borrowings.

As a debut, this remarkable *tour de force* would probably be short-listed for prizes and welcomed as a brave new voice. 'Promise' would flow off several typewriters. As it is, Miss Rhys came to London from the West Indies, as a girl, before the First World War; she was encouraged by Ford Madox Ford, and is the author of five [works] written in the Twenties and Thirties. These [...] were front-line reports from urban Bohemia. Underdogs abandoned by or abandoning inadequate male overdogs [...] revisit old haunts, look up old lovers, drift unsatisfactorily through a hostile world which stretches from Saint-Germain to Notting Hill Gate. The candour is complete but unostentatious; many of her contemporaries whose reputations have survived far more widely look dated by comparison.

Now Miss Rhys has returned to the lush pastures of the Caribbean. She does so with no sentimentality. The pretty dresses, the spindly furniture, the decanters of rum and the blazing landscapes are all there, but the style is utterly sparse (not for nothing did she inhabit the Paris of Ford, [Ezra] Pound [1885–1972] and Gertrude Stein [1874–1946]). The extreme economy of form masters and even implicitly rejects the tropical exuberance of content. 'Everything is too much', reflects the young husband, 'Too much blue, too much purple, too much green. The flowers too red, the mountains too high, the hills too near' [WSS, p.42]. Too much for reason – for his Creole wife's reason, certainly. Her interior monologues have the bright inconsequence of a child's perceptions in a garden – look at this flower, catch this butterfly. Touching enough in a child, it becomes gruesome in a woman whom circumstances and heredity together keep permanently childish. As in [William Faulkner's] The Sound and the Fury [1929], her scatterbrained narrative is a commentary on itself. It is also a work of some power, and some poetry. ☐

This review is much indebted to the image of Rhys initially fashioned by Ford and is duly marked, as it were, by its own critical 'resonances', if not 'borrowings', from Rhys's metropolitan mentor. In his Preface to The Left Bank, Ford famously (or perhaps infamously) praises Rhys for having 'a terrific – an almost lurid! – passion for stating the case of the underdog', together with a 'singular instinct for form'.[6] Both of these qualities are similarly sensed and extolled by Hope in Wide Sargasso Sea: he classifies Antoinette as 'one of nature's victims', reinvokes the gendered overdog/underdog opposition and revels in the novel's 'style', which he finds 'utterly sparse'.

As Hope goes on to suggest, the novel's aesthetic qualities are a direct sign of Rhys's Modernist credentials and place her among the élite if eclectic Euro-American circle of 'Ford [himself], Pound and Gertrude Stein'. What is most suggestive about his brief analysis of the stylistic properties of Wide Sargasso Sea is the claim that these aspects of the text exist in a certain tension with the novel's subject matter, as an 'extreme economy of form masters and even implicitly rejects the tropical exuberance of content'. While this may well be the case, it is worth noting that such a conflict between form and content effectively restates or restages the central struggles of the content itself. Rhys's novel, after all, is precisely nothing if not a drama of mastery and rejection, pitting Rochester's stereotypically English restraint against the manifold excesses – whether sensory, sexual or even epistemological – to which his Caribbean sojourn exposes him. This creates a sharp and curious irony for Hope, who finds himself stylistically embracing the very discipline and rigour which make English masculinity, in Rhys's text, so suspect and troublesome. Hope, it would appear, not only reads Rhys through Ford but also from what might be called a Rochesterean perspective. His reflections on *Wide Sargasso Sea* offer themselves, to recall Savory, as a subtly coded instance of the politics of criticism.

The second extract included in this chapter is taken from 'A Fairy-Tale Neurotic', a long unsigned review first published in *The Times Literary Supplement* for 17 November 1966. As Carole Angier notes, for Rhys's text to receive this kind of 'serious' and 'enthusiastic' attention from such a source is in itself significant, since, in the 1960s at least, the journal was regarded as Britain's 'premier forum of establishment literary opinion'.[7]

■ The sharpest weight that modern fiction has to bear is the lady novelist's typical heroine – most usually unpleasant yet always demanding interest. At best one could say that this is evidence of integration, an awareness of the fact that you do not have to be nice in order to be loved; and that it is more credible than the manichean set-up that prevailed in so many nineteenth-century novels where the heroine is all virtue and her sister, mother, stepmother, cousin or friend all evil. In *Jane Eyre* the irreproachable heroine's counterpart is the first Mrs Rochester, the Creole heiress who was not merely ugly but also 'bad, mad, and embruted' [*JE*, p. 306].

This demon is quite transformed in the heroine of *Wide Sargasso Sea*. In Miss Rhys's imagining she is as far from the graceless neurotics of the 1960s as from Charlotte Brontë's Gothic monster – she is in fact a fairy-tale neurotic. While respecting the facts as given in *Jane Eyre*, Miss Rhys tells a quite different story. *Jane Eyre* is the happy tale of an English Cinderella, *Wide Sargasso Sea* the tragedy of a West Indian heiress. Although the origins of her main characters are in Charlotte Brontë, Miss Rhys's work exists entirely in its own right.

The novel is written in three parts. The first is the heroine's account of her life before the advent of Mr Rochester. In the second, Mr Rochester describes their honeymoon on one of the Windward Islands. A brief final section, written again in the heroine's words, is set in England. The changeover in the narration from the heroine to Mr Rochester and back again gives the tragedy its moral perspective. Antoinette Cosway [...] was born at the time of the emancipation of the slaves in the West Indies; and her hopeless, ruined family – once notorious slave-owners – are now despised by Negroes and Europeans alike. Her heritage was, to say the least, inauspicious; her father died a drunkard leaving half-caste children all over the island; her mother eventually became insane; her brother was a congenital idiot. She grew up in isolation on an overgrown estate exposed to the beguiling spell of the West Indian landscape and to the treacherous influence of the Negro servants. She herself was beautiful and unprotected – as clearly marked for doom as the heroine of any melodrama but far too subtly portrayed to be a melodramatic heroine.

Her marriage to Mr Rochester is a marriage of convenience, arranged by her stepfather, who provided the dowry. Antoinette thought that Rochester only wanted her money; but he did not even want that. A downtrodden younger son, he had acted on his father's instructions. Antoinette in fear of him resorted to Negro sorcery: Rochester – equally terrified – took his revenge in the colonial way with a servant girl. When the honeymoon ends, the final outcome is already apparent. The last section shows Antoinette, demented with cold and misery, imprisoned in the attic at Thornfield Hall under the supervision of Grace Poole. Only the lighted candles are able to evoke the warmth and beauty she used to know.

In sensibility, Antoinette recalls the heroines of [Rhys's] inter-war novels. [...] [H]er alienation is to a large extent aesthetic. A Creole narcissus, she sees the world in terms of its beauty, but the only beauty she understands derives from the experiences and fantasies of her own childhood; and above all from the exotic landscape. It is that which gives her a sense of herself and of her own beauty; and with it belongs safety and happiness. [...] Mr Rochester, then, is very much the intruder. For him the West Indian landscape is unbearably wild and menacing. He destroys Antoinette because she belongs with everything he cannot understand:

> I hated the sunsets of whatever colour. I hated its beauty and its magic and the secret I would never know. I hated its indifference and the cruelty which was part of its loveliness. Above all I hated her. For she belonged to the magic and the loveliness. [WSS, p. 111]

He starts on the process of destruction by calling her Bertha (her mad mother's name and the name by which she is known in *Jane Eyre*). In Thornfield Hall, she recalls the effect: 'I saw Antoinette drifting out of the window with her scents, her pretty clothes and her looking-glass' [WSS, p. 117]. The image is gone and there is nothing left to replace it. Madness follows.

Antoinette becomes mad because she is dispossessed. Like the heroines of the novels which Jean Rhys published in the 1930s, her purpose is to love and be loved. If she does not please, she is nothing. Her predecessors were contemporary heroines belonging to the demi-monde of feminine emancipation. Independent of society, their lack of education and of financial resources made them all the more dependent on their men. It was the situation of their times but accentuated by their own fear of the world and unwillingness to meet it. Their commitment to the man is absolute. When they are abandoned, which they always are, their unhappiness is equally unyielding. They are romantic figures given up to sentiment and haunted by its transience.

Plainly, life is loaded against Miss Rhys's heroines. [...] Reduced to the bare narrative outline, her novels are about the injustice done by cruel men to lovely women. Even the disagreeable Grace Poole has suffered. That is why she accepts the job of supervising Antoinette: *'After all the house is big and safe, a shelter from the world outside which, say what you like, can be a black and cruel world to a woman'* [WSS, pp. 115–16]. The heroines fail because they are too gentle (or passive, depending on the extent of one's sympathies for them); it is always pointed out to them that they lack the guts needed to survive. [...] However, in all the novels and in this one particularly, the mixture of compassion and objectivity in the author's attitude is so subtle, the heroine's attractions are so skilfully combined with her shortcomings, the man's limitations portrayed with so much restraint that the issue of who is to blame remains quiescent.

In *Wide Sargasso Sea* the heroine's difficulties are placed in a larger perspective than in the other novels. The earlier heroines existed in a social vacuum, whereas Antoinette's tragedy is in part at least the tragedy of the society to which she belongs. Also Mr Rochester is the only one of the men in her novels who is 'presented live'; and not merely as the object of the heroine's affection and the agent of her unhappiness. Miss Rhys makes us understand his bewilderment as clearly as hers. He is the victim of a society where 'Gold is the idol they worship' [WSS, p. 122] and is dispatched against his will to a country that terrifies him. She is the victim of wild and tantalizing decadence; and the difference is that she is endowed with what Henry James [1843–1916] called 'the iridescence of decay' whereas he is the traditional insensitive Englishman abroad. In mood and style *Wide Sargasso Sea* achieves a rare synthesis of the baroque and the precise, the coolly empirical and the lushly pretty and most of this poetry, of course, belongs with Antoinette. She is, to use the author's own image, the orchid which Mr Rochester tramples into the mud. ▫

Despite the confident opening gesture of its title, which relates *Wide Sargasso Sea* to the traditional narrative form of the fairy tale, this review is particularly striking because of the problems it seems to encounter in maintaining the stability of its generic focus. The first hint of this occurs in the second paragraph of the review, where Antoinette is initially figured as 'a fairy-tale neurotic', only for her story to be swiftly reclassified as 'the tragedy of a West Indian heiress'. The category of tragedy itself proves to be not quite adequate and is replaced by another, which turns out, similarly, to fall just short of critical requirements: Antoinette is, on the one hand, 'as clearly marked for doom as the heroine of any melodrama' even as she is simultaneously 'far too subtly portrayed to be a melodramatic heroine'. Such breathless critical attempts to fix Rhys's text themselves begin to seem a little neurotic. This effect is compounded by the further allusion to Antoinette as 'Creole narcissus' (linking her to the world of Greek myth – see Gayatri Chakravorty Spivak's discussion in Chapter Two of this Guide) and the closing claim that the novel's 'mood and style' entail 'a rare synthesis of the baroque and the precise'.

Although the review does not itself make this point, the generically mixed and elusive nature of *Wide Sargasso Sea* is implicitly related to Rhys's larger exploration of Antoinette's predicament as a white Creole subject: just as the novel slips constantly between genres (fairy tale, tragedy, melodrama), so Antoinette inhabits the volatile space between English and African Caribbean cultures which colonial history has set violently in conflict. The generic uncertainty of *Wide Sargasso Sea* is not a matter of form exclusively, but indirectly linked to the porosity of its heroine's racial location.

The critical approbation of *The Times Literary Supplement* is mirrored by that of the *New York Times Book Review*, which published Walter Allen's 'Bertha the Doomed' in its issue for 18 June 1967. This review is reproduced below, making up the third and final piece in this section of the chapter.

■ This is Jean Rhys's first novel since 1939. Before then, she had written five works of fiction, the first of which, a collection of stories called *The Left Bank*, appeared in 1927 with an enthusiastic preface by Ford Madox Ford. *Wide Sargasso Sea* has a no less enthusiastic preface by the English critic Francis Wyndham. In many ways, it is very perceptive. Yet I think he tends to exaggerate both the indifference with which her prewar fiction was received and its ultimate value.

She was, in fact, much admired by other contemporary novelists. Mr Wyndham admits that her novels had a critical success, but adds: 'their true quality had never been appreciated. The reason for this is simple: they were ahead of their age, both in spirit and in style'.[8] For me, when I last read her some years ago, she seemed very much a writer of her period, one who had come to maturity in the 1920s and whom one might expect to be taken up by Ford. It seemed to me that it was there, as a period writer, that her main interest lay.

But this doesn't mean one shouldn't be grateful to Mr Wyndham for his generous partisanship – or for her new novel, which is a considerable tour de force by any standard. Readers of Charlotte Brontë will recall Jane Eyre's first glimpse of the mysterious prisoner in the garret of Thornfield. 'In the deep shade, at the further end of the room, a figure ran backwards and forwards. What it was, whether beast or human being, one could not, at first sight, tell: it grovelled, seemingly, on all fours; it snatched and growled like some strange wild animal: but it was covered with clothing; and a quantity of dark, grizzled hair, wild as a mane, hid its head and face' [JE, p. 307].

It is the Creole Bertha Mason, of course, the first Mrs Rochester, the announcement of whose existence, just as the wedding ceremony is about to be performed, prevents Mr Rochester's marriage to Jane. It is Bertha Mason who is the heroine and, for the greater part of the novel, the narrator of Wide Sargasso Sea; and she is indeed a plausible re-creation and interpretation of the one character in Jane Eyre that Charlotte Brontë tells us next to nothing about, presumably because she knew next to nothing about her. Jean Rhys, who herself comes from the Caribbean, convinces us that she does, and she does so because of her extraordinarily vivid rendering of life in Jamaica in the early nineteenth century, immediately after the emancipation of the slaves.

The novel is a triumph of atmosphere – of what one is tempted to call Caribbean Gothic atmosphere – brooding, sinister, compounded of heat and rain and intensely colored flowers, of racial antagonisms and all-pervasive superstition. It has an almost hallucinatory quality – and this is Bertha Mason's contribution, for it is through her mind, from childhood to her incarceration at Thornfield and her dreams of firing the house, that we view the action.

From the beginning she reveals herself as beautiful, pathetic and doomed, doomed both by heredity and environment. She is the child of generations of slave-owners who have suddenly been plunged in poverty by the emancipation and become objects of contempt for the freed Negroes, who call them 'white niggers' [WSS, p.64], and the English alike. Her younger brother is dumb and bed-ridden, her mother distraught by circumstances to the point finally of madness.

What I find especially interesting in Wide Sargasso Sea, apart from the relationship with Jane Eyre, is that Bertha Mason seems to sum up in herself, more closely than ever before, the nature of the heroine who appears under various names throughout Jean Rhys's fiction. She is a young woman, generally Creole in origin and artistic in leanings, who is hopelessly and helplessly at sea in her relations with men, a passive victim, doomed to destruction. It is remarkable that after so many years Miss Rhys should have pinned her down in a character, however sketchily presented, from another novelist.

It is here that the critical problem arises. Francis Wyndham rightly says that Miss Rhys's book is in no sense a pastiche of Charlotte Brontë. But does it exist in its own right? I think not, for the reason that her Mr Rochester is almost as shadowy a figure as Charlotte Brontë's Bertha Mason. One still, in other words, needs *Jane Eyre* to complement it, to supply its full meaning. □

As this review's penultimate paragraph makes clear, *Wide Sargasso Sea* constitutes, for Allen, the point at which Rhys's writing reaches its culmination. The representation of Antoinette, he declares, is definitive. It 'seems to sum up [...] the nature of the heroine who appears under various names throughout Jean Rhys's fiction': 'hopelessly and help-lessly at sea in her relations with men', Antoinette is the ultimate instance of the 'passive victim, doomed to destruction'.

The category of 'passive victim' to which Allen wishes to consign Antoinette and her fictional forebears is one that recent feminist critics have questioned and resisted. As Helen Carr points out, the heroine of *Wide Sargasso Sea* is far from passive, not only 'bit[ing] her husband and threaten[ing] him with a broken rum bottle',[9] but also finally resolving, it should be added, to set fire to his mansion. This action reduces Thornfield Hall to a 'blackened ruin' (*JE*, p.447), leaving its master per-manently disfigured. As Carr goes on to suggest, the most pernicious consequence of viewing Rhys's women as 'passive victim[s]' is that it blocks critical analysis of the larger power relations which those women must negotiate:

■ the emphasis on the passive victim has made it harder, or less neces-sary, to acknowledge the intensity of Rhys's attack on social injustice: a victim who is passive is by common consent [...] to a great extent to blame for her fate. The phrase implies that 'passivity' is an innate char-acteristic of that particular victim, and not that there could be social, cultural or historical conditions which have driven this 'victim' into an impasse.[10] □

The inscription of such power relations is itself legible in the insouciant linguistic habits of Allen's own review, which refers throughout to Rhys's Antoinette as Brontë's Bertha. This detail may at first seem rather trivial – no more than an excusable, if irritating, critical lapse. It gains in signifi-cance, however, when it is remembered that a similar misprision is per-formed by Rochester, the 'fine English gentleman' (*WSS*, p.80) of Rhys's text. In renaming her as Bertha, Rochester subjects Antoinette to a triple violence. He severs his wife from her cultural origins, dissolves her link to her mother and fractures her already precarious sense of identity. As she herself understands: 'Names matter, like when he wouldn't call me

Antoinette, and I saw Antoinette drifting out of the window with her scents, her pretty clothes and her looking-glass' (*WSS*, p.117). Considered in this embattled light, Allen's persistent misnaming of Antoinette offers an ironic trace of the very structures of colonial and patriarchal domination interrogated by Rhys's novel. Like Hope, he reads the text in a way which is peculiarly Rochesterean.

Early Criticism

The first of the three extracts in this section of the chapter comes from Wally Look Lai's 'The Road to Thornfield Hall: An Analysis of Jean Rhys' *Wide Sargasso Sea*'. This article was originally published in 1968 in *New Beacon Reviews*, a major contemporary locus, in Savory's phrase, for 'intra-Caribbean literary debate'.[11] The article is generally regarded as foundational to the critical exchanges which have since developed around Rhys's text. The main reason for its importance is that it represents the earliest sustained attempt to locate Rhys's novel within the specific context of an emergent Caribbean literary tradition, hailing it as 'one of the truly great novels to have ever emerged out of the West Indies'.[12]

In making this momentous claim, Look Lai directly challenges contemporary accounts of *Wide Sargasso Sea*, as produced in the 'English critical world'.[13] The problem with these accounts, in Look Lai's opinion, is that they fail to register the extent to which Rhys's novel signals a new direction in her writing, preferring to see the text merely as a 'continuation' – albeit a 'brilliant' one – of earlier concerns with 'the plight of the rejected woman, tragically isolated in a world in which she is at the complete mercy of men'. For Look Lai, by contrast, *Wide Sargasso Sea* does not simply repeat and refine the one-sided sexual politics of Rhys's previous work. Rather, it should be read, he argues, as a text in which gender conflicts take on a symbolic dimension: Antoinette's fraught encounter with Rochester is not in the end reducible to the issue of patriarchal oppression alone, but functions as a medium through which the racial tensions between white Creole and English identities are dramatized. Look Lai argues that it is these larger tensions – ultimately the product of English colonial history – which constitute the 'fundamental preoccupation' of *Wide Sargasso Sea*, 'distinguish[ing] this novel radically from [Rhys's] others'.[14] At the same time, he rightly points out that the conflict between white Creole and English worlds does not exhaust the novel's overall meaning but is complicated by Antoinette's equally vexed entanglement in a third world in the text. This third or alternative realm takes the form of the ex-slave community, which Antoinette repeatedly wishes to embrace and yet from which she remains permanently excluded.

■ *Wide Sargasso Sea* [...] has had a curious history since its publication in England in October 1966. On the one hand, it was acclaimed almost immediately by the English critical world as a literary masterpiece, and has since been the recipient of several distinguished literary awards. In West Indian literary circles, on the other hand, it has remained largely ignored, despite the enthusiasm with which it was greeted in England. Certainly, not a single review of the novel has ever appeared in any West Indian newspaper or periodical, and the result is that its existence is virtually unknown among the small but growing West Indian reading public. This is a really unfortunate state of affairs, because there can be little doubt that a serious reading will reveal *Wide Sargasso Sea* to be one of the genuine masterpieces of West Indian fiction, one of the truly great novels to have ever emerged out of the West Indies. In this article we shall attempt to examine for the first time the theme and structure of this novel, in an effort to establish the claims made here on its behalf and to hasten its recognition in the West Indies as a major work of art, an event which we feel to be long overdue.

The fact that *Wide Sargasso Sea* has so far failed to attract the serious attention of the West Indian critic may be due, not so much to insensitivity on his part, as to certain peculiar difficulties with which he is faced when he attempts to assess the status of this work in relation to the body of West Indian literature. In the first place, there is the difficulty of determining whether Jean Rhys can rightly be classed as a West Indian writer at all, despite the fact of her West Indian birth. Miss Rhys was born in Roseau, Dominica, the daughter of a Welsh father and a white West Indian mother, but she has lived for most of her life in Europe; she came to England some time before the First World War, when she was only sixteen, and has not returned to the West Indies since.[15] During the 1920s and 1930s, she wrote and published her first five [works] [...]. Miss Rhys' world in all these early [works] is the world of modern, urban Europe; her people are the people who live perpetually on the fringes of urban society – faceless, nomadic creatures inhabiting that transient world which is a permanent feature of modern urban life in Europe. Their experiences are evoked with a poetic sensitivity and familiarity which reflect the emotional involvement of the participant, rather than the detachment of the outside observer. On the basis of these [works] – their subject-matter, and the nature of the artist's relation to this subject-matter – one would certainly be justified in classing Jean Rhys as more of a European than a West Indian writer. To claim that *Wide Sargasso Sea* is a West Indian novel, therefore, is to claim that the whole artistic intention underlying this new work is different from that shown in any of her previous works, and that there is a fundamental preoccupation here which distinguishes this novel radically from the others.

This brings us on to the second difficulty, which is the more substantial one: the question of interpreting the artistic preoccupations in this new novel, and of showing their relation to the substance of West Indian life and experience. What is very evident so far (and perhaps detrimental as far as West Indian appreciation of the novel is concerned) is that *Wide Sargasso Sea* is being appreciated in England largely as a brilliant continuation of a theme which has tended to dominate all of Jean Rhys' work so far: the transience and instability of personal relationships, and the plight of the rejected woman, tragically isolated in a world in which she is at the complete mercy of men. In all her novels, and this one is no exception, this essential situation has always formed the basis of her stories, and her heroines have always been essentially the same kind of person: lonely, dispossessed and rejected, a passive victim of events over which she has no real control. In *Wide Sargasso Sea*, this same situation reappears, but in a different setting: we are no longer in the anonymous fringe world of urban Europe, but in the West Indies, just after Emancipation. *Wide Sargasso Sea* is the story of one of the key figures in Charlotte Brontë's *Jane Eyre*, Bertha Antoinette Mason, the mad Creole heiress who is Mr Rochester's first wife, and whose existence he tries to conceal from the world by keeping her under permanent confinement in the attics of Thornfield Hall. Jane Eyre, we remember, only becomes aware of her existence when Antoinette's brother reveals Rochester's secret at the abortive wedding ceremony between Jane and Rochester. Thereupon, she abandons Thornfield Hall, and is only able to resume her relationship with Rochester towards the end when she returns to Thornfield and learns that Antoinette has in the meantime burnt the Hall down and leapt to her death from the battlements. Taking over the elements of this story, Jean Rhys has recreated the life story of Antoinette, and the whole process – especially her disastrous relationship with Rochester – which culminates in her madness, and in her imprisonment at Thornfield Hall.

Despite the change of setting, there is an obvious similarity between this novel and the earlier ones: the interpersonal situation is the same, the tragic consequences are the same – the woman is rejected, the relationship comes to an unhappy end. It is tempting, therefore, to construe *Wide Sargasso Sea* as simply a triumphant restatement of an old preoccupation, placed in a different social context and presented with a greater complexity and sophistication. It is precisely this reading, however, which may have been responsible for the West Indian critic's reluctance to accept this novel as having any major relevance to West Indian life and experience, since on this interpretation there would be no real break between this novel and the earlier ones, and the West Indian social setting would be reduced to being a mere incidental background to the working out of an established concern with rejected womanhood. But whatever validity there may be in the orthodox reading of *Wide Sargasso Sea*, it is essentially a limited interpretation; the similarity between this novel and the earlier ones is no more than superficial, for the real greatness of this novel lies, not in the way in which Jean Rhys has restated an old theme of hers (however accomplished this may have been in itself), but in the way in which she has *made use of* this theme in order to convey a totally different reading of experience, one which is much more profound and ambitious than any she has ever attempted before. It is with this more fundamental reading that we are concerned, for this is what constitutes the essentially West Indian nature of the novel. The West Indian setting, far from being incidental, is central to the novel: it is not that it provides a mere background to the theme of rejected womanhood, but rather that the theme of rejected womanhood is utilized symbolically in order to make an artistic statement about West Indian society, and about an aspect of the West Indian experience.

For the first time in any of Jean Rhys' novels, character and situation are explored, not for their own sakes, but for their symbolic significance. The encounter between Antoinette and Rochester is more than just an encounter between two people: it is an encounter between two whole worlds; and the description of the relationship between the two persons is an artistic exploration of the relationship between these two worlds. In the story of Antoinette's relationship with Rochester, Jean Rhys attempts to explore a theme which transcends the purely personal nature of their encounter – the theme of the white West Indian's relation to England, the nature and consequences of his involvement with the world from which his ancestors came. Antoinette, the white West Indian, finds herself driven by the circumstances of her life into the arms of Rochester, the Englishman, and by the nature of the circumstances in which she finds herself coming to him, she is totally dependent on him for her happiness and personal salvation. But the relationship is doomed to failure from the very start: both parties are so rooted in their separate worlds, the difference between their respective pasts, and the sensibilities born of that past, is so great, that throughout the relationship they remain complete strangers to each other. For each of them, the world of the other is like some mysterious and inaccessible dream. [...] It is this haunting sense of strangeness, this existential distance between the two parties, which pervades the entire relationship, and which is ultimately responsible for its failure. For Rochester is unable to accept, or come to terms with, the alien nature of the woman who has become his wife. [...] He rejects her finally, and she goes mad, as her last hope of salvation from a hostile world is destroyed. He returns to England with her, and keeps her for the rest of her life hidden away inside the attics of Thornfield Hall, which is where we first meet her in *Jane Eyre*.

Antoinette's tragic fate, and the history of her relationship with Rochester, assume a symbolic significance in relation to the theme which Jean Rhys is attempting to explore in this novel – the theme of the existential chasm that exists between the white West Indian and his ancestors, and the tragic fate which awaits any attempt to bridge this chasm by an emotional involvement with this world. This is the theme which gives the novel its title: physically situated between the West Indies and England, the Sargasso Sea becomes a symbolic dividing line between two whole worlds, and two people whose spirits belong so totally to their own worlds that they are never able to meet each other in any fundamental sense. It is only at the end of their disastrous relationship that Antoinette becomes fully aware of her real relation to Rochester's world: 'We lost our way to England. When? Where? I don't remember, but we lost it' [*WSS*, p. 117].

But if, within the total meaning of the novel, Antoinette's symbolic meeting with Rochester is seen as bound to end in disaster, what is just as inevitable is that she should have been forced to seek happiness from him in the first place. For their encounter with each other is not of her own choosing, but the result of a whole process in which she finds herself caught up. Within the context of West Indian history, and the definitions born of that history, she is a descendant of the white masters, and in a world in which the slaves have just been emancipated, she becomes an outcast, a victim of the definitions into which she has been born. It is because she is an unhappy stranger in her own world, therefore, that she finds herself impelled in the direction of Rochester and his world, who become under these circumstances her last hope of salvation. And her real tragedy is that the reasons for which Rochester rejects her – her fundamental oneness with the people of her own world, and thus her strangeness to him – are not reasons which her own world will accept, because here other definitions are operative. The essence of Antoinette's dilemma, therefore, is that she finds herself spiritually alone, defined out of both worlds in her life:

'Did you hear what that girl was singing?' Antoinette said.

'I don't always understand what they say or sing.' Or anything else.

'It was a song about a white cockroach. That's me. That's what they call all of us who were here before their own people in Africa sold them to the slave traders. And I've heard English women call us white niggers. So between you I often wonder who I am and where is my country and where do I belong and why was I ever born at all.' [*WSS*, p. 64]

The logical result of this dual rejection, and the isolation thus imposed upon her, is madness. The story of Antoinette's life, therefore, and its tragic ending is not simply the life history of an individual, but a symbolic reconstruction of a plight into which history has thrown the white West Indian: his sense of spiritual displacement, caught as he is between two worlds, without being able to find a place in either. Far from being a story of a personal relationship, *Wide Sargasso Sea* is a profound statement about identity, and about the existential dilemma of a minority condemned by history to a claustrophobic existence which can end only in madness. Antoinette's imprisonment in Thornfield Hall becomes, on this reading, a symbol of the total spiritual isolation which is the white West Indian's historical destiny. □

In a section of his article not cited here, Look Lai suggests that in Rhys's text it is possible to discern 'the germs of the neurotic type of personality which [Antoinette's] isolation and the hostility of her environment gradually impose on her'.[16] This statement looks back to the fleeting construction of Antoinette as 'fairy-tale neurotic' already advanced by the anonymous reviewer in *The Times Literary Supplement*. It also anticipates the position on *Wide Sargasso Sea* adopted by Kenneth Ramchand in 'Terrified Consciousness', an article first published in the *Journal of Commonwealth Literature* in 1969 and later reprinted as the final chapter of Ramchand's innovative and substantial *The West Indian Novel and its Background* (1970). In common with Look Lai, Ramchand is eager to situate Rhys's text squarely in relation to other Caribbean writings, comparing and contrasting it to three contemporary novels produced by 'writers belong[ing]' – like Rhys – 'to a minority group called white West Indians'. The novels in question are Phyllis Shand Alfrey's *The Orchid House* (1953), Geoffrey Drayton's *Christopher* (1959) and J.B. Emtage's *Brown Sugar* (1966). Quickly dismissing *Brown Sugar* for its 'reactionary political stance',[17] Ramchand goes on to argue that the texts by Alfrey, Drayton and Rhys 'relate to West Indian society in more interesting ways'. Here Ramchand again follows Look Lai by directing critical attention to the plight of the white Creole subject, caught up in a 'socioeconomic situation that is recognizable as the fall of the planter class'.[18] What is distinctive about Ramchand's approach is the theoretical framework which he gives it, deriving both the title of his article and overall focus from the Martinique-born anticolonial thinker Frantz Fanon (1925–61) and, in particular, Fanon's *The Wretched of the Earth* (1961). Although principally concerned with theorizing colonialism from the perspective of the colonized, Fanon's text also gives some space to the effects that it produces upon the colonizers themselves. This is evidenced even in its opening paragraph, which Ramchand cites at the beginning of his article:

■ [D]ecolonization is always a violent phenomenon. ... Its unusual importance is that it constitutes, from the very first day, the minimum demands of the colonized. To tell the truth, the proof of success lies in the whole social structure being changed from the bottom up. The extraordinary importance of this change is that it is willed, called for, demanded. The need for this change exists in its crude state, impetuous and compelling, in the consciousness and in the lives of the men and women who are colonized. *But the possibility of this change is equally experienced in the form of a terrifying future in the consciousness of another 'species' of men and women: the colonizers.*[19] ☐

It is this 'terrifying future', Ramchand claims, which is differently confronted in each of the texts he analyzes. In the case of *Wide Sargasso Sea* – examined at the greatest length in the second half of Ramchand's article – such a prospect accounts for the 'sense of menace and persecution'[20] which pervades the novel as a whole.

■ *Wide Sargasso Sea*, which is set in the 1830s, opens with the girl Antoinette and her mother living on a derelict plantation. They are avoided by the rest of the whites and derided by the Negroes in the neighbourhood. Antoinette's mother is then saved by her marriage with a rich Englishman, Mr Mason, only to be plunged into madness after a Negro rising. Later, it is a letter from an embittered mulatto that destroys Antoinette's marriage and leads to her removal and confinement in an attic in England. It is not difficult to recognize in *Wide Sargasso Sea* the plight of some white Creoles at Emancipation, caught up between social forces and with nowhere to belong to [...].

But *Wide Sargasso Sea* is only incidentally about the dilemma of a class. Nor does it have the political drive of *The Orchid House* or the concern for social rapprochement that may be noticed in *Christopher*. Although the novel is much more 'historical' than *The Orchid House* or *Christopher* it creates out of its raw material an experience that we like to think of as essentially modern.

The Emancipation Act functions as a root of insecurity and the cause of despair. In a scene of throw-away violence, Antoinette, the torpid Creole narrator of Part One, recounts the death of a ruined planter: 'One calm evening he shot his dog, swam out to sea and was gone for always. No agent came from England to look after his property – Nelson's Rest it was called – and strangers from Spanish Town rode up to gossip and discuss the tragedy' [*WSS*, p. 5]. The new speculators and the English in the islands are presented as alien invaders, like Antoinette's husband, out of sympathy with people and place: 'Everything is too much, I felt as I rode wearily after her. Too much blue, too much purple, too much green. The flowers too red, the mountains

too high, the hills too near. And the woman is a stranger' [WSS, p.42].
The smouldering Negroes become a nightmare avenging force:

> we could not move for they pressed too close round us. Some of
> them were laughing and waving sticks, some of the ones at the
> back were carrying flambeaux and it was light as day. Aunt Cora
> held my hand very tightly and her lips moved but I could not hear
> because of the noise. And I was afraid, because I knew that the
> ones who laughed would be the worst. I shut my eyes and waited.
> [WSS, p.22]

In The Orchid House, the Madam's increasing apathy, and in Christopher,
Mrs Stevens's constriction and sense of being at bay, both suggest the
dramatic possibilities of the female character as a suffering, vulnerable
agent. In Wide Sargasso Sea these possibilities are exploited to their
limits. Through the singular narrating consciousness of Antoinette
Cosway, as girl and as married woman, Jean Rhys creates a pattern of
alienation within alienation, distress multiplied upon distress, as first
mother and then daughter are pushed towards inevitable madness and
despair:

> It was too hot that afternoon. I could see the beads of perspiration
> on her upper lip and the dark circles under her eyes. I started to fan
> her, but she turned her head away. She might rest if I left her alone,
> she said.
> Once I would have gone back quietly to watch her asleep on the
> blue sofa – once I made excuses to be near her when she brushed
> her hair, a soft black cloak to cover me, hide me, keep me safe.
> But not any longer. Not any more. [WSS, pp.8–9]

The novel's peculiar quality lies in this, that the emotional intensities
in which Jean Rhys involves us are being explored for their own
sakes, and are, as in [William Shakespeare's] King Lear [1605], in excess
of any given determinant.
A sense of being menaced, literally established in relation to the
rising Black population, is rendered again and again in oppressive
tactile detail:

> Then the girl grinned and began to crack the knuckles of her fin-
> gers. At each crack I jumped and my hands began to sweat. I was
> holding some school books in my right hand and I shifted them to
> under my arm, but it was too late, there was a mark on the palm of
> my hand and a stain on the cover of the book. The girl began to
> laugh, very quietly. [WSS, p.27]

A childhood episode when the Great House is ablaze and the Cosways about to take to flight, suggests not only Antoinette's hopeless identification with her native place and the loss of individual choice when violent socio-historical forces are at work, but also the dark image of the self that broods over the novel:

> Then, not so far off, I saw Tia and her mother and I ran to her, for she was all that was left of my life as it had been. We had eaten the same food, slept side by side, bathed in the same river. As I ran, I thought, I will live with Tia and I will be like her. Not to leave Coulibri. Not to go. Not. When I was close I saw the jagged stone in her hand but I did not see her throw it. I did not feel it either, only something wet, running down my face. I looked at her and I saw her face crumple up as she began to cry. We stared at each other, blood on my face, tears on hers. It was as if I saw myself. Like in a looking-glass. [WSS, p. 24]

Antoinette's childhood alienation comes over strongly in the novel as a recoil from a lush absorbent landscape suddenly gone rank and threatening:

> Our garden was large and beautiful as that garden in the Bible – the tree of life grew there. But it had gone wild. The paths were overgrown and a smell of dead flowers mixed with the fresh living smell. Underneath the tree ferns, tall as forest tree ferns, the light was green. Orchids flourished out of reach or for some reason not to be touched. One was snaky looking, another like an octopus with long thin brown tentacles bare of leaves hanging from a twisted root. Twice a year the octopus orchid flowered – then not an inch of tentacle showed. It was a bell-shaped mass of white, mauve, deep purples, wonderful to see. The scent was very sweet and strong. I never went near it. [WSS, p. 6]

Over against this sense of recoil, however, is a revulsion from people that turns into self-mutilation and a desire for annihilation or transcendence:

> I took another road, past the old sugar works and the water wheel that had not turned for years. I went to parts of Coulibri that I had not seen, where there was no road, no path, no track. And if the razor grass cut my legs and arms I would think 'It's better than people.' Black ants or red ones, tall nests swarming with white ants, rain that soaked me to the skin – once I saw a snake. All better than people.

Better. Better, better than people.

Watching the red and yellow flowers in the sun thinking of nothing, it was as if a door opened and I was somewhere else, something else. Not myself any longer. [*WSS*, p. 12]

The terms in which Antoinette's childhood alienation is expressed, and the sensuous immediacy with which it is done, make it clear that history and place, however accurately evoked, are being used only to lend initial credibility to a mood that establishes itself in the novel as a way of experiencing the world. In Antoinette's nightmares at the convent school, a desire for annihilation, or a death wish, becomes associated [...] with a magnetized anticipation of sexual experience:

I am wearing a long dress and thin slippers, so I walk with difficulty, following the man who is with me and holding up the skirt of my dress. It is white and beautiful and I don't wish to get it soiled. I follow him, sick with fear but I make no effort to save myself; if anyone were to try to save me, I would refuse. This must happen. Now we have reached the forest. We are under the tall dark trees and there is no wind. 'Here?' He turns and looks at me, his face black with hatred, and when I see this I begin to cry. He smiles slyly. 'Not here, not yet,' he says, and I follow him, weeping. Now I do not try to hold up my dress, it trails in the dirt, my beautiful dress. [*WSS*, p. 34]

The nightmare in Jean Rhys's novel is used to point the work towards the relationship between Antoinette and her husband that is the baffling substance of Part Two. [...]

Having established Antoinette's desolation, Miss Rhys proceeds to marry her in Part Two to the embittered younger son of an English gentleman: 'Dear Father. The thirty thousand pounds have been paid to me without question or condition. . . . I have a modest competence now. I will never be a disgrace to you or to my dear brother the son you love. No begging letters, no mean requests. None of the furtive shabby manoeuvres of a younger son' [*WSS*, p. 42]. Once again it is obvious that the novelist is building upon a type situation in island history – the marrying of Creole heiresses for their dowry by indigent younger sons – but this is used merely as a credible background 'explanation' of the twistings and turnings of love that the fiction now begins to explore. It is in this section of the novel that Jean Rhys makes maximum use of the chemical properties of a sensuous correspondent land. On the simplest level, we and the husband (with whose narration Part Two opens) are made to see Antoinette's 'blank face' [*WSS*, p. 56] and protective indifference giving way to animation, as she and her husband move on the long journey through virgin land to the cool remote estate in the hills, further and further away from the scenes of her earlier distress. At the 'sweet honeymoon house' [*WSS*, p. 39], a drugging sexuality associated with the sensuous land brings happiness at last to Antoinette. From the point of view of Christophine, the nurse, and it is also the point of view of an obeah woman [...] the husband has bewitched the vulnerable girl: 'you make love to her till she drunk with it, no rum could make her drunk like that, till she can't do without it. It's *she* can't see the sun any more. Only you she see' [*WSS*, p. 98]. But although this is true, it is only one side of the author's design.

Cruel and bitter though the young man may be, the novelist's purpose is not to lead us into an easy moral judgment. It is, rather, to explore the depths of his longing and frustrations too. This is reflected in the dividing of the narrative in Part Two between Antoinette and the husband. But it is largely done through his changing attitudes to a seemingly changing land. At first it is menacing: 'Those hills would close in on you' [*WSS*, p. 42]; then it is 'too much'; then sensuously overpowering; then charged with 'a music [...] never heard before' [*WSS*, p. 56], sounding intimations of a wished-for unknown: 'It was a beautiful place – wild, untouched, above all untouched, with an alien, disturbing, secret loveliness. And it kept its secret. I'd find myself thinking, "What I see is nothing – I want what it *hides* – that is not nothing"' [*WSS*, p. 54]. By allowing the husband to identify Antoinette with the secret land in this movement of the novel, the author invests love or the sensual relationship between the characters with supreme possibilities. The husband's disappointment at the end issues in hate for Antoinette and the land:

> I hated the mountains and the hills, the rivers and the rain. I hated the sunsets of whatever colour, I hated its beauty and its magic and the secret I would never know. I hated its indifference and the cruelty which was part of its loveliness. Above all I hated her. For she belonged to the magic and the loveliness. She had left me thirsty and all my life would be thirst and longing for what I had lost before I found it. [*WSS*, p. 111]

Since for Antoinette too the land becomes a hated place, to correspond with her unhappiness and her hate for her husband, it is possible to see that the author is less interested in a specific view of the place itself, than in using it as a subjective landscape [...] upon which the impersonal and obscure forces at work in the characters of love may be projected.

[...] Jean Rhys does not see the fierce sexuality between the characters as destructive. It is, indeed, the means by which each of the broken characters can abandon defensive postures: 'If I have forgotten caution, she has forgotten silence and coldness' [WSS, p. 56]. It is, however, part of the unsentimentality with which the author explores the terrified consciousness, and her fidelity to the facts of her fictional world, that the young man's extreme self-consciousness and his susceptibility to intrusions from outside love's retreat should frustrate his yearning to possess and be possessed.

In the husband's long period of vacillation following Daniel Cosway's accusations against Antoinette, Jean Rhys conveys the buffeting feel of love's uncertainties, and it is worth noting that when the decision to hate is taken it is love's tyranny rather than its absorbing power of which we are reminded: 'Even if she had wept like Magdalene it would have made no difference. I was exhausted. All the mad conflicting emotions had gone and left me wearied and empty. Sane' [WSS, p. 111]. Yet in the 'sweet honeymoon house' episodes Jean Rhys is driven to posit the value of even an annihilating love; and with less emphasis, but never beyond the characters' consciousness, a visionary love that promises to disclose itself only upon the surrender of our conventional premises in an increasingly materialistic world. The placing of these only fleetingly realized possibilities within the characters' reach intensifies the pattern of deprivation, insecurity, and longing that Miss Rhys sees in our own time and recognizes in the historical period in which the novel is set. The kind of transference or concurrency achieved in this way is reflected in the history of the person when Antoinette's resentful firing of her tyrannical husband's house is made to parallel the Negro burning of the Great House which had lodged in her childhood memory. In *Wide Sargasso Sea* at last, the terrified consciousness of the historical white West Indian is revealed to be a universal heritage. □

The final extract in this chapter is taken from Edward Kamau Brathwaite's *Contradictory Omens: Cultural Diversity and Integration in the Caribbean* (1974). In this complex work, Brathwaite ranges far beyond the precincts of literary criticism, offering a historically based and interdisciplinary account of the multiple and conflicting racial and cultural forces out of which Caribbean societies have been shaped. Nonetheless, he briefly turns to *Wide Sargasso Sea* at one point and, in particular, the work of Look Lai and Ramchand. This 'analytical diversion'[21] provides him with an effective means of illuminating 'The nature of West Indian cultural pluralism'[22] which is his main topic. As if anticipating Savory, Brathwaite contends that the meanings critics attribute to the texts they read are inevitably inflected by their own cultural and racial affiliations, explicitly announcing his own 'point of view' to be 'black West Indian'.[23] The engagement with Ramchand (somewhat ponderously described as 'a critic of East Indian derivation, whose orientation is "West Indian"') is fairly perfunctory and restricted to questioning Ramchand's final claims about the novel's universalism. The response to Look Lai, 'a West Indian of Chinese derivation',[24] is, on the other hand, rather more sustained and indeed overtly sceptical. Brathwaite argues that Look Lai significantly underplays the problems inherent in the 'black/white [...] relationships'[25] represented in Rhys's novel, an accusation also implicitly levelled at Rhys herself. This becomes especially clear, according to Brathwaite, in Look Lai's reading of the ending of *Wide Sargasso Sea*. For Look Lai, the novel's closing dream-sequence is a triumphant one, spiritually uniting Antoinette, through death, with Tia, who is both the young black confidante of her childhood and the daughter of an ex-slave. While Brathwaite concedes that such a racially harmonious reading is indeed tempting, he insists that it must ultimately be rejected as naïve, a wishful repression of the social and historical realities that necessarily keep the two figures – white and black – apart. This largely negative response to Look Lai's utopianism is a key moment in *Wide Sargasso Sea*'s critical history and, as Savory notes, 'has reverberated in West Indian criticism ever since'.[26]

■ The nature of West Indian cultural pluralism [...] can, I think, be effectively illuminated by discussion of [*Wide Sargasso Sea*] [...]. It was almost unanimously welcomed and praised by metropolitan critics who were impressed by its *fin-de-siècle* quality and the inventive variation it brought to the *Jane Eyre* story.[27] The concern here was not so much with fidelity to the West Indian experience, as with style. Among West Indian critics, on the other hand, there was no such unanimity, because here one's sympathies became engaged, one's cultural orientations were involved; one's perception of one's personal experience in its relationship to what one conceived to be one's history. It is dishonest, I think, to try to hold that it is possible to be an impartial critic in cases where one's historical and historically received image of oneself is under discussion.

[...] Kenneth Ramchand, a critic of East Indian derivation, whose orientation is 'West Indian', sees the novel as an illustration of the 'terrified consciousness' (the tag is from Fanon's *The Wretched of the Earth*) of white West Indians in a black West Indies, especially since emancipation; but goes on, through an appreciation of the art of the novel, to see this consciousness, somewhat ambiguously, as 'a universal heritage'.

Wally Look Lai, a West Indian of Chinese derivation, is anxious to take the novel out of the boudoirs of the English critics and place it firmly in the West Indies where he maintains it belongs. He is anxious to convince West Indians that the novel is as much for them as for anybody and that its 'greatness' lies connected with its 'West Indianness'. [...]

But what really interests Look Lai about *Wide Sargasso Sea* is not the deep subtle hopeless black/white 'West Indian' relationships [...] but the relationship between Creole and metropole – which was clearly Jean Rhys's concern also:

> 'Is it true,' she said, 'that England is like a dream? Because one of my friends who married an Englishman wrote and told me so. She said this place London is like a cold dark dream sometimes. I want to wake up.'
> 'Well,' I answered annoyed, 'that is precisely how your beautiful island seems to me, quite unreal and like a dream.'
> 'But how can rivers and mountains and the sea be unreal?'
> 'And how can millions of people, their houses and their streets be unreal?'
> 'More easily,' she said, 'much more easily. Yes a big city must be like a dream.'
> 'No, this is unreal and like a dream,' I thought. [*WSS*, p. 49]

Mad and in England, Antoinette, the novel's heroine continues to dream – of metropole/plantation:

> There were more candles on a table and I took one of them and ran up the first flight of stairs and the second. On the second floor I threw away the candle. But I did not stay to watch. I ran up the last flight of stairs and along the passage. I passed the room where they brought me yesterday or the day before yesterday, I don't remember. Perhaps it was quite long ago for I seemed to know the house quite well. I knew how to get away from the heat and the shouting, for there was shouting now. When I was out on the battlements it was cool and I could hardly hear them. I sat there quietly. I don't know how long I sat. Then I turned round and saw the sky. It was red and all my life was in it. I saw the grandfather clock and Aunt Cora's patchwork, all colours, I saw the orchids and the stephanotis and the jasmine and the tree of life in flames. I saw the chandelier and the red carpet downstairs and the bamboos and the tree ferns, the gold ferns and the silver, and the soft green velvet of the moss on the garden wall. I saw my doll's house and the books and the picture of the Miller's Daughter. I heard the parrot call as he did when he saw a stranger, *Qui est là? Qui est là?* and the man who hated me was calling too, Bertha! Bertha! The wind caught my hair and it streamed out like wings. It might bear me up, I thought, if I jumped to those hard stones. But when I looked over the edge I

saw the pool at Coulibri. Tia was there. She beckoned to me and when I hesitated, she laughed. I heard her say, You frightened? And I heard the man's voice, Bertha! Bertha! All this I saw and heard in a fraction of a second. And the sky so red. Someone screamed and I thought, *Why did I scream?* I called 'Tia!' and jumped and woke. [*WSS*, pp. 123–4]

The 'jump' here is a jump to death; so that Antoinette wakes to death, not to life; for life would have meant dreaming in the reality of madness in a cold castle in England. But death was also her allegiance to the carefully detailed exotic fantasy of the West Indies. In fact, neither world is 'real'. They exist inside the head. Tia was not and never could have been her friend. No matter what Jean Rhys might have made Antoinette think, Tia was historically separated from her [...].

From my (black West Indian) point of view, therefore, Wally Look Lai's very 'West Indian' conclusion that:

What is unmistakable, however, and in the final analysis much more important, is [Antoinette's] own readiness, once called upon to do so, to make the crucial leap; her own final realization that personal salvation, if it is to come at all, will come, not from the destructive alien embrace of Thornfield Hall, but only from a return – however difficult – to the spiritual world on the other side of the Wide Sargasso Sea.[28]

is hopeful and optimistic, but totally lacking in recognition of the realities of the situation. Like all of us, he is looking forward to cultural integration. But to posit this through interpretation of a fictional statement that ignores vast areas of social and historical formation, is to run an obstacle race in the dark or blindfolded. White Creoles in the English and French West Indies have separated themselves by too wide a gulf and have contributed too little culturally, as a *group*, to give credence to the notion that they can, given the present structure, meaningfully identify or be identified, with the spiritual world on this side of the Sargasso Sea. ◻

In juxtaposing initial English and Caribbean responses to *Wide Sargasso Sea*, this chapter has traced a path which is marked, broadly speaking, by a shift in critical attention from the sexual to the racial politics of Rhys's text. These issues remain central to much subsequent critical debate on the novel and are addressed, in the next chapter, from an explicitly intertextual perspective. Here critics consider *Wide Sargasso Sea* as a rewriting of Brontë's *Jane Eyre* and examine the problems to which its status as an instance of '*canonical counter-discourse* '[29] has given rise.

CHAPTER TWO

'The Creole is of Course the Important One': Rewriting *Jane Eyre*

■ When I read *Jane Eyre* as a child, I thought, why should [Charlotte Brontë] think Creole women are lunatics and all that? What a shame to make Rochester's first wife, Bertha, the awful madwoman, and I immediately thought I'd write the story as it might really have been. She seemed such a poor ghost. I thought I'd try to write her a life. □

Jean Rhys[1]

Following the burning down of Coulibri, her childhood home, by a riotous crowd of ex-slaves, Antoinette is sent for a period of 'nearly eighteen months' (*WSS*, p. 33) to the Mount Calvary convent school in Spanish Town, Jamaica. One of her earliest experiences at this 'refuge' (*WSS*, p. 31) takes place in a 'hot classroom', where she and other pupils embroider 'silk roses on a pale background' (*WSS*, p. 29) while Mother St Justine reads them 'stories from the lives of the Saints'. The life of the convent's own saint – Innocenzia – remains mysteriously untold, however. The only sign of the past existence of this 'girl of fourteen' is the 'skeleton' buried 'under the altar of the convent chapel'. 'We do not know her story, she is not in the book', Antoinette comments, offsetting Innocenzia's absence from the official hagiographic record with her own private speculations. These turn, in particular, on the dismal logistics of conveying Innocenzia's 'Relics' to their final resting place: 'how did the nuns get them out here [...]?', Antoinette wonders, 'In a cabin trunk? Specially packed for the hold? How?' (*WSS*, p. 30).

Antoinette's attempted reconstruction of Innocenzia's unwritten narrative provides a lightly stated allegory for Rhys's own rewriting of *Jane Eyre*, which transforms the silent and marginalized Other of Brontë's 'reactionary 19th century romance'[2] into a central narrating 'I'. The intertextual relation between *Wide Sargasso Sea* and *Jane Eyre* is a question addressed, to a greater or lesser degree, by almost all critics of Rhys's novel. It is also the burning topic of many of Rhys's letters, which repeatedly express consternation at the distorted colonial visions of Brontë's text, with its '"paper tiger" lunatic [and] all wrong creole scenes'.[3] This chapter provides a cross-section of critical explorations of Rhys's engagement with her Victorian pre-text, as they have developed – and become increasingly theoretical – between the mid-1970s and the late 1980s. It features extracts from the work of four critics – Dennis Porter, Elizabeth R. Baer, Gayatri Chakravorty Spivak and Benita Parry.[4]

Porter's 'Of Heroines and Victims: Jean Rhys and *Jane Eyre*' was first published in the *Massachusetts Review* in 1976, during a decade which witnessed the emergence of Anglo-American feminism as a major new form of literary analysis. The influence of these critical developments is plainly detectable throughout Porter's article, whose beginning sets the tone by defining 'the mad captive of [Brontë's] Thornfield Hall [...] as the most hideous example of the power exercised by men over women'.[5] For Porter, as for Rhys, the madness of this 'subhuman creature' – whom Brontë names Bertha and Rhys renames as Antoinette – is emphatically not the result of a 'degenerate heredity', as is the case in *Jane Eyre*. It is, rather, an effect of patriarchal oppression: 'Bertha', Porter insists, in a still more forthright early formulation, is 'not born mad but made so, and made so, both singly and collectively, by men'.[6] Yet even as he stresses the destructive potential of patriarchy for women, Porter makes it clear that Antoinette's deterioration is equally the consequence of her location in a 'colonial society' which has 'institutionalized slavery' and is 'founded on gradations of skin color and place of birth'.[7] This pathological order of things makes Antoinette, despite her whiteness, 'less than "English"'.[8] *Wide Sargasso Sea*, in Porter's view, privileges neither gender nor race as axes of domination, but is better understood as 'a subtle analysis of the relations between the sexes in the age of colonialism'.[9] By adopting such a position, Porter goes some way towards synthesizing the competing emphases of the English and Caribbean criticism outlined in Chapter One of this Guide.

This rapprochement between opposing critical perspectives is similarly discernible in Porter's analysis of the text's style – an issue which is as much foregrounded by Rhys's English reviewers as it is sidelined by Look Lai, Ramchand and Brathwaite. While the reviewers tend to content themselves simply with identifying and applauding Rhys's style as a late example of a coveted Modernist technique, Porter offers a much more nuanced and historically informed account which draws attention to the heterogeneous and shifting nature of linguistic forms in *Wide Sargasso Sea*. In particular, he underlines the uneasy and deliberate interplay between Rhys's use of standard English, associated mainly with Rochester, and 'the Creole speech of the black population',[10] deployed, especially by Christophine, at critical moments in the text. This juxtapositioning of textual voices is immediately apparent in the novel's abrupt first paragraph: 'They say when trouble comes close ranks, and so the white people did. But we were not in their ranks. The Jamaican ladies had never approved of my mother, "because she pretty like pretty self" Christophine said' (*WSS*, p. 5). As Spivak points out in the extract discussed later in this chapter, Western readers, in her experience, typically disregard the sudden change of register that occurs here and are seemingly unconcerned as to the meaning of Christophine's 'so-called incorrect English'.[11] For Porter, however, it is less the meaning than the very presence of the Creole phrases and exchanges in Rhys's text that is significant. The strange and hybrid verbal forms that repeatedly fracture the novel's conventional surfaces are a stubborn material testimony to the complex patterns of colonial encounter out of which the Caribbean has historically been forged.

Porter's article is divided into three sections, the first two of which provide the basis for the following extract. In the opening section, Porter discusses *Wide Sargasso Sea* in some detail, while the second goes on to consider the 'latent meanings' and 'hidden implications'[12] that the advent of Rhys's novel makes visible within *Jane Eyre*. Porter concludes his article with a brief reflection on the ways in which *Wide Sargasso Sea* itself similarly 'gives fresh significance to [Rhys's] whole *oeuvre*'.[13]

■ Unlike her other novels with a contemporary setting, *Wide Sargasso Sea* derives its leading characters and their situation from another work of art. *Jane Eyre* provides the impulse for an imaginative *tour de force* and at the same time dictates a mode and a style that are new in Jean Rhys's fiction. This time she has written an historical novel with an exotic setting [...]. And the reasons for such a setting and such a mood are clear. In order to comment effectively on *Jane Eyre* and extend its meaning in previously unperceived ways, Jean Rhys had to create a novel that would be largely continuous with Charlotte Brontë's work in terms of style and period and would stand comparison with the original. Thus although *Wide Sargasso Sea* is not a fully autonomous novel because an understanding of its meaning depends on our knowledge of *Jane Eyre*, it achieves its purpose because it is a remarkable work of art in its own right.

To begin with, since in Jean Rhys's striking interpretation the anguish which only ends with the burning of Thornfield has its origins in the realities of colonial society, she had to find a way of suggesting the deep differences and the hidden connections between nineteenth-century England and the Antilles. The Gothic of moor and manor in *Jane Eyre* had to be set off against the lush and stranger horror of the Caribbean islands during the heyday of colonialism. And just as Charlotte Brontë found it appropriate to use the first person in order to heighten the suggestiveness of her work, so Jean Rhys recreates the islands in the consciousness of her two narrators. She invents a prose not for Jane Eyre but for the first Mrs Rochester and Rochester himself, one that would differentiate their voices from each other and from that of Charlotte Brontë's heroine. The nature of the Creole girl and of the husband she will share with the English governess are to be revealed as significantly different from the way they seem in the original work.

As a result, there emerges a subtle analysis of the relations between the sexes in the age of colonialism, of the multiple hidden connections among class, race, and sex. That Jean Rhys succeeds so well is due in the first place to a use of the language that is new for her. Thus, on the one hand, *Wide Sargasso Sea* often employs a lyricism that is resolutely avoided in the novels set between the wars, but it is a functional lyricism that incorporates both beauty and terror and simultaneously defines the limited consciousness of the two narrators. The speech of the girl who will become the first Mrs Rochester is generally swift and elliptical. It is in no way that of a madwoman, but is shaped by the author to suggest the naiveté and the hope, the terrors and the longings that haunt her.

On the other hand, at the same time that Jean Rhys invents a language that expresses the form and content of the consciousness of her two leading characters, she also uses extensively the Creole speech of the black population. Whether or not it is historically accurate insofar as it is a precise transcription of the spoken language of black Jamaicans and others in the nineteenth century, Jean Rhys's Creole convinces of its authenticity both because it possesses the characteristic of all pidgin and Creole language to simplify and eliminate redundancies in the standard language, and because it has the energy and precision of a vehicle that satisfies all the communication needs of its speakers. As used particularly by the black servant, Christophine, and by Antoinette Cosway's self-proclaimed half-brother, Daniel, it establishes itself as an alien and powerful medium when set against the relatively pedestrian standard English of Rochester.

Central to Jean Rhys's vision of the nineteenth-century Antilles is her sense of the ubiquity of suspicion, fear, and hate. A colonial society that had institutionalized slavery means a society deeply divided according to a complicated caste system founded on gradations of skin color and place of birth. Colonialism fosters the myth of irreconcilable differences between groups, objectified, for the writer, in the very speech which is the medium of her art. Jean Rhys gives a specific concrete form to the knowledge that the history of colonialism is written into the varieties and levels of human speech. In the words of a contemporary linguist, the very existence of pidgins and Creoles is 'largely due to the processes – discovery, exploration, trade, conquest, slavery, migration, colonialism, nationalism – that have brought the peoples of Europe and the peoples of the rest of the world to share a common destiny'.[14]

That experience which is mirrored in [the] language of races thrust together but culturally and socially separate within the same limited living space is also present in the earliest perceptions of the little girl whose life will end in Thornfield Hall in faraway England. Her earliest consciousness is of differentness and isolation. As a Creole girl whose mother is from another island, she is despised not only by blacks and the native-born English but also by the Creole ladies of Jamaica. She is a 'white cockroach' [WSS, p. 64] to the former and a 'white nigger' [WSS, p. 10] to the latter. For Antoinette Cosway, in the beginning is a sense of loss and degradation: though white, she is less than 'English'; as the daughter of a former slave-owning planter, she is mocked by the ex-slaves as a poor white; finally, her mother rejects her female off-spring in favor of the half-wit brother.

When Rochester comes into her life, she is an odd blend of know-ledge and innocence, having perceived far more than she can fully apprehend. And Rochester's failure to care enough for the feelings and the fate of his vulnerable child-bride is represented by Jean Rhys as a paradigm of male cruelty towards women. For in her version, it is not Rochester who is the innocent party; it is not he who is deceived and trapped into an alliance with a mad heiress, but she who is sought out by a fortune hunter and his family, sexually exploited for a time, and when once she has grown dependent on his love and his lovemaking, rejected [...].

In *Wide Sargasso Sea*, therefore – and here the facts are taken straight from *Jane Eyre* – Rochester provides an example of how the colonial system operated for the benefit of England's established families. As the younger son of a father determined to preserve the integrity of his wealth and property by bequeathing it all to his first male child, Rochester is required to seek his own fortune by marrying the daughter of a wealthy plantation-owner from the West Indies. Marriage to Antoinette Cosway is looked upon as a business arrange-ment by means of which caste and class are traded off against a sub-stantial sum of cash. The fortune of the plantation-owner's daughter is exported to the homeland after having first been 'washed' through marriage into an appropriate family. Rochester's affluence will in part be founded on slavery.

If the fate of the first Mrs Rochester is bound up with her colonial origins, as is barely hinted in *Jane Eyre*, it is also determined by the character of male sexuality and the cultural modes through which such sexuality finds expression. Rochester, of course, has been taken to be the most conventional figure in Charlotte Brontë's novel, an embodiment of the darkly brooding Byronic hero stricken with romantic melancholy, on the one hand, and as a wish-fulfillment figure, a dominant highly sexualized male, on the other. By the very fact that she adopts his point of view, Jean Rhys to some extent demythifies the figure; to see the West Indies through his eyes is to see what a relatively conventional and class-conscious nineteenth-century English gentleman might well have perceived. But Jean Rhys is not simply reductive. The journey to the Antilles to procure a rich wife is also in her handling a journey to Rochester's own heart of darkness – a journey for which even in *Jane Eyre* he will eventually be called to account.

The two themes of colonialism and male sexuality come together most strikingly during the meeting between Rochester and the demonic Daniel Cosway. The latter's letter is by itself a brilliant piece of writing that suggests the profound deviousness and complex self-hate of the social outcast which turns him into an informer and a destroyer of other people's happiness. It is, in any case, Daniel's function to play Iago to Rochester's swaggering Othello, only on this occasion, in terms of color, the roles are reversed. It is Daniel who confirms the white male's buried fears in relation to his colonial bride. Thus, the concluding remarks of Rochester's embittered interlocutor reverberate in a mind that is suspicious both of his wife's blood and of her physical attractiveness: "'Give my love to your wife – my sister," he called after me venomously. "You are not the first to kiss her pretty face. Pretty face, soft skin, pretty colour – not yellow like me. But my sister just the same ..."' [*WSS*, p. 80].

Daniel's claims mean that for Rochester his wife is doubly contaminated. In the first place, she is henceforth associated with the yellow-skinned Daniel; she is derived at the very least from a perverted source, from a lecherous, alcoholic father who had sexual relations with black women. In the second place, he is haunted with the idea that she was not pure but sexually experienced before he married her. The play on the word 'pretty' suggests the psychic mechanism through which he will now reject her. Hers is a prettiness made squalid by his own obsessions, that face which had made her attractive to him is now her ugliest feature; since it arouses desire, it becomes the face of desire. To look at her is to be reminded of her double impurity. Therefore, since he cannot be rid of her, she will be shunned, broken and finally shut away.

Although the relationship of *Jane Eyre* to *Wide Sargasso Sea* is not entirely reciprocal – the one is fully autonomous, the other is not – there is reciprocity to the degree that Jean Rhys's novel constitutes a formidable critical essay on the nineteenth-century work. The modern author alerts us to latent meanings in the original that remind us of its singular power. *Wide Sargasso Sea* may develop hints from her own work in ways that would have surprised Charlotte Brontë, but it is the genius of the nineteenth-century novelist to have created a symbolic structure that accommodates itself easily to the insights of the twentieth-century writer. Now that the shibboleths of nineteenth-century realism have been discarded and the rather narrow modernist view of 'the art of the novel' significantly modified, it is impossible to dismiss *Jane Eyre* patronizingly as a form of Gothic sport or as the wish-fulfillment of frustrated sexuality. *Wide Sargasso Sea* pays homage to what modern French critics refer to as 'the plurality' of substantial literary texts by bringing to consciousness some of the hidden implications of *Jane Eyre*, which it both develops and challenges.

To begin with, the secret that is for so long hidden away at Thornfield is finally revealed to Jane, but its meaning is not interpreted. From Jean Rhys's point of view, Jane Eyre's own question concerning the mystery receives no satisfactory answer in Charlotte Brontë's novel: 'What crime was this, that lived incarnate in this sequestered mansion, and could neither be expelled nor subdued by the owner? – What mystery, that broke out, now in fire and now in blood, at the deadest hours of night? – What creature was it, that, masked in an ordinary woman's face and shape, uttered the voice, now of a mocking demon, and anon of a carrion-seeking bird of prey?' [*JE*, p. 221]. Jean Rhys's answer [...] is that the 'creature' was once an ordinary woman, who had the misfortune to be raised in Jamaica in the 1830s and 1840s, a white planter's white daughter, who discovered she did not belong where she was born and had no place else to go, a woman put up for sale by one man and purchased for his own purposes by another.

In the light of *Wide Sargasso Sea*, the mad Bertha Rochester of *Jane Eyre* can be seen as a living image of Rochester's shame and guilt that he can neither destroy nor forget, though he has the power to lock it away out of sight of the world. As a member of the colonial *nouveaux riches*, she is felt to be inferior to England's fine old families; as a daughter of a former slave-owning plantation-owner, she is a living reminder of the sordid origins of his affluence; as an exotic and beautiful woman raised on a tropical island, she is associated with a sensuality that both tempts and torments Rochester; as a Creole, the racial purity of her blood will always remain suspect in Rochester's eyes. No wonder Thornfield (Thorn-field, Thorn-filled) appears so malevolent; its grandeur disguises greed and concupiscence and pride. The purifying fire that destroys it and the incarnation of Rochester's guilt is in *Jane Eyre* a necessary prelude to the harmonious relationship achieved at the end. Rochester has to be punished and Jane herself put to a further test before their successful union is possible. It is a remarkable tribute to the force of Charlotte Brontë's insights that in spite of her professed Toryism she intimates how the manor house is a monument raised on the foundation of human exploitation. For the sake of his soul Rochester has to give up his baronial dwelling, the symbol of a power rooted in sex and class arrogance. The difference between Charlotte Brontë and Jean Rhys as far as Rochester is concerned is, first, that the latter explicitly adds race, where the former perceives sex and class, and second, that the modern author sees him as unredeemable, whereas her nineteenth-century predecessor demonstrates how he might be reformed. The harsh pessimism of Jean Rhys concerning relations between the sexes confronts a relative optimism in the Victorian author that is founded on faith in moral energy and the regenerative power of human feelings. Charlotte Brontë's mythic tale embodies the tragedy of an overreacher, a Byronic rebel, who like Faust himself is saved through the power of a woman's love. The robust originality of the English novelist's work, however, resides in the fact that her heroine is far more complex than Goethe's loving and passively suffering Gretchen, and if she avoids the fate of Jean Rhys's women, it is because in her own patiently determined way she learns how to resist and survive. It is paradoxically the Victorian author who furnishes the model of a woman who triumphs in a male-dominated society, triumphs, moreover, in ways that are not attributable to authorial wish-fulfillment, but to a series of concrete choices that the heroine makes on the basis of her sense of what is right for herself.

Above all, the secret of Jane Eyre's triumph resides in her instinctive understanding of the fact that, especially when coupled with a sense of class superiority, male sexuality is a potentially destructive force. She is both drawn to and frightened by the energy of the wild rider who falls from his horse in an opening encounter that prefigures the end. But until what is merely a temporary physical disability in the beginning becomes a permanent condition of the whole man at the denouement, she never fully gives herself to Rochester. For a long time her apparent submissiveness as social inferior and as a woman disguises a determination not to submit to his will to possess and dominate. The sexual teasing to which she subjects him during the period of their first engagement is not simply a matter of Victorian hypocrisy. She does not shelter behind the exigencies of nineteenth-century morality merely to excite the more. The game she plays is vital, since it enables her to retain control over a potentially dangerous situation; it is dictated by an instinct for self-preservation. And the same thing is true of her decision not to become Rochester's mistress. To have yielded to him in that way would have been to give herself completely into his power. As the fate of Jean Rhys's Antoinette Cosway suggests, under such circumstances Rochester could not be trusted not to break what he so completely possessed.

It is not finally until Thornfield has been destroyed and Rochester has been obliged to put away the aggressive accoutrements of his sex and class – the horse and those weapons, spurs, boots and crop, by means of which one mounts and dominates it – that Jane Eyre finally consents to be his bride. Consequently, the blindness and maiming that Rochester experiences as a consequence of the burning of Thornfield are not simply a matter of his punishment for past sins – whether those committed in connection with Bertha, as Jean Rhys would have it, or, in the more conventional view, because of his decision to commit bigamy. Rochester has to be spiritually humbled and physically impaired before a marriage between him and Jane Eyre on the basis of equality is possible.

The form the punishment takes is itself significant because it suggests that in Charlotte Brontë's work, too, the cause of the suffering in the past and its avoidance in the future are related to the character of Rochester's sexuality. The fire in the blood which drew him to his Creole wife and later to his foreign mistresses [...] has to be controlled without being extinguished. Yet the idea of an asexual, passionless marriage that St John Rivers proposes is felt by Jane Eyre to be as sad as the merely sexual unions that characterize Rochester's past. The implication is that love without sexual consummation is as destructive of human happiness as the sexual drive that seeks to dominate and humiliate and finds its ultimate expression in a rape. Sex, as both Charlotte Brontë and Jean Rhys remind us, *can be* dehumanizing and demonic. Consequently, Rochester loses the sight of those eyes which saw and in seeing, desired, and one of the two hands that caressed and overpowered. From henceforth the only beauty he will experience is that which can be felt and heard; he will know only the warmth of a physical presence and the sweetness of a disembodied voice. Rochester's is such an extreme case that it requires the radical surgery of blindness before he can see fully through Jane's outward plainness in order to appreciate an inner beauty that is nevertheless of the body.

Whether or not we approve of all the implications of Rochester's impaired potency, Jane Eyre is no simple 'castrating female'. She is prepared to have Rochester only on terms of equality. Only a marriage founded on mutual respect and mutual need could hope to prove happy and durable. Before he could become a husband and a father – see in this respect his previous treatment of Adèle – Rochester had first to suffer and to be taught how to love. In her novel of the orphan/governess turned wife, therefore, Charlotte Brontë creates one of the great portraits of women in literature, next to whom Jean Rhys's characters appear as almost willing victims. In Jane Eyre's extraordinary instinct for survival and self-affirmation, a balance is struck between spirited independence and loving solicitude, tough-mindedness and generosity. She has the strength of character to resist the powers of men in a society dominated by men and to choose the right man at the right time on terms that fulfill her own deepest needs.

It may be, as *Wide Sargasso Sea* provocatively implies, that Jane Eyre's ultimate happiness is founded on the suffering of another woman, that Bertha Rochester's madness and horrible death were necessary in order to chasten Rochester's male arrogance. There is certainly something uncharacteristic about the way in which Jane Eyre leaves her husband's version of his first wife's past unexamined. It may even be that she herself unconsciously harbors a combination of nineteenth-century parochialism and racism that made it normal for her to associate colonial living with the idea of degeneracy and madness. Nevertheless, the man she marries is profoundly different from the one whom Jean Rhys regards as the tormentor of Bertha.

Whether Jean Rhys fully intended it or not, the contrast between the two women characters is, in any case, highly instructive. Although Jane Eyre begins as apparently the more disadvantaged, she has a resourcefulness and a positive sense of self that are altogether lacking in Antoinette Cosway. It is perhaps providential that she is without face or fortune and, as a consequence, is the object of neither male cupidity nor, for a long time, of desire. But there is far more than providence involved. From the memorable opening chapter of Charlotte Brontë's novel, Jane Eyre is revealed as someone who knows she must fight back to survive. At the same time, although the English girl may be an unloved orphan, she has the rich cultural resources of the Victorian middle-class available to her – in that same opening chapter, in resisting her tyrannical boy cousin she can call upon [Oliver] Goldsmith's *History of Rome* [1769] for support. The Creole girl, on the other hand, grows up in a milieu without books and finds support in a traditional value system only briefly during the years of her convent education. Elsewhere she encounters the bitter cultural conflicts and moral ambiguities of colonial life.

There is thus a singular appropriateness in Jane Eyre's situation as *govern-ess*, since the very word implies the way in which she finally forces respect for her situation and her sex. The enlightened self-discipline of her conduct invests the word's root with an unexpected significance, and the suffix itself is suggestive of a proud acceptance of her womanhood. Unlike the heiress, whose status derives from another and is therefore alienable, the penniless orphan is self-possessed as well as self-made; since she owes nothing to anyone, she is owned by no one. Her triumph is perhaps all the more remarkable, but it is grounded in Charlotte Brontë's firm sense of the complex interrelatedness of socio-economic and psychic realities. Jane Eyre is not, as has sometimes been suggested, the heroine of a fairy tale. Hers may be the triumph of a plain, middle-class woman over the obstacles of wealth and class and beauty, as well as over the antithetical demons of aggressive male sexuality (Rochester) and inhuman religious fervor (St John Rivers), but it is a triumph that is fully motivated in psychological and socio-economic terms. If Jane Eyre negotiates a course that leads to self-fulfillment in the face of great odds, it is because she is first made independent by circumstances – a poor orphan is socially and economically as well as psychologically a completely autonomous individual – and learns the difficult art of maintaining will, intelligence, and feelings in delicate equilibrium. Unlike Antoinette Cosway, Jane Eyre knows how to govern as well as to give and which, under changing circumstances, is the humanly appropriate choice. □

The second extract in this chapter comes from Baer's 'The Sisterhood of Jane Eyre and Antoinette Cosway'. This was originally published in *The Voyage In: Fictions of Female Development* (1983), an innovative collection of feminist essays on the nineteenth- and twentieth-century female *bildungsroman* (or 'novel of growth'), edited by Elizabeth Abel, Marianne Hirsch and Elizabeth Langland. Baer's feminism is more refined than Porter's, informed, as it is, by theoretical insights on the problems and possibilities of women's writing derived from a galaxy of influential American co-feminists: Sandra M. Gilbert and Susan Gubar, Nancy K. Miller, Adrienne Rich and Judith Fetterley. Her main argument is that the respective heroines of *Wide Sargasso Sea* and *Jane Eyre* are not rivals or antagonists but 'doubles' and 'sisters'[15] to one another. The racial difference that might have divided Antoinette and Jane historically is, for Baer at least, ultimately less important than their struggle against the patriarchal order which oppresses them both.

Baer supports these claims by spending a good deal of time, in the early part of her essay, charting the multiple parallels between Rhys's text and Brontë's, eventually focusing on the two sets of dreams experienced by Antoinette and Jane as her central interpretative framework. Antoinette's three dreams form a sequence 'roughly equivalent to the traditional three stages of the quest and the three parts of the novel itself: separation, descent/initiation [and] return'.[16] Their greater significance lies, however, in the ways in which they debunk and demystify the stories of fairy-tale romance with which patriarchy invites – or incites – its female subjects to identify. As Baer notes, what happens to Antoinette in *Wide Sargasso Sea* is an inversion of the suasive pattern of the traditional fairy tale. Rochester, the 'stranger from an exotic land', is no Prince Charming: he 'does not rescue [Antoinette] but imprisons her; does not bring her back to life but kills her; is not kind and noble but self-serving'.[17] This is what Baer calls the novel's 'surface text'. Antoinette's dreams themselves compose its 'submerged text',[18] prefiguring, with increasing clarity, the finally lethal threat to female autonomy housed beneath the patriarchal conventions of the romantic plot into which she is inveigled. The five dreams recounted by the heroine of *Jane Eyre* are equally premonitory. They are warnings to Jane of the dangers and duplicities of being seduced by 'a sugary romance that ends "happily ever after"'.[19] This is one of the senses in which Antoinette and Jane can be seen as 'sisters'. The two figures are further allied in terms of Antoinette's actions, which include, for example, the tearing in half of Jane's wedding veil, two nights before her marriage to Rochester is due to take place (*JE*, p. 297). Rather than competing against one another for Rochester's love, Antoinette and Jane are, in Baer's analysis, more profoundly connected – like Rhys and Brontë indeed – by strategies of patriarchal subversion and resistance.

The extract which follows examines Antoinette's three dreams in detail, making an interesting and original contribution to the critical debate on Rhys's intertextual dialogue with Brontë.

■ Looking [...] at the dreams in *Wide Sargasso Sea*, we see that each of Antoinette's three dreams is triggered by an event that brings her closer to her imprisonment, and ultimate death, in Thornfield tower. The first dream occurs when she is still a young girl at Coulibri. Visitors, unusual at Coulibri, have stopped by to introduce themselves to Antoinette's mother. These new neighbors will be the vehicle of her remarriage to Mr Mason, whose son Richard is responsible for arranging Antoinette's and Rochester's marriage. Antoinette recalls the dream:

> I went to bed early and slept at once. I dreamed that I was walking in the forest. Not alone. Someone who hated me was with me, out of sight. I could hear heavy footsteps coming closer and though I struggled and screamed I could not move. I woke crying ... . I woke next morning knowing that nothing would be the same. It would change and go on changing. [*WSS*, pp. 11–12]

This is a dream of menace, of foreboding. Antoinette finds herself in a forest, the scene of evil and vulnerability in many fairy tales. She senses a dreaded presence but is powerless to control or escape the approach of that presence. She and Rochester have begun their doomed and ineluctable journey toward each other.

If, however, we accept Nancy K. Miller's suggestion that 'the heroine's destiny ... is a form of insistence about the relation of women to writing',[20] then this dream and the two that succeed it are less a formula about Antoinette's life than they are her [...] realization that the first stage of her development, the 'separation', is about to occur. She relinquishes the comfortable security of childhood. She acknowledges that the plots will 'change and go on changing'. Her story will not end 'happily ever after'.

The second dream/chapter in Antoinette's life/novel occurs during her stay at the Mt. Calvary convent; again the dream is triggered by strangers. Her stepfather has visited her and announced his intention to withdraw her from the convent and introduce her to some 'English friends' [WSS, p. 33]. He refers, of course, to Rochester. Although Antoinette cannot consciously or rationally know what her fate will be as a result of this meeting, she has a strong sense of foreboding. In this second dream, Antoinette again leaves Coulibri in the night and walks toward the forest. This time she can see the face of the man, a face 'black with hatred'. The man is leading her and she acknowledges a sense of helplessness: 'I follow him, sick with fear but I make no effort to save myself; if anyone were to try to save me, I would refuse. This must happen.' Antoinette wears a white dress, symbolic of her vulnerability, her virginity, her wedding. They reach the forest; Antoinette does not know where she is being taken. 'Here?' she asks. Suddenly the forest turns into an enclosed garden: West Indian landscape becomes Thornfield. Then Antoinette is brought to a set of steps leading upward:

> It is too dark to see the wall or the steps, but I know they are there and I think, 'It will be when I go up these steps. At the top.' I stumble over my dress and cannot get up. I touch a tree and my arms hold on to it. 'Here, here.' But I think I will not go any further. The tree sways and jerks as if it is trying to throw me off. Still I cling and the seconds pass and each one is a thousand years. 'Here, in here,' a strange voice said, and the tree stopped swaying and jerking. [WSS, p. 34]

The 'tree' of course is Rochester as he carries Antoinette up the stairs to the third floor of Thornfield. Here, as throughout her novel, Rhys subtly mirrors the imagery of Brontë: both Brocklehurst and Rochester are described by Jane in phallic terms, as pillars and trees. This dream, far more concrete and threatening than the first, warns of the quickening approach of Rochester. It (p)revises the fairy-tale marriage and honeymoon of Antoinette and Rochester, revealing the bride's sexual initiation to be a loss of power and control. The sudden transformation, a commonplace in fairy tales, turns the natural forest into a cultivated garden: her marriage is a trap, an imprisonment. Ultimately, it is a descent into madness. Antoinette awakens and tells the nun in the dormitory 'I dreamed I was in Hell.' The nun advises her: 'That dream is evil. Put it from your mind' [*WSS*, p. 34]. But Antoinette will dream yet another dream, an evil dream, evil because the fairy-tale innocence of the surface text must be re-vised.

That incident closes Part One of *Wide Sargasso Sea*. Part Two is narrated by Rochester (except for a short hiatus by Antoinette). [...] Because Part Two of the novel is narrated by Rochester, we get no account of Antoinette's dreams in this section. Just as Rochester, in *Jane Eyre*, tries to 'own' Jane after their engagement by coy comments and elaborate gifts, so Rochester here signals his possession of Antoinette by appropriating her voice [...] and this section of the novel records Antoinette's 'death' before her rebirth in Part Three. During Part Two, Antoinette herself says to Rochester, 'There are always two deaths, the real one and the one people know about' [*WSS*, p. 81].

On their first evening at Granbois, Antoinette and Rochester have a tragically sad conversation:

'Is it true,' she said, 'that England is like a dream? Because one of my friends who married an Englishman wrote and told me so. She said this place London is like a cold dark dream sometimes. I want to wake up.'
'Well,' I answered annoyed, 'that is precisely how your beautiful island seems to me, quite unreal and like a dream.' [*WSS*, p. 49]

Aside from the obvious connection of Antoinette's query with her own dreams (in which England figures as something from which she wants to wake up), this exchange between husband and wife reveals each one's inability to accept the reality of the other's world. Rochester admits this. 'I did not love her. I was thirsty for her, but that is not love. I felt very little tenderness for her, she was a stranger to me, a stranger who did not think or feel as I did' [*WSS*, p. 58].

Shortly after their arrival at the honeymoon house, one afternoon Rochester follows a path into the forest. 'It is hostile' [*WSS*, p. 65], he muses, reiterating his usual failure to be at ease in nature. What he finds in the forest reverberates strangely with Antoinette's dream sequence. He stumbles first upon what was once a paved road, then upon the ruins of a stone house, and finally upon trees with bunches of flowers surrounding them. Remembering Antoinette's despair at the crumbling road [*WSS*, p. 5] and the burning of Coulibri, the reader wonders if Rochester has passed into a time warp; this sense is intensified when, as darkness comes on, he sees a little girl: 'I met her eye and to my astonishment she screamed loudly, threw up her arms and ran' [*WSS*, p. 65]. Rochester has somehow blundered into Antoinette's first dream: here is Antoinette as a young girl, encountering the stranger in the forest. Surface text and subtext merge briefly here. When Rochester returns home, he pulls out a book on obeah that offers the following explanation:

> 'A zombi is a dead person who seems to be alive or a living person who is dead. A zombi can also be the spirit of a place, usually malignant but sometimes to be propitiated with sacrifices or offerings of flowers and fruit.' [WSS, p. 67]

The little girl in the forest, then, is a zombi; Antoinette, having lost her parents, her money, her identity, her autonomy, is in a sense dead already.

The name of the honeymoon house, Granbois, links it with the great woods of Antoinette's dreams. Rochester's narration tells of growing alienation between the newly married couple. Rochester, the menacing figure of the dream, refuses to call his wife by her given name and instead provides her with a stout English name, Bertha. Antoinette later recalls, 'Names matter, like when he wouldn't call me Antoinette, and I saw Antoinette drifting out of the window with her scents, her pretty clothes and her looking-glass' [WSS, p. 117]. Antoinette's identity, her sense of herself, slips further and further from her grasp. She experiences a growing division – Antoinette/ Bertha, dead/alive – which Rhys deftly mirrors in the two texts. Bertha emerges in the surface text; Antoinette keeps her identity alive only in her dreams.

Antoinette makes one final desperate effort to heal the split of herself and her marriage: she obtains an aphrodisiac from Christophine. In an inversion of many fairy-tale plots, Antoinette administers the magic potion instead of taking it herself. The magic does not work. The following morning, Rochester awakens, a feeling of cold his strongest sensation: he is calm, rational, emotionless. He goes to the bedside of the sleeping Antoinette. Instead of awakening her with a kiss, as the prince is supposed to do, '[he draws] the sheet over her gently *as if [he] covered a dead girl*' [WSS, p. 88; emphasis added]. Destructive rather than chivalrous, Rochester does the reverse of what men do in fairy tales. Part Two is a narrative of foreboding. It is important to note that this is *Rochester's* narrative. He is the instrument of descent/ initiation, of death. His forebodings become a self-fulfilling prophecy. Antoinette, as we have seen, 'dies'. But the very fact that she narrates Part Three, that she again revives her voice, is an act of assertion, a rebirth, a return.

Antoinette's first words to us as the 'madwoman in the attic' concern awakening to the chill of early morning. She waits for Grace Poole to light the fire in the fireplace: 'In the end flames shoot up and they are beautiful' [*WSS*, p. 116]. Antoinette associates warmth and fire with the West Indies, with passion, with freedom, with the past. The final conflagration becomes then an assertion of her colonial identity and of release. She has been given a grey wrapper to wear in the attic but much prefers a red dress brought with her from the West Indies. She describes the dress as 'the colour of fire and sunset. The colour of flamboyant flowers'; it 'has a meaning'. 'The scent that came from the dress was very faint at first, then it grew stronger. The smell of vetivert and frangipani, of cinnamon and dust and lime trees when they are flowering. The smell of the sun and the smell of the rain' [*WSS*, p. 120]. Like warmth and fire, the dress represents her home, her past, her identity; now Antoinette seeks to recover these. When the dress fuses with the fire in her mind, Antoinette determines what she will do:

> But I looked at the dress on the floor and it was as if the fire had spread across the room. It was beautiful and it reminded me of something I must do. I will remember I thought. I will remember quite soon now. [*WSS*, pp. 121–2]

This passage is followed immediately by the third and final installment of Antoinette's recurring and prophetic dream, in which she fantasizes/foresees the end. The dream begins in the tower in which Antoinette had implicitly been confined at the end of her last dream, the tower in which she is actually imprisoned now. Her first act in this dream is to take candle and keys from the snoring Grace Poole, and let herself out of the tower: a dream of escape, of liberation. 'I walked as though I were flying.' In the ensuing [...] dream, Antoinette frequently describes the sensation of floating or flying. She becomes a bird, a reincarnation of Coco, the parrot of her childhood. As she proceeds along the corridors of Thornfield, Antoinette never looks behind her for, as she explains, '[she does] not want to see that ghost of a woman who they say haunts this place' [*WSS*, p. 122]. The 'ghost' is, of course, herself. She enters a large room decorated in red and white, suggesting the clash between herself and Rochester. Here she starts the fire. She returns to the hall. 'It was then that I saw her – the ghost. The woman with streaming hair. She was surrounded by a gilt frame but I knew her.' In a sense, then, Antoinette has exchanged places with her alter ego: she has re-entered her real self. Earlier in the novel, she saw the real Antoinette drift out of a window and she became Bertha, the identity Rochester imposed upon her. Now, she sees the ghost ('who they say haunts this place') in a mirror; by exteriorizing the image imposed on her, she reclaims herself.

Immediately following this vision, Antoinette (still in the dream) climbs to the third story and out onto the battlements. 'Then I turned round and saw the sky. It was red and all my life was in it' [WSS, p. 123]. Again, red is connected with her past, her real self. She goes on to recount the conclusion of the dream:

> I heard the parrot call as he did when he saw a stranger, *Qui est là? Qui est là?* and the man who hated me was calling too, Bertha! Bertha! The wind caught my hair and it streamed out like wings. It might bear me up, I thought, if I jumped to those hard stones. But when I looked over the edge I saw the pool at Coulibri. Tia was there. She beckoned to me and when I hesitated, she laughed. I heard her say, You frightened? And I heard the man's voice, Bertha! Bertha! All this I saw and heard in a fraction of a second. And the sky so red. Someone screamed and I thought, *Why did I scream?* I called 'Tia!' and jumped and woke. [WSS, pp. 123–4]

In this final passage, then, Antoinette becomes the parrot who jumped with clipped wings on fire to its death at Coulibri. Antoinette, too, jumps to her death. Just as the parrot saved Antoinette's family, Antoinette's jump saves Jane. Her presence in the tower has served as a warning to Jane to leave Rochester; now, in Jane's absence, she destroys the tools given Rochester by the patriarchy, the tools of authority and power. Although Jane and Antoinette are both orphans, their 'sisterhood' becomes the means of survival.

Also in this passage, Antoinette sees Tia, her childhood friend, once again, and her name is the last word she speaks. Here, Antoinette enacts the rebellion of the oppressed; setting Rochester's house afire, she follows the model of the rebellious servants of her childhood. Antoinette's death is an act of self-destruction. But it is also clearly an act of assertion, of reconnection with the warmth, red, beauty, and passion of her West Indian identity. Her third dream is the dream of return. And it is a dream of escape. For finally, Antoinette refuses to live out her life, confined to a tower, labeled insane. She will not be Bertha. [...]

In an essay entitled 'Jane Eyre: The Temptations of a Motherless Woman', Adrienne Rich describes Jane as resisting four temptations on her quest: first, that of victimization and hysteria at Gateshead; next, that of self-hatred and self-immolation at Lowood; third, that of romantic love and surrender at Thornfield; and, finally, that of passive suicide at Marsh End.[21] Just as Rich sees Jane resisting temptation, so Rhys's novel encourages us to see Brontë, Antoinette, and all women dreamers/writers as resisting temptation, the temptation of writing a sugary romance that ends 'happily ever after'. Rhys depicts Antoinette in the very throes of this struggle as she muses about England on the

day she obtains the love potion from Christophine. She daydreams/
writes the conclusion of her life/story:

> After summer the trees are bare, then winter and snow. White
> feathers falling? Torn pieces of paper falling? They say frost makes
> flower patterns on the window panes. I must know more than I
> know already. For I know that house where I will be cold and not
> belonging, the bed I shall lie in has red curtains and I have slept
> there many times before, long ago. How long ago? In that bed I
> will dream the end of my dream. But my dream had nothing to do
> with England and I must not think like this, I must remember
> about chandeliers and dancing, about swans and roses and snow.
> And snow. [*WSS*, p.70]

Antoinette juxtaposes here two versions of England: the fairy-tale
version of 'swans and roses', which is the version she has been taught
as a colonial child, and the version of her dreams, the England of cold
and confinement.

We see Antoinette, in this passage, with both her vision and
revision of England, the two texts of *Wide Sargasso Sea*. These two texts
merge at the conclusion of the novel when Antoinette herself finally
rejects the fairy-tale text and heeds the dream text. It is at that moment
that she, like Jane, recovers her childhood, her identity. The dream,
not the fairy tale, becomes the instrument of her awakening, her assertion, her autonomy.

Wide Sargasso Sea is a 're-vision', then, in several senses. It encourages us to be 'resisting readers'[22] toward *Jane Eyre* by warning us of the
dangers of misreading it as a romance with marriage as the solution.
The point of *Jane Eyre*, according to Rhys, is that Jane's transformation
is not magical, temporary, and external, as was Cinderella's, but internal and thorough. And that she gains equality with Rochester not by
having the correct shoe size but by heeding the warning of Bertha and
refusing marriage until it is based on equality. *Wide Sargasso Sea* also
revises our perceptions of Antoinette/Bertha. She and Jane are not
polar opposites, nor a handy dichotomy, but sisters, doubles, orphans
in the patriarchy. Each woman, in her own way, resists temptations,
rejects 'swans and roses', and wrests her identity from the patriarchal
hypocrisy of 'happily ever after'.

Though it is certainly elegant and illuminating, Baer's analysis of the
relation between Antoinette and Jane in terms of sisterhood is not
without its problems. Not the least of these is the way in which, in order
to maintain the coherence of her argument, Baer must in effect elide the
colonial realities in which both fictional heroines are implicated,

whether directly, in Antoinette's case, or indirectly, in Jane's. In this respect, her reading represents something of a retreat from Porter's, with its more flexible and encompassing recognition of 'the multiple hidden connections among class, race, and sex'. It is also a perfect example of what Penny Boumelha calls the 'narrowly [...] race-blind interpretations'[23] often produced by feminist critics in the 1970s and early 1980s. Such interpretations have themselves prompted a number of critics to become 'resisting readers', to recall the phrase Baer takes from Fetterley, particularly those working under the aegis of postcolonial theory, which had already begun to establish itself at the time when Baer was writing. One of the most eminent of these critics is Spivak who, along with Edward W. Said and Homi K. Bhabha, forms part of postcolonialism's so-called 'Holy Trinity'.[24] Spivak examines the politics of feminist interpretation in 'Three Women's Texts and a Critique of Imperialism', using *Jane Eyre* and *Wide Sargasso Sea* (as well as Mary Shelley's *Frankenstein* [1817]) as her main points of reference. This theoretically dense and searching article was originally published in *Critical Inquiry* in 1985 and has been subsequently much anthologized.

Spivak's position on *Jane Eyre* is close to Rhys's own, showing how Brontë's novel encourages – or perhaps coerces – readers to identify with its heroine by representing her colonial counterpart in purely negative terms: English is to white Creole, Jane to Antoinette, the text implies, as human is to bestial/monstrous. For Spivak, as indeed for other post-colonial critics, it is this kind of hierarchical opposition that indicates the violent complicity between 'nineteenth-century British literature' and 'the imperialist project'. Yet it is not only *Jane Eyre* itself which thus blithely 'reproduces the axioms of imperialism'.[25] Such a process is also troublingly evident in the work of Brontë's Anglo-American feminist critics. To illustrate this latter point, Spivak turns not to Baer herself but to Gilbert and Gubar's reading of *Jane Eyre* in *The Madwoman in the Attic: The Woman Writer and the Nineteenth-Century Literary Imagination* (1979). By seeing Antoinette 'only in psychological terms, as Jane's dark double',[26] Spivak argues, these highly influential critics repeat the very denial of Antoinette's status as an autonomous subject performed by *Jane Eyre* itself.

It is the recovery of just such autonomy which is, of course, the driving concern of *Wide Sargasso Sea*. This is made clear, for example, in Rhys's letter to Selma Vaz Dias of 9 April 1958:

■ I've read and re-read 'Jane Eyre' [...] and I am sure that the character [of Antoinette] must be 'built up'. [...] The Creole in Charlotte Brontë's novel is a lay figure – repulsive which does not matter, and not once alive which does. She's necessary to the plot, but always she shrieks, howls, laughs horribly, attacks all and sundry – *off stage*. For me [...] she must be right *on stage*.[27] □

As Spivak suggests, however, Rhys's revision of Brontë generates its own problematic politics. On the one hand, the emergence of Antoinette 'right *on stage*' is designed to free her not only from *Jane Eyre*'s third-storey attic, but also from the space of the nineteenth-century colonial discourse in which she is incarcerated as 'awful madwoman'. Yet on the other hand, even as it carries out this act of intertextual liberation, *Wide Sargasso Sea* remains caught within its own discursive limits. These are most clearly revealed, for Spivak, in the novel's representation of Christophine, figured as 'good servant'.[28] In resorting to such a stereotype, *Wide Sargasso Sea* shows itself to be ironically 'bound by the reach of the European novel'[29] that it sets out to contest, even as it simultaneously appears to recognize its own predicament. As Christophine removes herself from the novel, towards the end of Part Two, she offers a precise allegory for the discursive exclusion or foreclosure of the black female subject performed by the text as a whole. It is in these broad and complex terms that Spivak approaches *Wide Sargasso Sea* in the middle section of her article.

■ When Jean Rhys, born on the Caribbean island of Dominica, read *Jane Eyre* as a child, she was moved by Bertha Mason: 'I thought I'd try to write her a life.' *Wide Sargasso Sea*, the slim novel published in 1966, at the end of Rhys' long career, is that 'life'.

I have suggested that Bertha's function in *Jane Eyre* is to render indeterminate the boundary between human and animal and thereby to weaken her entitlement under the spirit if not the letter of the Law. When Rhys rewrites the scene in *Jane Eyre* where Jane hears 'a snarling, snatching sound, almost like a dog quarrelling' [*JE*, p. 219] and then encounters a bleeding Richard Mason, she keeps Bertha's humanity, indeed her sanity as critic of imperialism, intact. Grace Poole, another character originally in *Jane Eyre*, describes the incident to Bertha in *Wide Sargasso Sea*: 'So you don't remember that you attacked this gentleman with a knife? ... I didn't hear all he said except "I cannot interfere legally between yourself and your husband." It was when he said "legally" that you flew at him' [*WSS*, pp. 119–20]. In Rhys' retelling, it is the dissimulation that Bertha discerns in the word 'legally' – not an innate bestiality – that prompts her violent reaction.

In the figure of Antoinette, whom in *Wide Sargasso Sea* Rochester violently renames Bertha, Rhys suggests that so intimate a thing as personal and human identity might be determined by the politics of imperialism. Antoinette, as a white Creole child growing up at the time of emancipation in Jamaica, is caught between the English imperialist and the black native. In recounting Antoinette's development, Rhys reinscribes some thematics of Narcissus.

There are, noticeably, many images of mirroring in the text. I will quote one from the first section. In this passage, Tia is the little black servant girl who is Antoinette's close companion: 'We had eaten the same food, slept side by side, bathed in the same river. As I ran, I thought, I will live with Tia and I will be like her ... . When I was close I saw the jagged stone in her hand but I did not see her throw it ... . We stared at each other, blood on my face, tears on hers. It was as if I saw myself. Like in a looking-glass' [WSS, p. 24].

A progressive sequence of dreams reinforces this mirror imagery. In its second occurrence, the dream is partially set in a *hortus conclusus* or 'enclosed garden' – Rhys uses the phrase – a Romance rewriting of the Narcissus topos as the place of encounter with Love. In the enclosed garden, Antoinette encounters not Love but a strange threatening voice that says merely 'in here', inviting her into a prison which masquerades as the legalization of love [WSS, p. 34].

In Ovid's *Metamorphoses*, Narcissus' madness is disclosed when he recognizes his Other as his self [...]. Rhys makes Antoinette see her *self* as her Other, Brontë's Bertha. In the last section of *Wide Sargasso Sea*, Antoinette acts out *Jane Eyre*'s conclusion and recognizes herself as the so-called ghost in Thornfield Hall: 'I went into the hall again with the tall candle in my hand. It was then that I saw her – the ghost. The woman with streaming hair. She was surrounded by a gilt frame but I knew her' [WSS, p. 123]. The gilt frame encloses a mirror: as Narcissus' pool reflects the selved Other, so this 'pool' reflects the Othered self. Here the dream sequence ends, with an invocation of none other than Tia, the Other that could not be selved, because the fracture of imperialism rather than the Ovidian pool intervened. [...] 'That was the third time I had my dream, and it ended ... . I called "Tia!" and jumped and woke' [WSS, pp. 122–4]. It is now, at the very end of the book, that Antoinette/Bertha can say: 'Now at last I know why I was brought here and what I have to do' [WSS, p. 124]. We can read this as her having been brought into the England of Brontë's novel: 'This cardboard house' – a book between cardboard covers – 'where I walk at night is not England' [WSS, p. 118]. In this fictive England, she must play out her role, act out the transformation of her 'self' into that fictive Other, set fire to the house and kill herself, so that Jane Eyre can become the feminist individualist heroine of British fiction. I must read this as an allegory of the general epistemic violence of imperialism, the construction of a self-immolating colonial subject for the glorification of the social mission of the colonizer. At least Rhys sees to it that the woman from the colonies is not sacrificed as an insane animal for her sister's consolation.

Critics have remarked that *Wide Sargasso Sea* treats the Rochester figure with understanding and sympathy.[30] Indeed, he narrates the entire middle section of the book. Rhys makes it clear that he is a victim of the patriarchal inheritance law of entailment rather than of a father's natural preference for the firstborn: in *Wide Sargasso Sea*, Rochester's situation is clearly that of a younger son dispatched to the colonies to buy an heiress. If in the case of Antoinette and her identity, Rhys utilizes the thematics of Narcissus, in the case of Rochester and his patrimony, she touches on the thematics of Oedipus. [...]

In place of the 'wind [fresh] from Europe' scene [*JE*, pp. 324–5], Rhys substitutes the scenario of a suppressed letter to a father, a letter which would be the 'correct' explanation of the tragedy of the book. 'I thought about the letter which should have been written to England a week ago. Dear Father ...' [*WSS*, p. 40]. This is the first instance of the letter not written. Shortly afterward:

> Dear Father. The thirty thousand pounds have been paid to me without question or condition. No provision made for her (that must be seen to) .... I will never be a disgrace to you or to my dear brother the son you love. No begging letters, no mean requests. None of the furtive shabby manoeuvres of a younger son. I have sold my soul or you have sold it, and after all is it such a bad bargain? The girl is thought to be beautiful, she is beautiful. And yet ... [*WSS*, p. 42]

This is the second instance: the letter not sent. The formal letter is uninteresting; I will quote only a part of it:

> Dear Father, we have arrived from Jamaica, after an uncomfortable few days. This little estate in the Windward islands is part of the family property and Antoinette is much attached to it .... All is well and has gone according to your plans and wishes. I dealt of course with Richard Mason. ... he seemed to become attached to me and trusted me completely. This place is very beautiful but my illness has left me too exhausted to appreciate it fully. I will write again in a few days' time. [*WSS*, p. 46]

And so on.

Rhys' version of the Oedipal exchange is ironic, not a closed circle. We cannot know if the letter actually reaches its destination. 'I wondered how they got their letters posted', the Rochester figure muses. 'I folded mine and put it into a drawer of the desk .... There are blanks in my mind that cannot be filled up' [*WSS*, p. 46]. It is as if the text presses us to note the analogy between letter and mind.

Rhys denies to Brontë's Rochester the one thing that is supposed to be secured in the Oedipal relay: the Name of the Father, or the patronymic. In *Wide Sargasso Sea*, the character corresponding to Rochester has no name. His writing of the final version of the letter to his father is supervised, in fact, by an image of the *loss* of the patronymic: 'There was a crude bookshelf made of three shingles strung together over the desk and I looked at the books, Byron's poems, novels by Sir Walter Scott, *Confessions of an Opium Eater* ... and on the last shelf, *Life and Letters of* ... The rest was eaten away' [*WSS*, pp. 45–6].

Wide Sargasso Sea marks with uncanny clarity the limits of its own discourse in Christophine, Antoinette's black nurse. We may perhaps surmise the distance between *Jane Eyre* and *Wide Sargasso Sea* by remarking that Christophine's unfinished story is the tangent to the latter narrative, as St John Rivers' story is to the former. Christophine is not a native of Jamaica; she is from Martinique. Taxonomically, she belongs to the category of the good servant rather than that of the pure native. But within these borders, Rhys creates a powerfully suggestive figure.

Christophine is the first interpreter and named speaking subject in the text. 'The Jamaican ladies had never approved of my mother, "because she pretty like pretty self" Christophine said' [*WSS*, p. 5], we read in the book's opening paragraph. I have taught this book five times, once in France, once to students who had worked on the book with the well-known Caribbean novelist Wilson Harris, and once at a prestigious institute where the majority of the students were faculty from other universities. It is part of the political argument I am making that all these students blithely stepped over this paragraph without asking or knowing what Christophine's patois, so-called incorrect English, might mean.

Christophine is, of course, a commodified person. 'She was your father's wedding present to me' explains Antoinette's mother, 'one of his presents' [*WSS*, p. 8]. Yet Rhys assigns her some crucial functions in the text. It is Christophine who judges that black ritual practices are culture-specific and cannot be used by whites as cheap remedies for social evils, such as Rochester's lack of love for Antoinette. Most important, it is Christophine alone whom Rhys allows to offer a hard analysis of Rochester's actions, to challenge him in a face-to-face encounter. The entire extended passage is worthy of comment. I quote a brief extract:

'She is Creole girl, and she have the sun in her. Tell the truth now. She don't come to your house in this place England they tell me about, she don't come to your beautiful house to beg you to marry with her. No, it's you come all the long way to her house – it's you beg her to marry. And she love you and she give you all she have.

Now you say you don't love her and you break her up. What you
do with her money, eh?' Her voice was still quiet but with a hiss in
it when she said 'money'. [*WSS*, p. 102]

Her analysis is powerful enough for the white man to be afraid: 'I no
longer felt dazed, tired, half hypnotized, but alert and wary, ready to
defend myself' [*WSS*, p. 102].

Rhys does not, however, romanticize individual heroics on the part
of the oppressed. When the Man refers to the forces of Law and Order,
Christophine recognizes their power. This exposure of civil inequality
is emphasized by the fact that, just before the Man's successful threat,
Christophine had invoked the emancipation of slaves in Jamaica by
proclaiming: 'No chain gang, no tread machine, no dark jail either.
This is free country and I am free woman' [*WSS*, p. 103].

As I mentioned above, Christophine is tangential to this narrative.
She cannot be contained by a novel which rewrites a canonical
English text within the European novelistic tradition in the interest of
the white Creole rather than the native. No perspective *critical* of
imperialism can turn the Other into a self, because the project of
imperialism has always already historically refracted what might have
been the absolutely Other into a domesticated Other that consolidates
the imperialist self. [...]

Of course, we cannot know Jean Rhys' feelings in the matter. We
can, however, look at the scene of Christophine's inscription in the
text. Immediately after the exchange between her and the Man, well
before the conclusion, she is simply driven out of the story, with
neither narrative nor characterological explanation or justice. '"Read
and write I don't know. Other things I know." She walked away without looking back' [*WSS*, p. 104]. □

Since its publication, Spivak's essay has assumed landmark status,
becoming central both to critical analyses of *Jane Eyre* and *Wide Sargasso
Sea* and more general theoretical debates within the field of postcolonialism. Yet the responses it has elicited have frequently been quite questioning. One of the earliest of these occurs in the second section of Benita
Parry's 'Problems in Current Theories of Colonial Discourse'. This article
first appeared in the *Oxford Literary Review* in 1987 and is the source for
the final extract in this chapter. For Parry, Christophine is anything but
the 'domesticated Other' Spivak would have her be. Instead Christophine
offers a powerful critique of the 'patriarchal, settler and imperialist'[31] discourses which she confronts in the text.

■ Spivak argues that because the construction of an English cultural
identity was inseparable from othering the native as its object, the

articulation of the female subject within the emerging norm of feminist individualism during the age of imperialism necessarily excluded the native female, who was positioned on the boundary between human and animal as the object of imperialism's social mission or soul-making. In applying this interactive process to her reading of *Wide Sargasso Sea*, Spivak assigns to Antoinette/Bertha, daughter of slave-owners and heiress to a post-emancipation fortune, the role of the native female sacrificed in the cause of the subject-constitution of the European female individualist. Although Spivak does acknowledge that *Wide Sargasso Sea* is 'a novel which rewrites a canonical English text within the European novelistic tradition in the interest of the white Creole rather than the native', and situates Antoinette/Bertha as caught between the English imperialist and the black Jamaican, her discussion does not pursue the text's representations of a Creole culture that is dependent on both yet singular, or its enunciation of a specific settler discourse, distinct from the texts of imperialism. The dislocations of the Creole position are repeatedly spoken by Antoinette, the 'Rochester' figure and Christophine; the nexus of intimacy and hatred between white settler and black servant is written into the text in the mirror imagery of Antoinette and Tia, a trope which for Spivak functions to invoke the other that could not be selved [...].

But while themselves not English, and indeed outcastes, the Creoles are Masters to the blacks, and just as Brontë's book invites the reader via Rochester to see Bertha Mason as situated on the human/animal frontier ('One night I had been awakened by her yells ... it was a fiery West-Indian night. ... those are the sounds of the bottomless pit!' [*JE*, p. 324]), so does Rhys' novel via Antoinette admit her audience to the regulation settler view of rebellious blacks: 'the same face repeated over and over, eyes gleaming, mouth half open' [*WSS*, p. 22], emitting 'A horrible noise ... like animals howling, but worse' [*WSS*, p. 20].

The idiosyncrasies of an account where Antoinette plays the part of 'the woman from the colonies' are consequences of Spivak's decree that imperialism's linguistic aggression obliterates the inscription of a native self: thus a black female who in *Wide Sargasso Sea* is most fully selved, must be reduced to the status of a tangential figure, and a white Creole woman (mis)construed as the native female produced by the axiomatics of imperialism, her death interpreted as 'an allegory of the general epistemic violence of imperialism, the construction of a self-immolating colonial subject for the glorification of the social mission of the colonizer'. While allowing that Christophine is both speaking subject and interpreter to whom Rhys designates some crucial functions, Spivak sees her as marking the limits of the text's discourse, and not, as is here argued, disrupting it.

What Spivak's strategy of reading necessarily blots out is Christophine's inscription as the native, female, individual Self who defies the demands of the discriminatory discourses impinging on her person. Although an ex-slave given as a wedding-present to Antoinette's mother and subsequently a caring servant, Christophine subverts the Creole address that would constitute her as domesticated Other, and asserts herself as articulate antagonist of patriarchal, settler and imperialist law. Natural mother to children and surrogate parent to Antoinette, Christophine scorns patriarchal authority in her personal life by discarding her patronymic and refusing her sons' fathers as husbands; as Antoinette's protector she impugns 'Rochester' for his economic and sexual exploitation of her fortune and person and as female individualist she is eloquently and frequently contemptuous of male conduct, black and white. A native in command of the invaders' language – 'She could speak good English if she wanted to, and French as well as patois' [*WSS*, p.7] – Christophine appropriates English to the local idiom and uses this dialect to deride the post-emancipation rhetoric which enabled the English to condemn slavery as unjust while enriching themselves through legitimized forms of exploitation: 'No more slavery! She had to laugh! "These new ones have Letter of the Law. Same thing. They got Magistrate. They got fine. They got jail house and chain gang. They got tread machine to mash up people's feet. New ones worse than old ones – more cunning, that's all"' [*WSS*, p.11]. And as obeah woman, Christophine is mistress of another knowledge dangerous to imperialism's official epistemology and the means of native cultural disobedience.

Christophine's defiance is not enacted in a small and circumscribed space appropriated within the lines of the dominant code, but is a stance from which she delivers a frontal assault against antagonists, and as such constitutes a counter-discourse. Wise to the limits of post-emancipation justice, she is quick to invoke the protection of its law when 'Rochester' threatens her with retribution: 'This is free country and I am free woman' [*WSS*, p.103] – which is exactly how she functions in the text, her retort to him condensing her role as the black, female individualist: 'Read and write I don't know. *Other things I know*' [*WSS*, p.104; emphasis added]. In Spivak's reconstruction, Christophine's departure from the story after this declaration and well before the novel's end, is without narrative and characterological explanation or justice. But if she is read as the possessor and practitioner of an alternative tradition challenging imperialism's authorized system of knowledge, then her exit at this point appears both logical and entirely in character:

'England,' said Christophine, who was watching me. 'You think there is such a place?'

'How can you ask that? You know there is.'
'I never see the damn place, how I know?'
'You do not believe that there is a country called England?'
... 'I don't say I don't *believe*, I say I don't *know*, I know what I see with my eyes and I never see it.' [*WSS*, p. 70]

This articulation of empiricism's farthest reaches spoken by a black woman who *knows* from experience that her powders, potions and maledictions are effective in the West Indies, undoes through its excess the rationalist version valorized by the English, while at the same time acknowledging the boundaries to the power of her knowledge. Officially condemned and punishable in Jamaica – 'Rochester' tries to intimidate Christophine with mention of magistrates and police – this other wisdom of the black communities is assimilated into Creole culture – Antoinette calls on and has faith in its potency. But when the novel transfers to England, Christophine must leave the narrative, for there her craft is outlawed, which is why after making her statement, 'She walked away without looking back' [*WSS*, p. 104].

Spivak's deliberated deafness to the native voice where it is to be heard, is at variance with her acute hearing of the unsaid in modes of Western feminist criticism which, while dismantling masculinist constructions, reproduce and foreclose colonialist structures and imperialist axioms by 'performing the lie of constituting a truth of global sisterhood where the mesmerizing model remains male and female sparring partners of generalizable or universalizable sexuality who are the chief protagonists in that European contest'.[32] Demanding of disciplinary standards that 'equal rights of historical, geographical, linguistic specificity' be granted to the 'thoroughly stratified larger theatre of the Third World',[33] Spivak in her own writings severely restricts (eliminates?) the space in which the colonized can be written back into history, even when 'interventionist possibilities' are exploited through the deconstructive strategies devised by the post-colonial intellectual. ☐

As the exchange between Parry and Spivak indicates, the role of Christophine is a key (and contentious) issue in the critical assessment of Rhys's novel. Equally important, however, are the complex patterns of cross-racial identification which *Wide Sargasso Sea* establishes between Christophine (and other black figures) and its white Creole heroine. These patterns form the object of inquiry for the critics included in the next chapter.

CHAPTER THREE

'Like Goes to Like': Race and the Politics of Identification

■ I was curious about black people. They stimulated me and I felt akin to them. It added to my sadness that I couldn't help but realise they didn't really like or trust white people – white cockroaches they called us. Sick with shame at some of the stories of the slave days ... . Yet all the time knowing that there was another side to it. Sometimes seeing myself powerful ... sometimes being proud of my great grandfather, the estate, and the good old days ... . But the end of my thinking about them was always a sick revolt and I wanted to be identified with the other side which of course was impossible. ❑

Jean Rhys[1]

One of the peculiar coincidences of *Jane Eyre* is the way in which the domestic and textual locations of its madwoman seem to mirror one another. Secreted in the third storey of Rochester's manor-house, Bertha is introduced to the reader in the central third story of Brontë's novel, in which Jane recounts her dramatic experiences as governess at Thornfield Hall. These two locations belong to one who might herself be described as the novel's third person, constituting, as she does, the scandalous 'impediment' whose discovery ensures that the marriage between Jane and Rochester – the prospective happy couple – 'cannot proceed' (*JE*, p. 303).

In *Wide Sargasso Sea*, by contrast, Rhys's Antoinette figures as a third person in a different sense, occupying a space between the binaries of master and slave, the English sources and African resources out of which her colonial world is produced. The point is underlined as Antoinette explains the meaning of the words sung by Amélie, the 'little half-caste servant' (*WSS*, p. 39) in Part Two of the novel. 'It [is] a song', she tells Rochester:

■ about a white cockroach. That's me. That's what they call all of us who were here before their own people in Africa sold them to the slave traders. And I've heard English women call us white niggers. So between you I often wonder who I am and where is my country and where do I belong and why was I ever born at all. □

[*WSS*, p.64]

The principal characteristic of this interstitial space is its instability, as Antoinette moves constantly between identities, bearing out, as she does so, Maggie Humm's description of *Wide Sargasso Sea* as 'Rhys's most complex novel of border crossing in relation to colour'.[2] On several occasions, these movements take the form of an identification with images from the metropolis: Antoinette's 'favourite picture', for example, is 'The Miller's Daughter', with its figure of 'a lovely English girl with brown curls and blue eyes' (*WSS*, p.18). Yet the novel's dominant pattern enlists Antoinette into identifications with a range of black others, whether they be Tia, Christophine or, most spectacularly, the collective of ex-slaves who destroy Coulibri. Such identifications are integral, it might even be argued, to the intertextual or revisionary project of Rhys's novel as a whole. *Wide Sargasso Sea* releases Antoinette from the Anglocentric feminism of *Jane Eyre*, in which she is silently fixed and framed as Bertha, even as the moment of her inscription into narrative is coeval with the emancipation of slaves in British colonies in 1833–4. Rhys's reclamation of the voice of the white Creole woman coincides with and parallels the moment of black slave-liberation.

The question of Antoinette's identifications with her black others is one which has preoccupied a number of critics of Rhys's novel. This chapter examines the ways in which the question is approached in three articles, produced between the late 1970s and early 1990s, by Helen Tiffin, Lee Erwin and Maria Olaussen. The first of these offers a useful introductory guide to white/black identification in *Wide Sargasso Sea* and has the added virtue of showing how such an issue is already adumbrated in Rhys's earlier novels. In the end though, the claims Tiffin makes for the analogies between the position of the white female subject – 'whether ostensibly English or actually Creole'[3] – and the history of black colonial oppression seem both crude and overstated. This is certainly the implication of the articles by Erwin and Olaussen. Both of these later critics are much more sophisticated and indeed circumspect than Tiffin in their treatment of the dynamics of cross-racial identification in *Wide Sargasso Sea*, providing trenchant analyses of the ways in which it is both politically suspect and historically dubious. At the same time, their own positions are marked by some important differences. While Erwin sees *Wide Sargasso Sea* as itself problematizing white/black identification, Olaussen argues that Rhys's text is rather less self-questioning in its racial politics and needs, consequently, to be viewed with a degree of suspicion.

Tiffin's 'Mirror and Mask: Colonial Motifs in the Novels of Jean Rhys' was first published in *World Literature Written in English* in 1978. The article begins by taking issue with Look Lai and Porter's orthodox assumption that *Wide Sargasso Sea* represents a break from the earlier concerns of Rhys's fiction. In contrast to this view, Tiffin stresses continuity, arguing that – despite their overt differences of historical and geographical setting – Rhys's earlier work and final novel are closely linked. What unites them is the recurrent use of colonialism as a metaphor with which to represent gender relations. As Tiffin somewhat starkly summarizes: 'The parallel between destructive male/female relationships and [...] imperial nation and colonial underdog is obvious.'[4]

Tiffin briefly discusses Rhys's manipulation of this parallel in *Wide Sargasso Sea* in the closing pages of her article, from which the following extract is taken.

■ *Wide Sargasso Sea* provides the summation and climax of Rhys's explorations. In the marriage between Antoinette Cosway and Edward Rochester, the imperial/colonial relation is clear. What were purely metaphoric expressions for psychic states in the earlier novels are actual in *Wide Sargasso Sea*. Antoinette is literally Rochester's prisoner in England. She is friendless, has lost her own name, and is regarded as a wild animal who must be restrained by her captors. Earlier heroines felt they were being exposed in a zoo, but Antoinette actually has a keeper in the formidable Grace Poole, a confessed 'underdog' herself [*WSS*, pp. 115–16].

While the ultimate implications of that always-destructive colonial/ imperial relation are now laid bare, so too are the very real similarities between Antoinette's fate and that of black slaves in European hands. Antoinette is bought for profit, and is regarded as exotic, hysterical, and incomprehensible by her buyer. He changes her name to a more comfortably English one, and she is dependent on him for her very existence. When she seems to show signs of rebellion she is cruelly punished, though the evidence against her is at best circumstantial. Finally she is reviled as a wild animal and confined in a cruelly uncongenial prison. Antoinette Cosway is thus shown to share the history which apparently divided her from the Blacks.

As a child, Antoinette was pulled between the prejudices of the white and black communities [...] and though she subconsciously realizes her affinity with Blacks as victims of history, the divisive stereotypes created by that history continued to thwart her attempts at identification with them. Her embryonic relationship with Tia is shattered when, feeling cheated by Tia, she reacts with automatic white prejudice and dubs Tia 'cheating nigger' [*WSS*, p. 10]. Yet her conviction that Tia is her soul-mate persists, though Tia forcibly rejects her former playmate when Antoinette's family home is fired by the Blacks. Though Tia utterly rejects Antoinette here, it is noteworthy that in Antoinette's memory of the incident all violence is repressed, and what is shared is emphasized. Antoinette [...] can reach beyond the immediate violence of the relation between 'underdogs' to perceive their common condition. Victims of history, one is the true sacrificial mirror image of the other:

> As I ran, I thought, I will live with Tia and I will be like her ... .
> When I was close I saw the jagged stone in her hand but I did not
> see her throw it. I did not feel it either, only something wet, run-
> ning down my face. I looked at her and I saw her face crumple up
> as she began to cry. We stared at each other, blood on my face, tears
> on hers. It was as if I saw myself. Like in a looking-glass. [*WSS*, p. 24]

Here at last is an image in which Antoinette can perceive herself, not the English distortion of self.

After her confinement in Thornfield Hall, Antoinette has suffered in fact a fate comparable with the black Creole one, and her reaction to her confinement is [...] the typical slave retaliation in the firing of the great house. In this final, controversial section of the novel, Antoinette's red dress provides a striking and supremely important contrast to the black dress of the earlier Rhys heroines. Black there represented the ideal of male European taste: '"She wore black. Men delighted in that sable colour, or lack of colour."'[5] The women believed that the black dress provided camouflage, protecting them from the critical observation of others, and it was also frequently seen as a potential talisman which might ward off evil. But the black dress ultimately provides no armour against judging European eyes: it never provides the woman with the darker identity she seeks either. Her skin remains insistently pale, and the black dress only mirrors the cold, sad, northern world; it cannot invoke the warm gaiety of a tropical one.

The red dress is different. Beautiful, and strangely alive, it is both an effective mask and an integrated reflection of Antoinette's personality. [...] it is a satirical comment on an English character which fears and so represses any outbreak of spontaneous warmth, joy, or colour, and which tries, like Grace Poole, to force others into its 'grey wrapper' [*WSS*, p. 121]. The dress has its own obeah to ward off those who are now by *its* definition outsiders. Its charm works effectively against the English spell of darkness cast over former Rhys heroines, and which they were generally powerless to resist. [...] [Its] meaning is the unashamed expression of a tropical riot of felt experience, the sights, sounds, and scents of the West Indian environment [...] which so appalled Edward Rochester. This red dress which has been locked away by her English captors is the true and undistorted image of Antoinette's personality:

> As soon as I turned the key I saw it hanging, the colour of fire and sunset. The colour of flamboyant flowers. 'If you are buried under a flamboyant tree,' I said, 'your soul is lifted up when it flowers. Everyone wants that.'
> [Grace Poole] shook her head but she did not move or touch me.
> The scent that came from the dress was very faint at first, then it grew stronger. The smell of vetivert and frangipani, of cinnamon and dust and lime trees when they are flowering. The smell of the sun and the smell of the rain. [*WSS*, p. 120]

Significantly Grace Poole cannot 'touch her' while she communes with the dress which casts its charmed circle round her.

Though Antoinette's identification with Tia, and thus her genuine absorption by the black Creole community remains ambiguous to the end, the red flowers of fire and beauty which have blossomed out of Antoinette's actual experience of slave suffering promise that her choice of Tia's invitation to jump, rather than live as Rochester's captive, is the correct one. Though initially 'faint' the 'scent' of the red dress has been strengthened by this suffering, and in death she will at last be accepted and lifted up by her childhood environment through the myth of rebirth that 'Everyone' shares. The fire which consumes Thornfield Hall that Antoinette sees in her dream is both the promise of a flamboyant rebirth and the culmination of her shared slave experience with the Blacks. Jumping to the still slightly taunting Tia, she rejects Rochester and the old imperial associations, choosing instead the fate of her Carib 'ancestors'. Along the dark passage that has been the experience of England for the Rhys heroine, Antoinette has at last found, in the mask of the red dress, the talisman that lights her way. □

Apart from its repeated and disconcertingly faceless allusions to 'the Blacks', this extract from Tiffin is marked by a number of rhetorical flourishes and a generally declamatory tone which cannot quite conceal the contradictions of its main argument. These are particularly apparent in Tiffin's central claim that there are 'very real similarities between Antoinette's fate and that of black slaves in European hands'. To what extent does it make sense to say that 'similarities' of any kind are 'very real'? Precisely by using the intensifier 'very', Tiffin inadvertently casts her reading into doubt, as if the rhetorical excess of her formulation were designed to compensate for a certain lack of conviction as to its truth. The tension which this implies between an affirmation and a questioning of the resemblances between the racial and gender oppression suffered by Antoinette and a black slave-history is evident elsewhere in this extract, most notably in the discussion of *Wide Sargasso Sea*'s 'controversial' ending. In this part of her analysis, Tiffin makes two claims that do not mesh convincingly. On the one hand, she declares that Antoinette's fiery destruction of Thornfield Hall is a gesture of 'typical slave retaliation', by which its perpetrator gains full admission into the realms of 'slave experience'. Yet, on the other, she is prepared to concede that 'Antoinette's identification with Tia, and thus her genuine absorption by the black Creole community remains ambiguous to the end'. The consistency of Tiffin's argument is further compromised in her penultimate sentence. Here the meaning of Antoinette's final incendiary actions undergoes an unexpected change, as what is initially the definitive expression of a 'shared slave experience' is suddenly refigured as the sign of a mysterious and hitherto unmentioned Carib ancestry.

While these shifts and fluctuations in Tiffin's analysis create the impression of a certain critical imprecision, they are nonetheless true to *Wide Sargasso Sea*'s own ambivalence towards the issue of white/black identification. Such ambivalence is written into the language of Rhys's novel, an aspect of the text with which Tiffin largely fails to engage. It can be brought out by returning to the stone-throwing episode cited above in the extract's third paragraph. Far from revealing a 'common condition', as Tiffin claims, this episode only underlines the insuperable differences between its two protagonists. The authenticity of Antoinette's self-recognition in Tia is itself recognized by the text to be both illusory and implausible, discreetly blocked by the intrusion of Rhys's 'as if' formulation. The discrepancies between Antoinette and Tia are additionally highlighted in the 'looking-glass' simile. This rhetorical device necessarily makes Tia subordinate to Antoinette in the same way that a mirror image is dependent upon its object. It thus turns, paradoxically, into a specular metaphor for the enduring racial hierarchies whose demise it is meant, according to Tiffin at least, to signal.

The question of cross-racial identification addressed by Tiffin is also the focus of Lee Erwin's '"Like in a Looking-Glass": History and Narrative in *Wide Sargasso Sea*', an article originally published in *Novel* in 1989. In this widely cited and substantial piece, Erwin elaborates an argument which not only displays a much greater textual rigour than Tiffin's but also is much ampler in its consideration of the politics of Rhys's textual strategies. At first glance, the analogies that *Wide Sargasso Sea* repeatedly suggests between Antoinette and the novel's various black characters would appear to be highly questionable. From the vantage of the late 1980s, after the emergence of postcolonial and black feminist criticism,

they can only seem politically incorrect in the extreme, ironically trivial-
izing the realities of slavery from which they derive their force. The
potential dangers of such analogies are eloquently mapped by the
African-American critic bell hooks in *Ain't I a Woman: Black Women and
Feminism* (1982). Discussing the trope of the (white) woman-as-slave in
the feminist abolitionist discourses of antebellum America, hooks writes:

■ It did not enhance the cause of oppressed black slaves for white
women to make synonymous their plight and the plight of the slave.
[...] there was very little if any similarity between the day-to-day life
experiences of white women and the day-to-day experiences of the
black slave. Theoretically, the white woman's legal status under patriarchy may have been that of 'property,' but she was in no way subjected to the de-humanization and brutal oppression that was the lot of
the slave. When white reformers made synonymous the impact of
sexism on their lives, they were not revealing an awareness of or sensitivity to the slave's lot; they were simply appropriating the horror of
the slave experience to enhance their own cause.[6] □

As Erwin goes on to demonstrate, however, *Wide Sargasso Sea* is not to be
comfortably dismissed as a perfidious 'exercise in bad faith'.[7] The 'easy
equation between "woman" and "nigger"',[8] associated by Erwin (and
hooks) with the last 'vestige of bourgeois feminism',[9] is a seduction that
is as much resisted as it is courted by Rhys's text.

This textual tension is most strikingly dramatized, for Erwin, in terms
of the conflict between the two narratives, Antoinette's and Rochester's,
that structure the novel. These narratives are directed towards markedly
different goals. The ruling 'desire of [Antoinette's] narrative' is for a
'fantasized union with [...] blackness'[10] which will enable her to occupy the
place of the other. This wish to become 'like Tia' and 'Like Christophine'
(*WSS*, p. 53) involves a double repression. It constitutes a forgetting both
of Antoinette's true status as 'the daughter of a slave-owner' (*WSS*, p. 15)
and, more generally, of the realities of slavery itself, conceived as a system
reliant upon the institutionalization and maintenance of racial difference.
Yet as Erwin shows, the problem for Antoinette is that 'the history of
slavery'[11] she strives to repress is precisely what Rochester strives to
recover. As it pores over a range of materials – from local place-names
and ruins to Antoinette's complex family history and the African
Caribbean cult of obeah – Rochester's narrative engages in a project
whose aim is antithetical to that of his wife's. Its 'driving impulse is a
search for [a] past'[12] which Antoinette herself is determined to deny.

■ The dramatic appearance of Jean Rhys's *Wide Sargasso Sea* in 1966,
after a quarter-century of silence and obscurity for its author, has

tended to occult the less romantic facts of the book's two-decade-long gestation. That the novel had been partly written by 1945 is significant, however. The years between the mid-forties and the mid-sixties having encompassed much of the break-up of the British Empire, and *Wide Sargasso Sea* alone of all of Rhys's novels engaging fully (though at a certain historical remove) with her background in the British West Indies, we might look for a difference in the way the subject of a narrative written at one time or another reads itself into history by means of that narrative. Elizabeth Nunez-Harrell has suggested that *Wide Sargasso Sea* might be a 'response to the nationalistic mood [in the West Indies] of the late 50s and 60s', which could have led Rhys to wish 'to assume her place in West Indian literature'.[13] Yet the novel seems rather to inhabit a limbo *between* nationalisms; it exists as a response to the loss, rather than the recovery, of a 'place-to-be-from', enacting a struggle over identity which is a peculiarly modern rereading of West Indian history.

The historical circumstances that set the novel in motion are the Emancipation Act that in 1833 decreed the eventual freedom of the slaves in all of the British colonies and the racial conflicts and social and economic turmoil that surrounded it. As Gayatri Spivak has argued, Rhys takes the risks of writing from the point of view of 'the wrong side' in the novel's colonial setting, writing not only from the point of view of Antoinette, the white slave-owner's daughter, but from that of a white Englishman as well.[14] Yet, in my view, the greater risk Rhys takes is to suggest an identification between Antoinette (Rhys's revision of Bertha Mason in *Jane Eyre*) in her firing of Thornfield Hall and the ex-slaves who set fire to her family's estate. Besides drawing a parallel between the two events, the novel suggests that it is Christophine's obeah that guides the outcome. Before 'Rochester' leaves the West Indies, he is driven by his long last talk with Christophine to cry, 'I would give my eyes never to have seen this abominable place.' Christophine replies, 'You choose what you give, eh? Then you choose. You meddle in something and perhaps you don't know what it is' [*WSS*, p.104]. Thus, when Antoinette dreams her dream for the third and last time, in Thornfield Hall, she cries out to Christophine for help and sees that she has 'been helped' by 'a wall of fire' [*WSS*, p.123] – and we know from *Jane Eyre* that Rochester loses exactly what he 'chose' to lose. Laid out in this way, *Wide Sargasso Sea* may seem an exercise in bad faith, appealing only to any vestige of bourgeois feminism still able to accept an easy equation between 'woman' and 'nigger'; yet it is precisely the problematizing of that equation, and that because it is an aim of the narrative, that I will suggest drives the novel.

If we lay out the racial issues the novel addresses as they are manifested in its two major narratives, Antoinette's and Rochester's, settler woman and metropolitan man, it begins to appear that whereas Antoinette sees her own displaced, deracinated condition in terms of historically specific shifts in class and economic power, the Rochester figure refuses these categories and instead interprets racial difference in moral and sexual terms, specifically in terms of miscegenation and 'contamination'. Thus, Antoinette's discourse constantly suggests an interchangeability of racial positions, manifested most obviously in the play on such terms as 'white nigger' [WSS, p.10] and 'black Englishman' [WSS, p.22]: in a crucial scene, when in a moment of childhood conflict Antoinette calls her black playmate Tia a 'cheating nigger', Tia's response is:

> She hear all we poor like beggar ... . Plenty white people in Jamaica. Real white people, they got gold money. They didn't look at us, nobody see them come near us. Old time white people nothing but white nigger now, and black nigger better than white nigger. [WSS, p.10]

Thus, too, the burning of the restored estate house after Antoinette's mother's remarriage suggests that what might be called racial hatred is class-specific in origin: 'The black people did not hate us quite so much when we were poor. We were white but we had not escaped and soon we would be dead for we had no money left. What was there to hate?' [WSS, p.16].

The fantasmatic dimension of this notion of interchangeability becomes clear, however, when, as the house burns, Antoinette sees Tia in the crowd and runs toward her thinking, 'I will live with Tia and ... be like her':

> When I was close I saw the jagged stone in her hand but I did not see her throw it. I did not feel it either, only something wet, running down my face. I looked at her and I saw her face crumple up as she began to cry. We stared at each other, blood on my face, tears on hers. It was as if I saw myself. Like in a looking-glass. [WSS, p.24]

Having been subjected both to her mother's attempts to make her 'white' and to the metropolitan view that the effort is a failure, Antoinette will try to be black, not an anomalous 'white nigger'. But the violence with which her wish is met closes off that position as well.

The image of the looking-glass, a motif running throughout all of Rhys's fiction, has a particular resonance in Wide Sargasso Sea, where questions of identity are given the racial and national complications that can only act as a subtext in Rhys's 'English' novels. Here the image splits into its own reversal infinitely, as the identity Antoinette claims is also simultaneously the recognition of an unbridgeable difference. That is, even as she claims to be seeing 'herself', she is simultaneously seeing the other, that which only defines the self by its separation from it, in this case literally by means of a cut. History here, in the person of a former slave's daughter, is figured as refusing *Antoinette*.

The play between racial terms in Antoinette's narrative, each replacing and suppressing the other by turns, has implications for the novel's temporal structure as well. The linear time of history, which would inevitably recall the history of slavery to consciousness and thus restore the racial differentiation Antoinette's narrative seeks to disrupt, must be foreclosed. Thus her two narratives are defined by only two temporal points: 'now and the hour of our death ... that is all we have' [*WSS*, p. 32]. Such a foreclosure is most obvious in the chronology of Antoinette's early life: if she is nearly seventeen in 1839, as the date in an embroidery suggests, she would have been born in 1822 or 1823, well before the Emancipation Act, which did not go into effect for another year after its enactment in 1833 and even then decreed from four to six years' further service for slaves (now 'apprentices') before they were to be 'full free'. Any memory of slavery and, for that matter, any memory of her father – avatar of that history – whose death must also have been very recent ('Emancipation troubles killed old Cosway?' [*WSS*, p. 13]) is excised from Antoinette's narrative. This excision is duplicated in her mother's speech: 'Why do you pester and bother me about all these things that happened long ago?' [*WSS*, p. 8]. The subsequent traversal of that gap by Christophine's references to the old times, then ('New ones worse than old ones – more cunning, that's all' [*WSS*, p. 11]), only marks out what is not there and makes plain the impossibility of any appeal to the past against an equally feared future. It is a past only existing in the narrative in parenthesis: '(My father, visitors, horses, feeling safe in bed – all belonged to the past)' [*WSS*, p. 5]. [...]

The novel's figure for its own narrative is Antoinette's dream, with its twice-deferred (but foregone) conclusion ('Not here, not yet' [*WSS*, p. 34]) and its dreaded but inevitable forward propulsion. The dream in a sense suggests a subsuming of the 'Rochester' narrative under Antoinette's, her narrative enunciating a trajectory in the dreams that it will be the task of the Rochester narrative to fulfill. A notable feature of Rochester's narrative, especially in contradistinction to Antoinette's, however, is precisely its fascination with and search for the 'past'. His first words ('So it was all over .... Everything finished, for better or for worse') already suggest a backwards trajectory for his narrative; the difference between his and Antoinette's is encapsulated in their first recorded conversation:

> I looked at the sad leaning coconut palms, the fishing boats drawn up on the shingly beach, the uneven row of whitewashed huts, and asked the name of the village.
> 'Massacre.'
> 'And who was massacred here? Slaves?'
> 'Oh no.' She sounded shocked. 'Not slaves. Something must have happened a long time ago. Nobody remembers now.' [*WSS*, p. 39]

The shift to Rochester's voice upon their marriage suggests that Antoinette's own narrative is now ended, having reached its proper nineteenth-century conclusion ('for better or for worse'), and that his desire now drives the narrative. In these first moments, this shift also associates his pursuit of the 'truth' of the past with naming and with desire, in a revision of the Gothic that puts the male into a threatening and alien environment (if not house, the house at Granbois being a pathetically fragile excuse for a Gothic manse) to seek out its secret. 'What I see is nothing – I want what it *hides* – that is not nothing' [*WSS*, p. 54].

The association of sexuality with the history Rochester seeks to recover is not without precedent, given that a commonplace of British abolitionist writing [...] associates the institution of slavery with licentiousness:

> And what the hurricane [of 1831] did for the physical atmosphere ... emancipation effected for its moral and domestic atmosphere, it purified that in a remarkable manner, and to the matron ladies and their daughters, always exemplarily correct, was an incalculable comfort. Licentiousness, whatever it might have been before, was almost entirely banished from society: young men no longer exposed to the same temptations as before, acquired new ideas of correctness and purer tastes and habits, all of an elevating kind and favoring the developement [sic] of the higher energies.[15]

The gender division explicit here is also evident in *Wide Sargasso Sea*, in which Rochester's attempts to search out the 'truth' of the past are in part attempts to uncover the licentiousness that has marked the Cosways [...]: if his search uncovers the transgressions of the male subjected to the 'temptations' [noted above], it nonetheless ultimately displaces the responsibility for those transgressions onto the woman, guardian of 'exemplary correctness'. If Antoinette's racial imagination is metaphoric, based upon the wished-for substitution of one term for another, Rochester's is metonymic, constantly expressing itself as a perception of contamination from contiguity, one racial term slipping or 'leaking' into another through sheer proximity, obsessively perceived as sexual.

Thus, for Rochester, Antoinette's sexuality itself is an index of racial contamination: on their journey to their 'honeymoon house' [*WSS*, p. 39], Rochester looks at his wife's eyes and thinks, 'Long, sad, dark alien eyes. Creole of pure English descent she may be, but they are not English or European either. And when did I begin to notice all this about my wife Antoinette? After we left Spanish Town I suppose. Or did I notice it before and refuse to admit what I saw?' [*WSS*, p. 40].

Both fear of some unspeakable taint and an inadmissible desire are suggested here, an ambivalence ultimately worked through in Rochester's narrative by the construction of a relay of sexual contamination that circulates *through* males but is finally displaced *onto* females and exorcised. Thus the bizarre accusations of Daniel Boyd/Cosway, who claims that he is Antoinette's mulatto half-brother and that both she and her mother are 'Crazy and worse besides', are given immediate and otherwise unmotivated credence by Rochester: 'I folded the letter carefully and put it into my pocket. I felt no surprise. It was as if I'd expected it, been waiting for it' [*WSS*, p. 62]. His instant and apparently total alienation from Antoinette is only reinforced by a visit to Daniel in person, when the physical disgust aroused in Rochester by the man's 'yellow sweating face' [*WSS*, p. 79] and venomous abuse paradoxically seals his belief in all of Daniel's accusations of Antoinette. The paradox is only explicable if Rochester's contact with Daniel is itself a contamination that must immediately be passed on to the woman and thus transformed into *her* guilt. 'The "white *man*'s burden" thus becomes his sexuality and its control, and it is this which is transferred into the need to control the sexuality of the Other, the Other as sexualized female. The colonial mentality that sees "natives" as needing control is easily transferred to "woman"'.[16]

But if such a 'racial' taint is the fear evident in Rochester's narrative, what of its desire? I have said that its driving impulse is a search for the past; but Rochester's position, the narrative makes clear, is one of exclusion from his own origins, from what Jacques Lacan [1901–81] would term the Name-of-the-Father, cast in economic terms by the English system of primogeniture. Thus, as Gayatri Spivak has pointed out, he remains literally nameless in this text.[17]

Thus, too, the £30,000 Rochester gains in the West Indies only calls up its missing or shadowed origins, the missing name that alone could transform mere money ('They bought me, *me* with your paltry money' [*WSS*, p. 114]) into 'man's estate', motivating the search for the 'truth' of the past that drives Rochester's narrative. In fact, Rhys has made free with the Brontë text at exactly this point, with the effect of separating Antoinette's money from her *own* father's name and attaching it only to the name of her stepfather. The whole Cosway lineage is 'layered' onto a background that in *Jane Eyre* only includes the Masons, of whom 'Bertha' is a biological daughter and 'Richard' a son. The addition of the Cosway figure does two things in *Wide Sargasso Sea*: first, because Antoinette's mother is not even 'old Cosway's' first wife, but the wife of his late years, their marriage and thus Antoinette's and her brother's origins are already coded as 'sexual excess', which in fact killed the old man off; second, because Antoinette's mother then herself remarries, the name of the father, of Antoinette's father, that is, is lost. Thus, the problem of Rochester's search is that, unlike the English Name-of-the-Father, which is notable for its exclusive provenance, being assumable in its full privileges only by the first-born son, this name is nowhere and everywhere, disseminated all over the islands and yet vanishing again under scrutiny.

It is arguable, nonetheless, that Antoinette's dowry is Cosway money, although 'named' as Mason's: early on in the text, an overheard voice claims that Mason has come to the West Indies to make money by buying up for much less than their actual value estates that have been allowed to run down after the passage of the Emancipation Act. Thus, the 'natural' value of the Cosway property Mason acquires, its fertility, is translated into money by an Englishman not averse to profiting from, as well as moralizing about, the downfall of the slave system. Rochester's task, then, is to reattach his newly acquired money to its sources, which in a sense have become the 'secret', buried in the past, of the post-Emancipation Caribbean.

It is perhaps for this reason, then, that Daniel's narrative in his tête-à-tête with Rochester focuses only peripherally on Antoinette and her mother, except as a claim to knowledge about them allows him access to Rochester. The real center of his discourse is Antoinette's father, old Cosway, and his generation of innumerable mixed-race offspring, one of whom Daniel claims to be. The climax of the encounter is Rochester's reenacting the old man's refusal to give Daniel money:

'You believe me, but you want to do everything quiet like the English can. All right. But if I keep my mouth shut it seems to me you owe me something. What is five hundred pounds to you? To me it's my life.'

Now disgust was rising in me like sickness. Disgust and rage.

'All right,' he yelled … . 'Now it's me to say it. Get out. Get out. And if I don't have the money I want you will see what I can do.

'Give my love to your wife – my sister,' he called after me

venomously. 'You are not the first to kiss her pretty face. Pretty face, soft skin, pretty colour – not yellow like me. But my sister just the same ...' [WSS, p.80]

Later Rochester will significantly misremember those words as *'Give my sister your wife a kiss from me. Love her as I did – oh yes I did'* [WSS, p.102] – a malfunction of memory suggesting exactly the source of Antoinette's 'contamination' in Rochester's eyes. Not that she has been 'loved' by Daniel – there is no evidence for that, nor does Rochester require any. The 'contamination' Daniel represents is a metonymy, attaching to Antoinette and her mother by way of the real transgressor, old Cosway. That planters often raped (whether the word signifies physical, legal, or economic coercion) slave women and free women of color is history; but the moral categorization fundamental to the nineteenth-century English novel here speaks through Rochester tacitly to assign blame to the planters' wives as guardians of sexual morality. Perhaps it is no accident, then, that when Rochester next encounters Antoinette he notices that the white dress he has been fond of before is now 'too large' for her and has 'slipped untidily over one shoulder' [WSS, p.81] – no angel in the house this. Nor is the textual metonymy here without reference to another, historical, metonymy: the 'taint' of the Cosways, which has produced the idiot son Pierre and which the text codes as 'alcoholism' (or the more genteel 'inbreeding' Francis Wyndham mentions in his introduction to the novel),[18] is plainly congenital syphilis, a disease whose believed point of origin shifted in the nineteenth century to Africa. 'The association of the black, especially the black female, with the syphilophobia of the late nineteenth century was thus made manifest'.[19]

The only defense against such 'contamination' is the law, which alone can fix origins [...] and control the otherwise uncontrollable; Rochester's narrative seems to enact a constant punning on Christophine's phrase the 'Letter of the Law' [WSS, p.11], as he turns repeatedly to the scribal to fix his position vis-à-vis the father and the past. Thus, for example, the newly married Rochester imagines a letter to his father expressive of his rage at that father's rejection and manipulation of him, but then actually pens a quite different letter that is correct and lifeless in the extreme, expressive only of a submission to patriarchal authority. The scene of the letter's writing, moreover, is the 'little England' in the house at Granbois that acts as a patriarchal parody of the beleaguered heroine's room at the center of the Gothic castle:

It seemed crowded after the emptiness of the rest of the house. There was a carpet, the only one I had seen, a press made of some beautiful wood I did not recognize. Under the open window a small writing desk with paper, pens, and ink. 'A refuge' I was thinking when someone said, 'This was Mr Mason's room, sir, but he did not come here often. He did not like the place.' Baptiste, standing in the doorway to the veranda, had a blanket over his arm ... .

'It can be cold here at night,' he said. Then went away. But the feeling of security had left me. I looked round suspiciously. The door into her room could be bolted, a stout wooden bar pushed across the other. This was the last room in the house ... . There was a crude bookshelf made of three shingles strung together over the desk and I looked at the books, Byron's poems, novels by Sir Walter Scott, *Confessions of an Opium Eater*, some shabby brown volumes, and on the last shelf, *Life and Letters of* ... The rest was eaten away. [*WSS*, pp. 45–6]

Perhaps, then, the role of Daniel Cosway/Boyd in the narrative is almost literally a battle over the letter. He enters the narrative, of course, by *means* of a letter, perhaps explaining further why Rochester gives his accusations such immediate credence; after its receipt, Rochester's response is to leave the house, 'following the path [he] could see from [his] window', from the window of his dressing room, that is. The wanderings that follow repeat the Renaissance topos of the wood of error, as Rochester's search for the truth leads him into the past:

I had reached the forest and you cannot mistake the forest. It is hostile. The path was overgrown but it was possible to follow it ... . How can one discover truth I thought and that thought led me nowhere ... . A track was just visible and I went on ... . The track led to a large clear space. Here were the ruins of a stone house. [*WSS*, p. 65]

Père Lilièvre, whom Baptiste says lived in the house 'a long time ago' [*WSS*, p. 66], recalls Père Labat, who lived on Martinique and visited Dominica several times during the sixteenth century; his *Nouveau Voyage aux Isles de L'Amérique* was published in Paris in 1722, suggesting the volume that Rochester takes up to read about obeah from on his return to the house. Thus, Rochester's search for the 'truth' leads him not only to an artifact of the past but to yet another father and another scribal legacy. Here, however, Père Labat's conviction that 'the Negro [was] a natural child of the devil, a born sorcerer, an evil spirit wielding occult power'[20] might be said to have generated, ironically, only the bunches of flowers surrounding the ruins, the 'obeah-ization' of the father's legacy. The momentarily 'savage'-looking Baptiste's insistence that 'No road' [*WSS*, p. 66] led to the ruined house suggests a refusal by the freed blacks to acknowledge any retracing of that past on the part of the master, as when Antoinette's seeming to recapitulate her father's (alcoholic) violence inspires Rochester's ironic repetition of the phrase:

> [Baptiste] had opened the chest and taken out a bottle of rum … .
> 'Who is that for?' I said. He didn't answer.
> 'No road?' I said and laughed.
> 'I don't want to know nothing about all this,' he said. [WSS, p.92]

Nor does Daniel ultimately offer any clearer 'road' to the truth of the past; although his use of the name Cosway and his ability to 'read write and cypher a little' [WSS, p.61] give him access to Rochester, the past he describes reveals rather his exclusion from the patronymic than his place in its inscription. Not only does the portrait of his father that he has hanging on his wall reveal a more properly imaginary doubling in the image of, not Cosway, but a 'coloured' father, but his recital also reveals his exclusion from the symbolic order, inscribed, literally, on Cosway's tomb:

> 'My father old Cosway, with his white marble tablet in the English church at Spanish Town … . It have a crest on it and a motto in Latin and words in big black letters. I never know such lies … . "Pious," they write up. "Beloved by all".
> Not a word about the people he buy and sell like cattle.' [WSS, p.77]

Thus the Name-of-the-Father, graven in stone and in the English church, closes off the history of slavery days as thoroughly as does Antoinette's narrative, its refusal to inscribe the history of the Daniels and *their* origins being figured in old Cosway's silencing Daniel by hurling an inkstand at him [WSS, p.78].

The 'trouble' [WSS, p.5], finally, in which Rochester's narrative finds itself, then, is that, as in his visit to Daniel, his attempts to fix any 'authorized' history are repeatedly lost again in the slipperiness of 'mere' orality; just as Père Lilièvre's house, another stone monument, is obeah-ized, and its history transmuted into a little black girl's scream, so the authority of the book Rochester takes up upon his return to Granbois slides away into the bafflement it expresses at the 'lies', 'nonsense', and finally 'poison' ('which cannot be traced') of obeah itself [WSS, p.67]. In the same way, then, Rochester's narrative itself immediately gives way again to Antoinette's, which recounts her visit to Christophine to ask for exactly that obeah potion/poison, which will make Rochester love her again upon swallowing it.

His reaction, however, both to the 'poison' and to her words is momentarily to *lose* his literacy – 'I thought, I have been poisoned. But it was a dull thought, like a child spelling out letters of a word which he cannot read' [*WSS*, p.88] – but then to vomit, rejecting both Antoinette's story and the racially tainted sexuality the potion and their resultant lovemaking represent to him. Afterwards, he retraces without difficulty the path from the ruined house back to Granbois ('I never stumbled once' [*WSS*, p.89]), suggesting a restoration of scribal history; in fact, practically the next thing he does is to write the letter that will set in motion the final triumph of the law:

I wrote a cautious letter to Mr Fraser on the third day.
I told him that I was considering a book about obeah and had remembered his story of the case he had come across. Had he any idea of the whereabouts of the woman now? Was she still in Jamaica? [*WSS*, p.91]

Yet first Rochester must perform another purification; his making love to Amélie suggests a final attempt to displace the contamination he has taken from Antoinette back onto her across the 'thin partition' dividing them from her bedroom, where he knows she is lying and hearing all. No wonder then that afterwards he finds Amélie's skin 'darker, her lips thicker than [he] had thought' [*WSS*, p.89] and that he has 'no wish to touch her' [*WSS*, p.90].

Amélie's subsequent exit from the novel anticipates the more significant departure of Christophine herself, who is both the locus of a powerful orality and the purveyor of its materialization as what is poison to '*béké*'; it is Rochester's effort to bring that 'poison' into the provenance of the law ('I kept some of that wine' [*WSS*, p.103]) that finally drives Christophine out of the novel. Rochester's letter to Mr Fraser has, in fact, called up what might literally be termed the 'Letter of the Law' that his narrative has sought:

I read the end of Fraser's letter aloud: '*I have written very discreetly to Hill, the white inspector of police in your town. If [Christophine] lives near you and gets up to any of her nonsense let him know at once. He'll send a couple of policemen up to your place and she won't get off lightly this time ...*'
... 'So you send me away and you keep all her money. And what you do with her?' ...
'You can write to her,' I said stiffly.
'Read and write I don't know. Other things I know.'
She walked away without looking back. [*WSS*, pp.103–4]

Christophine's exit from the novel implies, if not the control, then the foreclosure of an impermissible discourse and leaves the way clear for Rochester's final control over Antoinette herself. Why this should be so, however, is not immediately clear even given the disjunction between the scribal history of paternity Rochester seeks and the oral history of 'licentiousness' he finds; it becomes so only if Christophine is seen not only as a figure around whom the novel's orality is 'distilled' into poison, as it were, but who is also capable of speaking Rochester's own desire. Thus, in their last long confrontation, her speech repeats itself within his mind, as if finding a responsive echo there, and continues to do so even after she has walked out of the text; thus, too, she restores to Rochester a portion of his own lost 'history', that of his final night with Antoinette, when he has assumed most completely the role of the 'licentious' slave-owners whose past he has been seeking. True to the opposition the text has set up between authorized and forbidden histories, Rochester has suppressed his own memories: 'that is all I remember. All I *will* remember of the night' [*WSS*, p. 87; emphasis added]. But Christophine restores them to him in speech, and what she 'speaks' suggests exactly the abandonment and even brutality that the rest of his narrative has both sought and feared to discover in the past:

> 'I undress Antoinette so she can sleep cool and easy; it's then I see you very rough with her eh?'
> At this point she laughed – a hearty merry laugh ... .
> 'So I give her something for love.'
> *(For love)*
> 'But you don't love. All you want is to break her up. And it help you break her up.'
> *(Break her up)*
> 'She tell me in the middle of all this you start calling her names. Marionette. Some word so ... . You want to force her to cry and to speak.'
> *(Force her to cry and to speak).* [*WSS*, pp. 97–9]

Antoinette makes the same point explicitly: 'You abused the planters and made up stories about them, but you do the same thing' [*WSS*, p. 94], suggesting that the exclusion of such 'stories' from (scribal) history leaves them all the more susceptible to an imaginary reduplication.

Thus, the 'taint' Antoinette carries is not unspeakable after all, but only 'uninscribable'; after Christophine's exit, the only task left for Rochester's narrative is to silence Antoinette herself and everything she represents. His final 'writing' seems almost to reduce Antoinette herself to a kind of hieroglyph: 'a child's scribble, a dot for a head, a larger one for the body, a triangle for a skirt, slanting lines for arms and feet' [*WSS*, pp. 105–6].

The aim of the 'Rochester' narrative [...] thus becomes clear. In *Jane Eyre*, Rochester's father must be dead in order for Rochester to return to England and thus for Antoinette/Bertha to be locked away, that is, to come to occupy 'Jane's space'. In *Wide Sargasso Sea*, the causality is reversed, and Antoinette must be put away [...] in order for the father to die, for Rochester to assume that father's position and his own patrimony. The renunciation demanded in such an assumption of the Name-of-the-Father is evident most of all in the final few pages of Rochester's narrative, in which Antoinette's *voice* [...] reemerges more often, and more seductively, than anywhere else in Part Two, and in which she is implicitly metaphorized as the 'treasure' about which it is 'Better not to tell' [*WSS*, p. 109]. ⊡

One of the most illuminating of the many insights contained in this extract relates to the nature of Antoinette's 'racial imagination', which Erwin describes as 'metaphoric' in form and function. What is curious about this claim is that it could equally well be applied to *Jane Eyre*. Like *Wide Sargasso Sea*, Brontë's novel is organized, as several recent critics have shown, in terms of a series of metaphorical identifications between its eponymous narrator/heroine and the figure of the black slave, deploying such strategies as a powerful means of critiquing the gender and class relations of early Victorian England.[21] This congruence between the operations of the 'racial imagination' in Rhys's text and Brontë's leads to a certain irony. Antoinette's drive to identify herself with blackness turns out to have the opposite effect, as she becomes Jane Eyre's intertextual double, tethered all the more firmly to the whiteness she wishes to escape. In this respect, to recall Spivak, *Wide Sargasso Sea* does indeed reveal itself to be 'bound by the reach of the European novel'.

The final extract in this chapter is from Maria Olaussen's 'Jean Rhys's Construction of Blackness as Escape from White Femininity in *Wide Sargasso Sea*', first published in *Ariel* in 1993. In a lively and provocative analysis, Olaussen agrees with Erwin that it would be reductive to dismiss *Wide Sargasso Sea* as a naïve celebration of a "women and blacks" equation'.[22] At the same time, however, she is considerably more negative than Erwin in her assessment of the politics of Rhys's text. The main problem with *Wide Sargasso Sea*, Olaussen argues, lies in its representation of the black female subject, particularly Christophine. Drawing on the insights of black feminist criticism, Olaussen suggests that the images of black women in Rhys's novel can be usefully read alongside the stereotypical constructions to be found in white portrayals of slavery in the American South. The two stereotypes on which Olaussen focuses in most detail are those of the black woman as whore and as mammy, neither of which, she claims, are adequately questioned by the text.

While these stereotypes may not appear especially appealing in themselves, they become more attractive when set in relation to the constraints of the future that Antoinette faces as wife to Rochester in Victorian England. These constraints are both literal and metaphorical: Antoinette's confinement in the attic at Thornfield Hall simultaneously functions as a harrowing trope for the limits that the patriarchal ideology of the Victorian period imposes upon white women. It is in this bleak light, Olaussen contends, that the novel's investment in blackness can be accounted for. The images of 'black womanhood' that inform the text offer the promise of 'exactly that which is desirable and lacking in the white woman's position',[23] whether this be an unbridled sexual freedom or a liberation from familial ties, associated with the figures of the whore and the mammy respectively.

In reproducing rather than displacing such stereotypes, Wide Sargasso Sea contributes to what Homi K. Bhabha calls 'a conspiracy of silence around the colonial truth',[24] working to mystify the 'systematic oppression of black women'.[25] By sexualizing the black female (whether she be the marginal figure of Daniel Cosway's mother or Amélie), Rhys's text fashions a fictional image that inverts the routine historical truth of white male violations of black female bodies. Similarly, in its promotion of Christophine as an isolated mammy figure – protector, surrogate mother and nurse to Antoinette above all others – the novel diminishes the struggles of black women to maintain the family structures that slavery sought to disrupt. In these ways, Wide Sargasso Sea emerges as a text marked by a troubling irony. Antoinette's identification with blackness is motivated by a desire for flight from the ideologically determined limits of her own femininity. Yet its consequence, for the black woman, is only a form of discursive servitude, enslaving her to the narcissistic sway of the racial stereotype. Olaussen offers the following analysis:

■ Although Rhys's novel starts with Antoinette's childhood in Coulibri, its boundaries lie outside the novel in another woman's text. In Jane Eyre we have the madwoman Bertha locked up in the attic of Thornfield Hall. We know the ending of the story and thus the restrictions placed on both the narrative and the main character. The significant title Wide Sargasso Sea refers to the dangers of the sea voyage. Rochester first crosses the Atlantic alone to a place which threatens to destroy him, then once more, bringing his new wife to England. Both Rochester and Antoinette are transformed through this passage. Rochester gives Antoinette a new name, Bertha, and in England she finally is locked up as mad. [...] In her challenge to Jane Eyre, Rhys draws on the collective experience of black people as sought out, uprooted, and transported across the Middle Passage and finally locked up and brutally exploited for economic gain. She uses this experience and the black forms of resistance as modes through which the madwoman in *Jane Eyre* is recreated.

[...] Rhys constructs black womanhood as exactly that which is desirable and lacking in the white woman's position. Here many critics actually repeat Rhys's wishful thinking, equating British colonial rule over all inhabitants of the colonies with the specific situation of slavery. Mary Lou Emery writes: 'The protagonist of *Wide Sargasso Sea*, Antoinette (Bertha) Cosway Mason (Rochester), undergoes sexual and class enslavement as a white Creole woman'.[26] Such a definition of slavery disregards the actual, historical institution of slavery as experienced by black people under the domination of their white owners. That these white slave owners could also be oppressed and excluded by metropolitan politics and the fact that patriarchal oppression took on a specific meaning for a white Creole woman still did not make her share the experience of slavery. [...]

With the imprisoned madwoman in Thornfield as both starting point and end, Rhys starts her own narrative. The narrator is the madwoman but her tale is the young Antoinette's. The theme is the fear and the possibility of losing one's whiteness. The very first sentences of the novel set the tone: 'They say when trouble comes close ranks, and so the white people did. But we were not in their ranks' [*WSS*, p. 5]. Also the black people point out that they now lack real whiteness: 'Real white people, they got gold money. They didn't look at us, nobody see them come near us. Old time white people nothing but white nigger now, and black nigger better than white nigger' [*WSS*, p. 10].

The lack of real whiteness gains increasing significance when Antoinette grows up. The meaning of her sexual identity is what ultimately determines her racial identity and vice versa. Antoinette recollects an incident where she returned home in her black friend Tia's dress to find that they had beautifully dressed white visitors. Antoinette's appearance in a black girl's torn and dirty dress causes a great deal of disturbance; it shows that she is not part of the real white people. The black servant Christophine is the one who points to the necessity for change when she says: 'She run wild, she grow up worthless' [*WSS*, p. 11]. Tia's dress has to be burned, and Antoinette's mother comes out of her passive state and tries to provide Antoinette with new clothes. Antoinette remembers this change in her mother: 'it was my fault that she started to plan and work in a frenzy, in a fever to change our lives' [*WSS*, p. 84]. Here Antoinette has a dream which is then repeated twice in the novel, each time with more clarity and detail:

I dreamed that I was walking in the forest. Not alone. Someone who hated me was with me, out of sight. I could hear heavy footsteps coming closer and though I struggled and screamed I could not move. [*WSS*, p. 11]

This dream suggests fear of sexual violation. Antoinette fears her future when it becomes clear that she cannot grow up like Tia.

The real change, however, comes with Mr Mason, Antoinette's mother's second husband. He sees himself as a liberator; he 'rescues' Antoinette from growing up worthless, from being a 'white nigger'. This he does by reestablishing the black-white dichotomy, reintroducing the connection of white with wealth and domination, and the connection to England. For Antoinette the meaning of being a woman is firmly placed within a colonial context. Growing up worthless, on the other hand, is the result of a situation where the black-white dichotomy no longer exists.

The most important black character in *Wide Sargasso Sea* is the servant Christophine. She is the first character to speak within Antoinette's narrative and her voice is used to explain the behaviour of the white people. 'The Jamaican ladies had never approved of my mother, "because she pretty like pretty self" Christophine said' [*WSS*, p. 5]. A description of Christophine, again, is given by Antoinette's mother Annette. Antoinette wants to know who Christophine is, her origin and her age. Annette tells her that Christophine was a wedding present from her first husband; she knows that Christophine comes from Martinique, but she doesn't know her age. Annette says:

'I don't know how old she was when they brought her to Jamaica, quite young. I don't know how old she is now. Does it matter? Why do you pester and bother me about all these things that happened long ago? Christophine stayed with me because she wanted to stay. She had her own very good reasons you may be sure. I dare say we would have died if she'd turned against us and that would have been a better fate.' [*WSS*, p. 8]

Christophine's most important function as a powerful protector and nursing mother-figure is thus introduced against the backdrop of the information that she was a wedding gift. The life of the white family is now in the hands of a person who once was part of their property. The reasons for staying are Christophine's own, her age is unknown, her origin on another island. She is thus outside the sphere of what can be controlled and understood by the white family once slavery has ended.

Christophine is mentioned in her relation to Antoinette at a point in the narrative where Antoinette most clearly describes the indifference of her mother to herself: 'she pushed me away ... without a word, as if she had decided once and for all that I was useless to her'. When her own mother pushes her away and finds her 'useless', Antoinette turns to Christophine for the mothering she needs. It is Antoinette who finds Christophine useful. 'So I spent most of my time in the kitchen which was in an outbuilding some way off. Christophine slept in the little room next to it' [WSS, p. 7]. Antoinette's mother, the white lady, develops only her feminine qualities in spite of their distressing situation. These qualities, such as beauty, fragility, dependence, and passivity, make it impossible for her to change actively their situation. They also make her unable to care for her daughter or to perform the most necessary household tasks. Antoinette's mother concentrates her energies on survival in a feminine way in that she does everything to get a new husband.

Christophine's function in the novel has to be understood within the overall context of the white woman's tale. Antoinette's narrative in Part One is a reminiscence of her childhood which carries within it an awareness of the loss of place and identity which, for her, is the meaning of womanhood. Christophine belongs to her childhood, to a period of time which is lost even before the narrative begins. [...]

Black feminist critics in the United States have studied black female characters in texts by white authors and pointed to the way in which these characters are constructed to fit a view of history which mystifies the oppression of black people. Although there are important differences between the American South and the Caribbean, they have the history of slavery in common. Hazel Carby argues that stereotypes about black women have their origin in slavery and furthermore that these stereotypes do not exist in isolation but should be understood in connection with dominant ideas about white women. 'The dominating ideology to define the boundaries of acceptable female behavior from the 1820s until the Civil War was the "cult of true womanhood"'.[27] This ideology defined white women as physically delicate and saw this as an outward sign of chastity, sensitivity, and refinement; it also defined the black woman but in different terms. Here the physical strength and endurance necessary for the work required of black women were seen as signs of moral and spiritual depravity. The function of these stereotypes becomes clear only when the situation of the white slave-owning man is seen as the determining instance, the centre around which female identities were constructed. Carby writes:

The effect of black female sexuality on the white male was represented in an entirely different form from that of the figurative power of white female sexuality. Confronted by the black woman, the white man behaved in a manner that was considered to be entirely untempered by any virtuous qualities: the white male, in fact, was represented as being merely prey to the rampant sexuality of his female slaves. A basic assumption underlying the cult of true womanhood was the necessity for the white female to 'civilize' the basic instincts of man. But in the face of what was constructed as the overt sexuality of the black female, excluded as she was from the parameters of virtuous possibilities, these baser male instincts were entirely uncontrolled.[28]

In contrast to the stereotype of the black woman as a 'whore', another stereotype emerged, that of the 'mammy'. Barbara Christian points out that also this stereotyped role has to be looked at in the context of the role of the white woman. 'The mammy figure, Aunt Jemima, the most prominent black female figure in southern white literature, is in direct contrast to the ideal white woman, though both images are dependent on each other for their effectiveness'.[29] The mammy is the house slave or domestic servant, who is represented as being loyal to the white family and who has no ties to the black community; the needs of her own family do not interfere with her work for the white family. She is harmless or benevolent and can therefore be trusted with a great deal of responsibility when it comes to taking care of the white children. In this way the contradiction of considering black people less than human and at the same time entrusting the care of one's children to them is to some extent made less apparent. Christian argues that the mammy, the whore, and the conjure woman as stereotypical roles for the black woman are based on a fear of female sexuality and spiritual power. In the oral tradition of the slaves the mammy is still present as a stereotype:

> She is there as cook, housekeeper, nursemaid, seamstress, always nurturing and caring for her folk. But unlike the white southern image of mammy, she is cunning, prone to poisoning her master, and not at all content with her lot.[30]

The complexity of Christophine as a character does not challenge these stereotypes. Christophine's relations to her own children and to the rest of the community are made to fit the needs of the white family without making Christophine's own situation seem overly oppressive. Only one of her children survived and he is now grown. She does not have a husband having chosen to be independent. Although the family unit takes on different forms because of the situation of slavery, there is ample evidence to show that such units existed and were maintained and recognized as families by the black community.[31] Similarly, the fact that black women could have children on their own, and thus were not subject to the same rules as white settler women, does not mean that most black women did not, sooner or later, live together with men. According to Herbert S. Klein, it was common during slavery for black women in the Caribbean 'to engage in pre-marital intercourse on a rather free basis. This continued until the birth of the first child. At this point in time a woman usually settled down into a relationship which might or might not be with the child's father'.[32] As Hortense J. Spillers has written in an analysis of the meaning of black American kinship systems as determined by slavery:

> 'kinship' loses meaning, *since it can be invaded at any given and arbitrary moment by* [...] *property relations.* I certainly do not mean to say that African peoples in the New World did not maintain the power-ful ties of sympathy that bind blood-relations in a network of feel-ing, of continuity. It is precisely *that* relationship – not customarily recognized by the code of slavery – that historians have long identi-fied as the inviolable 'Black Family'.[33]

Rhys works within an ideological framework where property relations are given the meaning of blood-relations for black people. By describ-ing Christophine as perfectly free of social ties and responsibilities, she makes her primary attachment to the white family seem natural. Being a white Creole woman implies the necessity of securing a husband by clinging to a definition of womanhood which makes that husband necessary in the first place. The black woman is, however, free to work and support herself. She is furthermore in a position to help the white woman in distress until the husband is found. She is not able to prevent the ultimate disaster where the white woman is victimized precisely through her womanhood, but she herself is saved because as a black woman she is excluded from that definition of womanhood.

Black feminist critics claim that it is the mystification of sexual relations between white men and black women that has given rise to the stereotype of the black whore. We find two important incidents of this kind in *Wide Sargasso Sea*. Antoinette's father is said to have had several children by his black slaves; one of these children, Daniel Cosway, approaches Rochester with fatal information about the Cosway family. This he does in revenge for not having received proper recognition as one of the family. Daniel's mother is described as a liar, someone who tempted Mr Cosway and then tried to trick him into taking responsibility for her son.

The second incident concerns Rochester and the servant girl

Amélie on the honeymoon island. Amélie destroys what is left between Rochester and Antoinette by seducing Rochester at a crucial moment. She is scheming and finally manages to take advantage of the white man so that she can start a new life with the money she gets from him; at the same time, it is the 'white cockroach' [WSS, p. 64] that she is willing to harm most ruthlessly. Thus we have the white mistress, victimized by the black servant woman who takes advantage of the white master and husband. Christophine takes the side of the white mistress when she tells Rochester, 'Why you don't take that worthless good-for-nothing girl somewhere else? But she love money like you love money – must be why you come together. Like goes to like' [WSS, p. 96].

In both these incidents the victim is the white wife. The first incident causes suffering for Antoinette's mother and later destroys Antoinette's life; the second incident brings a great deal of pain to Antoinette and constitutes a turning point in her life. The black women are not seen to suffer; even the white men are to some extent victims of their own confusion caused by the cunning of the black women. The mammy turns against the whore in defending the white mistress. The identification of black with sexual power and white with innocent confusion is further underlined through the description of Antoinette's mother: mad and abandoned, being sexually abused by her black warden while his female mate watches them, smiling maliciously.

Significantly, Rochester is the narrator of Part Two of the novel, which describes his encounters with Daniel Cosway and Amélie. In this way his confusion and fear of the island, his desire for black women, and his guilt are all narrated from his point of view. This narrative also contains the possibility of blackness for Antoinette but here blackness is given an entirely new meaning. When Daniel Cosway visits Rochester he makes a clear link between sexual promiscuity and blackness: '"Give my love to your wife – my sister," he called after me venomously. "You are not the first to kiss her pretty face. Pretty face, soft skin, pretty colour – not yellow like me. But my sister just the same"' [WSS, p. 80]. Shortly afterwards, Rochester looks at Antoinette and thinks that she looks very much like Amélie. [...]

Antoinette's own wish to be part of the black people is thus supported by Rochester's fears. Rochester's narrative gives the British point of view. This point of view starts in *Jane Eyre* and we know that what really happens next is that Antoinette goes mad and has to be incarcerated in the attic of Thornfield Hall. We also know that she will set fire to the house, kill herself, and blind Rochester. By giving Rochester a voice in the narrative, Rhys shows that this is only his perception of events. If we complement the black feminist insight about race and gender construction with analyses of nineteenth-century British definitions of womanhood, we find that sexual desire and womanhood are defined as mutually exclusive. Furthermore, Victorian psychiatrists established a link between mental illness in women and the female reproductive system. Elaine Showalter has studied these discussions and concludes that:

> In contrast to the rather vague and uncertain concepts of insanity in general which Victorian psychiatry produced, theories of female insanity were specifically and confidently linked to the biological crises of the female life-cycle – puberty, pregnancy, childbirth, menopause – during which the mind would be weakened and the symptoms of insanity might emerge.[34]

In Victorian discussions, female sexuality exists as a symptom of mental illness. In 1857, William Acton found sexual desire in women only among low and immoral women whom he encountered in the divorce courts and the lunatic asylum. Not surprisingly, Charlotte Brontë describes her madwoman very much in accordance with the beliefs and attitudes of her time. *Jane Eyre* provides clear indications that Rochester fears Bertha's sexuality: 'Bertha Mason, – the true daughter of an infamous mother, – dragged me through all the hideous and degrading agonies which must attend a man bound to a wife at once intemperate and unchaste' [*JE*, p. 323]. In *Wide Sargasso Sea*, Rhys takes up this element but places it within Rochester's narrative. His encounters with the island, Amélie, Daniel Cosway, and finally Christophine's love-potion are described as a powerful illicit force, at once tempting and dangerous. The only escape is to project all the forbidden feelings onto Antoinette and define her as mad because of these feelings: 'She'll loosen her black hair, and laugh and coax and flatter (a mad girl. She'll not care who she's loving). She'll moan and cry and give herself as no sane woman would – or could. *Or could*' [*WSS*, p. 106]. Rochester experiences only a brief conflict about the reality of his vision. He is aware of all that he has to give up in order to keep his view of the world intact:

> I shall never understand why, suddenly, bewilderingly, I was certain that everything I had imagined to be truth was false. False. Only the magic and the dream are true – all the rest's a lie. Let it go. Here is the secret. Here. [*WSS*, p. 108]

In Antoinette's narrative, which continues in Part Three and gives the final meaning to the events taking place in Part One, the alternative vision is expressed. The vision can only exist if the reality of England

and the meaning of being a white woman in that context is denied. An identification with blackness is established as the only possible escape. In Part One, the burning of the great house at Coulibri is a final and clear manifestation of the hostility of the black people towards their oppressors. Antoinette's narrative is shaped around this event, in that everything that took place before it is reinterpreted and thus turns into premonitions. Everything that happened after the event is seen as resulting from this. The dead horse, poisoned by the black people, is one of the first signs of hostility. 'Now we are marooned' [WSS, p.6] is the reaction of Antoinette's mother. Emery argues that this term, referring to the Maroon communities of escaped slaves, might suggest for Antoinette a possible way out of the necessity of getting married and living the life of a white lady:

> Inadvertently Annette alludes to places in the island's history that Antoinette might inhabit and the wild, unexplored parts of the island that may help her to survive. And she suggests possible kinship with Christophine, who, as an obeah woman, practices a magic that enables survival in dangerous and hostile environments. [35]

When the black people burn the house and it becomes clear that white and black are irreconcilable, Antoinette chooses sides: she runs back to her black friend Tia:

> As I ran, I thought, I will live with Tia and I will be like her. Not to leave Coulibri. Not to go. Not. When I was close I saw the jagged stone in her hand but I did not see her throw it. [WSS, p.24]

Here Antoinette still believes that her racial identity is simply a matter of choice, that through an act of will she can make herself belong to the black community. The rejection by Tia places Antoinette firmly within the white community and thus secures her white female identity. Significantly, Antoinette's Aunt Cora later refers to the wound inflicted by Tia in this way: 'That is healing very nicely. It won't spoil you on your wedding day' [WSS, p.25]. The wound inflicted through the separation of white from black did not only not spoil her on her wedding day, it was in fact a necessary prerequisite for her wedding with a British gentleman. Without that separation she would not have been able to escape the risk of 'grow[ing] up worthless'.

The feeling of impending danger is momentarily relieved at the convent. The convent represents a world where definitions of womanhood are suspended and where the necessity of counteracting black hostility and fighting for a place among the black people is no longer present. As soon as Antoinette is visited by Mr Mason the security vanishes:

> It may have been the way he smiled, but again a feeling of dismay, sadness, loss, almost choked me. This time I did not let him see it.
>   It was like that morning when I found the dead horse. Say nothing and it may not be true.
>   But they all knew at the convent. The girls were very curious but I would not answer their questions and for the first time I resented the nuns' cheerful faces.
>   They are safe. How can they know what it can be like *outside*? [*WSS*, pp. 33–4]

Here Antoinette has her dream for the second time. This time the dream contains even more clearly the fear of sexual violation but also an active determination not to fight or try to escape. It is significant that the visit by Mr Mason is a premonition equal to the incident of the dead horse. In this way, fear of sexual violation is linked to the rejection by Tia: Antoinette is not a black person; thus she cannot escape what lies in store for all white women.

The theme of the burning of the Great House is repeated in the third part of the novel when Antoinette in a dream sets fire to Rochester's mansion in England. This dream is described by Antoinette when she has already lost her sanity and her ability to communicate her view of the world to other people. We arrive, then, back at *Jane Eyre*, from a world of relative clarity and sanity to a world of madness. This is the result of the passage across the Sargasso Sea and the other side of *Jane Eyre*. Rhys thus invites a comparison between Antoinette's situation and that of the slaves. Antoinette is captured, sold, given a new name, transported across the sea, and locked up. She does, however, offer passive resistance; the love-potion prepared by Christophine makes Rochester think he has been poisoned. Antoinette also resists in that she refuses her new identity. In *Wide Sargasso Sea*, Bertha remains Antoinette. For her to keep this identity she is compelled to remember and to perform an important task, something which she has seen coming to her ever since the house at Coulibri was burned:

> There is no looking-glass here and I don't know what I am like now. I remember watching myself brush my hair and how my eyes looked back at me. The girl I saw was myself yet not quite myself. Long ago when I was a child and very lonely I tried to kiss her. But the glass was between us – hard, cold and misted over with my breath. Now they have taken everything away. What am I doing in this place and who am I? [*WSS*, p. 117]

Shortly afterwards, Antoinette has her dream for the third time. Now the dream is clear; she knows why she was brought to England. Antoinette is far from a passive victim. She is determined to fulfill her mission even though its significance lies entirely in the West Indies of her childhood. The confrontation with her mirror image in the hall brings her great confusion, and it is only by escaping that image that she can hold on to the significance of her dream. She calls to Christophine for help and miraculously escapes 'the ghost' [WSS, p. 123] in the mirror.

The struggle for 'Antoinette' against 'Bertha' continues through the last part of the novel. 'Antoinette' is connected to the island and the power of Christophine's obeah, whereas Rochester's attempts to turn her into a Victorian woman are in Part Two rejected by Antoinette as just another form of obeah. In the dream, Antoinette sees the Coulibri of her childhood in the red sky:

> I saw my doll's house and the books and the picture of the Miller's Daughter. I heard the parrot call as he did when he saw a stranger, *Qui est là? Qui est là?* and the man who hated me was calling too, Bertha! Bertha! The wind caught my hair and it streamed out like wings. It might bear me up, I thought, if I jumped to those hard stones. But when I looked over the edge I saw the pool at Coulibri. Tia was there. She beckoned to me and when I hesitated, she laughed. I heard her say, You frightened? And I heard the man's voice, Bertha! Bertha! All this I saw and heard in a fraction of a second. And the sky so red. Someone screamed and I thought, *Why did I scream?* I called 'Tia!' and jumped and woke. [WSS, pp. 123–4]

The dream finally shows her what she is supposed to do: 'Now at last I know why I was brought here and what I have to do' [WSS, p. 124]. The second burning implies liberation and fulfillment and this meaning it derives by refusing the English context. At the event at Coulibri the whole family was saved by their parrot, which frightened the superstitious black people when it was falling off the railing with its clipped wings alight. Antoinette embodies the burning parrot when she jumps down from the battlement at Thornfield Hall, her hair aflame. As Wilson Harris suggests, Rhys here evokes the black legend of flying to freedom. In Virginia Hamilton's retelling of the legend 'The People Could Fly' some slaves knew how to fly already in Africa but had to shed their wings on the slave ship. They thus looked the same as all other slaves but owned the secret knowledge and flew away to freedom when the situation in the fields became unbearable. The Master 'said it was a lie, a trick of the light'.[36] Rhys similarly invokes a secret knowledge which changes the meaning of

[Antoinette's] actions, a mission which will give her a new identity outside of that prescribed for her by patriarchal demands. The Master will always have his own interpretation of events, but within this frame Antoinette creates her own alternative.

It is finally the combination of both Rochester's and Antoinette's narratives that points towards blackness as the escape from white femininity. [...] Antoinette's use of black strategies of resistance reinforces the meaning of blackness as freedom. In exploring the construction of a particular white female identity, Rhys denies the existence of systematic oppression of black women. □

Perhaps the most original aspect of the analysis provided by Olaussen in this extract is its use of work on white literary representations of black women in the American South as a touchstone for reading Rhys's novel. This approach proves to be a productive one, particularly in bringing to light the points where *Wide Sargasso Sea* fails to liberate itself from the conventions of a racially stereotyped discourse. At the same time, Olaussen's methodology courts the danger of obscuring the specificities of the black cultural traditions with which Rhys's text engages. These traditions are brought more sharply into focus by the critics featured in the following chapter, where the central concerns are with Rhys's fictional treatment of the African Caribbean folk practice of obeah and the related cult of the zombie.

CHAPTER FOUR

'There is Always the Other Side': African Caribbean Perspectives

■ This book should have been a dream – not a drama – I know. Still I want to make the drama *possible*, convincing.

The West Indies *had* a (melo?) dramatic quality. A lot that seems incredible could have happened. And did. Girls *were* married for their dots at that time, taken to England and no more heard of. Houses were burnt down by ex slaves, some servants *did* stick – especially children's nurses. I don't know if 'obeah' still goes on. But it did. And voodoo certainly does – Also anonymous letters – and still come tragedies. □

Jean Rhys[1]

At one point during their disastrous Dominican honeymoon, Rochester leaves his sleeping bride and ventures into the forest close to 'the shabby white house' (*WSS*, p.108) where he and Antoinette are staying. Following a 'paved road', he emerges in due course into 'a large clear space' on the forest's outskirts. Here he finds 'the ruins of a stone house', together with 'a wild orange tree', beneath which have been placed 'little bunches of flowers tied with grass' (*WSS*, p.65). Rochester speculates that the house, once the abode of a Roman Catholic priest, is now a site of obeah ceremonies and perhaps even haunted by 'a ghost' or 'zombi' (*WSS*, p.66), though his suspicions are neither confirmed nor denied by Baptiste, the servant sent to look for him when he becomes lost. On eventual arrival back at his own residence, Rochester continues, despite his weariness, to puzzle over the significance of the derelict building. Frustrated by Baptiste's reticence, he endeavours to penetrate the ruin's mysteries by turning to the archives of colonial historiography. Rochester consults neither Edward Long's *The History of Jamaica* (1774) nor Bryan Edwards's *The History, Civil and Commercial, of the British Colonies in the West Indies* (1793), both of which contain detailed accounts of obeah. Instead his point of reference is *The Glittering Coronet of Isles*. From this text – a source-book of Rhys's own invention – he gleans the following:

■ 'A zombi is a dead person who seems to be alive or a living person who is dead. A zombi can also be the spirit of a place, usually malignant but sometimes to be propitiated with sacrifices or offerings of flowers and fruit. [...] "They cry out in the wind that is their voice, they rage in the sea that is their anger."

So I was told, but I have noticed that negroes as a rule refuse to discuss the black magic in which so many believe. Voodoo as it is called in Haiti – Obeah in some of the islands, another name in South America. They confuse matters by telling lies if pressed. The white people, sometimes credulous, pretend to dismiss the whole thing as nonsense. Cases of sudden or mysterious death are attributed to a poison known to the negroes which cannot be traced. It is further complicated by ...' [*WSS*, p.67] □

In contrast to Rochester's own fragmentary inquiries into the motifs of obeah and the zombie, abruptly curtailed by an ellipsis as they are, fascination with these linked aspects of African Caribbean cultural tradition has remained a constant feature of critical work on *Wide Sargasso Sea*. This chapter brings together extracts from four quite varied but overlapping considerations of these topics, all of which appeared between the mid-1980s and mid-1990s.

The first extract is from Teresa F. O'Connor, who briefly discusses obeah in the final chapter of *Jean Rhys: The West Indian Novels* (1986). Here she argues that it functions as one of the main sources of the antipathy between Christophine and Rochester, as an African Caribbean spiritual system confronts and questions his Christian values, marking out the limits to their authority. The strength of her analysis lies in its awareness both of the historical dimensions underpinning the theological clashes between these two figures and of the ways in which questions of religious belief are bound up, in Rhys's Caribbean context, with issues of colonial power and anticolonial struggle. Drawing on Edward Kamau Brathwaite's *The Development of Creole Society in Jamaica, 1770–1820* (1971), O'Connor shows how the religious conflicts played out in the novel's post-emancipation present re-enact those between slaves and masters during the colonial period, in which obeah operates, as Markman Ellis has recently noted, as 'a byword for subversion as the most celebrated focus of African resistance to slavery'.[2] In striving 'to control and conquer' the 'mystery and power' embodied in Christophine, Rochester becomes, in O'Connor's phrase, 'much like the [...] white colonizers and missionaries'[3] who have gone before him.

■ Edward Brathwaite points out that perhaps the greatest conflict between the black and white Creoles arose over religion, an easily recognizable symbol of control and black autonomy overtly represented in the person of the obeah man or woman. Brathwaite writes:

> Equally significant were the black and/or slave preachers, doctors and obeah-men ... . [They] were almost entirely independent of white control and contributed enormously to the physical and psychological well-being of the slave population and therefore to the health of the society as a whole. Slave doctors usually confined their work to their own particular plantation. A good obeah-man would have influence throughout the district. These obeah men (and women) received a great deal of attention from the white legislators of the island.[4]

Brathwaite also discusses Clause X of the Acts of Assembly of 1769. [...] The purpose of Clause X was 'to prevent the many Mischiefs that may hereafter arise from the wicked Art of Negroes, going under the Appellation of Obeah Men and Women'. To that purpose, Clause X provided that:

> any Negro or other Slave, who shall pretend to any supernatural Power, and be detected in making use of any Blood, Feathers, Parrots Beaks, Dogs Teeth, Alligators Teeth, broken Bottles, Grave Dirt, Rum, Egg-shells or any other Materials relative to the Practice of Obeah or Witchcraft, in order to delude and impose on the Minds of others, shall upon Conviction thereof, before two Magistrates and three Freeholders, suffer Death or Transportation.[5]

That whites also used obeah at times, either because of their own belief in it or because it offered an easy way to control the blacks, seems to have been the case and provides another example of the ways in which black and white Creole cultures intermixed.

Part of the job of the European missionaries and priests in the West Indies was to convert the blacks to Christianity without raising questions about the rightness of slavery or apartheid. The greatest religious obstacle to this conversion was the obeah man or woman. Brathwaite writes:

> To achieve this [the conversion of the blacks], it was necessary for the missionaries to pluck out, root and branch, all vestiges of heathen (i.e., African) practices from those over whom they had acquired influence. The drum had to go. The dance had to go. A plurality of wives or women had to be put out of mind. Above all, obeah had to be confronted and defeated.[6]

In *Wide Sargasso Sea*, the conflict between Rochester and Christophine becomes more than a conflict of personality or personal interests. It includes the conflict between the underlying principles and aspects of their two societies, represented by their respective religions. Certainly, Christophine, who has already been persecuted for obeah under English law, must be well aware of this. It is through English law against obeah that Christophine is finally controlled by Rochester. And in their final and long confrontation, they actually argue about religion and the differences between Rochester's god and Christophine's 'spirits'. ☐

In contrast to O'Connor – who sees obeah as a site of white/black struggle – Alan Richardson offers a broadly intertextual or discursive approach to the subject in this chapter's second extract. Richardson's succinct reflections on obeah are to be found in his 'Romantic Voodoo: Obeah and British Culture, 1797–1807', an article originally published in *Studies in Romanticism* in 1993. At first glance, this source would seem to promise little of relevance to a reader of Rhys's novel. After all, as is to be expected from the article's subtitle, Richardson is primarily concerned with the early Romantic construction of obeah during the politically turbulent decade leading up to the abolition of the British slave trade. Yet his discussion also includes an intriguing coda that sketches some of the possible lines of connection – and contention – between the body of texts that is his central focus and Rhys's novel.

In the main part of the article, Richardson explores the representation of obeah in a variety of works, some of which are less well known than others. These range from William Shepherd's 'The Negro's Incantation' (1797) and *Obi; or, Three-Fingered Jack*, a popular melodrama first performed in 1800, to Maria Edgeworth's *Belinda* (1801) and 'The Grateful Negro' (1804) and *Furibond; or, Harlequin Negro* (1807).[7] Despite their diversity, these texts are united by their mutual reliance upon the treacherous stereotypes of colonial discourse, representing obeah as 'a mysterious cult of obscure African provenance, associated with fetishes, witchcraft, and poison, eroticism, and revenge'.[8] Such stereotypes are also to be found, Richardson suggests, in *Wide Sargasso Sea*, although, as he deftly goes on to argue, they are not endorsed by the novel. While Antoinette and Rochester both make assumptions about obeah that reflect the Eurocentric biases of early Romantic writing, the combined authority of their narratives is ultimately called into question. This becomes clear in Richardson's consideration of the scene – or rather non-scene – in Part Two, in which Christophine draws on obeah to prepare a love-potion for Antoinette to use on Rochester. In failing to describe either this scene or the exchange of knowledge it involves, *Wide Sargasso Sea* implicitly represents obeah as something which cannot be adequately contained within the two narrative frames – white Creole and English – available to it. Like the aphrodisiac itself, which Antoinette carries away from Christophine carefully 'wrapped in a leaf' (*WSS*, p.75), obeah remains textually occulted.

■ Set principally in Jamaica during the period immediately following the end of colonial slavery, *Wide Sargasso Sea* – Rhys's antithetical reworking of *Jane Eyre* – critically addresses the conventions for representing obeah developed by writers in the decade 1797–1807. Antoinette (Rhys' sympathetic elaboration of Brontë's Bertha Mason), a white Creole who has grown up in Jamaica, imagines a scene of obeah such as those displayed in 'The Negro Incantation' of *Three-Fingered Jack*: 'a dead man's dried hand, white chicken feathers, a cock with its throat cut' [*WSS*, p.14]. The unnamed Rochester figure, who has come from England in search of a West Indian heiress, reads a sensationalistic account of 'Obeah' in a book called *The Glittering Coronet of Isles*: 'Voodoo as it is called in Haiti – Obeah in some of the islands, another name in South America.' Rochester rationalizes obeah as a matter of poison but cannot help dreading it all the same; he claims to be writing a book about obeah in order to obtain incriminating information regarding Christophine [...] who protects Antoinette until threatened with police action and imprisonment. When Antoinette prevails against her better judgment, Christophine conjures up an aphrodisiac (Rochester's 'poison') with disastrous effect. But the narrative voice itself never presumes to represent obeah: rather, the practice (as Christophine intimates) signals what cannot be understood, or fully accepted, or assimilated by the white characters, Creole or English: 'So you believe in that tim-tim story about obeah, you hear when you so high? All that foolishness and folly. Too besides, that is not for *béké*. Bad, bad trouble come when *béké* meddle with that' [*WSS*, p.71]. In setting the standard Eurocentric approaches to obeah represented by Antoinette and Rochester – demonizing it, outlawing it, eroticizing it, conflating it with other Afro-Caribbean 'cults' – against the narrator's refusal to depict it at all (the scene in which Christophine produces Antoinette's love charm is pointedly ellipsed), Rhys effectively subverts the colonialist construction of obeah characteristic of romantic-era writing. In *Wide Sargasso Sea*, obeah represents what resists representation, what eludes containment; it negatively signifies the gulf that separates even a white Creole like Antoinette (the daughter of a slave-holder) from the island's black population and its living traditions. □

The third extract in this chapter comes from Regina Barreca's 'Writing as Voodoo: Sorcery, Hysteria, and Art', an essay originally included in Sarah

Webster Goodwin and Elisabeth Bronfen's edited collection entitled *Death and Representation* (1993). In this essay, Barreca sets *Wide Sargasso Sea* alongside a medley of other nineteenth- and twentieth-century texts by women writers as diverse as George Eliot (1819–80), Mary Webb (1881–1927), Colette (1873–1954) and Fay Weldon (1933–). Her approach to the inscription of obeah in Rhys's novel is noticeably less historically and culturally specific than that of the two previous extracts. Rather than grounding obeah in its colonial context, as O'Connor does, or considering its representation in relation to earlier discursive constructions, *à la* Richardson, Barreca takes Rhys's treatment of the practice as a cue for a more general theoretical reflection on women's writing, female sexuality and death, linking each of these phenomena to questions of patriarchal power and subversion.

■ Writing as voodoo: sorcery, hysteria, and art. What are the connections? *Wide Sargasso Sea*, Jean Rhys's revision of the story of Bertha from *Jane Eyre*, is laced with voodoo as well as replete with women's pain and women's art. Rhys's heroine, Antoinette (renamed Bertha by Rochester), consults her servant/surrogate mother Christophine to find out how to use magic to recapture Rochester's affection. Voodoo is the alternative text created by the islanders, the text placed up against the artificial, perhaps unreal text of this place called England, the place Antoinette/Bertha does not (in her saner moments) believe actually exists: '"England," said Christophine ... . "You think there is such a place?"' [*WSS*, p. 70].

Voodoo is fire and earth and air and water; mostly it is fire and earth. Voodoo as text is particularly interesting in terms of women's exclusion from the masculine 'high culture' script. Maya Deren, a dancer, filmmaker, and writer who went to Haiti in the late 1940s to record voodoo rituals as art, writes in *The Divine Horsemen*, 'I have come to believe that if history were recorded by the vanquished rather than by the victors, it would illuminate the real, rather than the theoretical means to power'.[9]

Jean Rhys's novel is the story written by the vanquished. Voodoo is the residual power of the vanquished held by Antoinette/Bertha. It is the power and magic behind the fire she calls down on the house of her husband and his mistress. Voodoo is the text constructed by Antoinette/Bertha. Voodoo – if we see it as the reaction of the vanquished to the victor, the skill adopted by the marginalized figure, the figure closest to banishment and death – is the power held by women in women's texts. [...]

But voodoo [also] works as an interesting metaphor for women's texts [themselves]: voodoo relies on the double frame whereby the 'true' power of the voodoo spirits is placed under the aegis of 'accepted' religion. Before a voodoo ceremony begins, there is an *action de grâce*, calling upon (usually) a Roman Catholic saint for a benediction on the ritual to follow. This creates an acceptable, decorous surface text that makes voodoo seem to be enfolded within the dominant religion. Behind this decorous surface supplied by the vigil candles around the plaster saints, by the superficial adherence to convention, there is hidden from the 'authorities' the nonbeliever, the true text of the ceremony. In the double frame of women's writing suggested by Gilbert and Gubar[10] we can see the parallels. Women writers are like voodoo practitioners in their nodding or kneeling toward convention even as they seek to dismantle the system by finding and using alternative sources of power. Women, needing to express their desires and anger in a language alien to them, must rely on ellipses and lacunae. As Rhys's Rochester says of the island: 'What I see is nothing – I want what it *hides* – that is not nothing' [*WSS*, p. 54].

Rhys makes this point most clearly when she describes the servant Christophine's room. Christophine is a slave, a present to Antoinette's mother on her wedding day. Christophine and Antoinette are very close – Christophine is more concerned with Antoinette's fate than anyone else in the book – yet Antoinette, when she comes near to understanding the source of her friend's power, is afraid to enter the servant's room: 'I knew her room so well – the pictures of the Holy Family and the prayer for a happy death. She had a bright patchwork counterpane, a broken-down press for her clothes, and my mother had given her an old rocking-chair' [*WSS*, p. 14].

Everything seems perfect for a servant's room. Religious, humble, used, useful, it appears both domestic and feminine. The passage continues, however:

> Yet one day when I was waiting there I was suddenly very much afraid. The door was open to the sunlight, someone was whistling near the stables, but I was afraid. I was certain that hidden in the room (behind the old black press?) there was a dead man's dried hand, white chicken feathers, a cock with its throat cut, dying slowly, slowly. Drop by drop the blood was falling into a red basin and I imagined I could hear it. No one had ever spoken to me about obeah – but I knew what I would find if I dared to look. [*WSS*, pp. 14–15]

After Antoinette asks Christophine to use her voodoo, known as obeah in Jamaica, she once again looks around the room: 'But after I noticed a heap of chicken feathers in one corner', she comments, 'I did not look round any more' [*WSS*, p. 74]. She understands without needing an explanation, and she is drawn to the possibility of employing voodoo for her own purposes. Why does Antoinette need voodoo? Rochester, after a period of intense desire and sexual exploration, no longer wants his wife in his bed. He is terrified by her sexuality, her intelligence, and her refusal to accept the role of a passive, conventional wife. Because he has discovered that she is named after her mad mother, Rochester always refers to her as Bertha. Changing both her names in marriage is also a form of magic. She tells him, 'Bertha is not my name. You are trying to make me into someone else, calling me by another name. I know, that's obeah too' [WSS, p. 94], but Rochester's is a form of black magic culturally sanctioned and translated into legal and religious terms. Rochester renames Antoinette and strips her of some of her power; yet he is intent on keeping her, despite his own lack of desire. 'Made for loving?', Rochester thinks of his wife: 'Yes, but she'll have no lover, for I don't want her and she'll see no other' [WSS, p. 107].

What recourse does Antoinette have? She asks Christophine to use magic to bring Rochester back to the marital bed. The servant at first refuses to use voodoo on Antoinette's behalf. Christophine explains, 'When man don't love you, more you try, more he hate you, man like that. If you love them they treat you bad, if you don't love them they after you night and day bothering your soul case out .... . A man don't treat you good, pick up your skirt and walk out. Do it and he come after you' [WSS, p. 69]. This is enormously sound advice, but Antoinette understandably wishes to employ more desperate measures. '[I]f he, my husband, could come to me one night. Once more. I would make him love me' [WSS, p. 71]. Christophine warns her of the possible consequences, but she performs the magic.

Her voodoo brings Rochester to his wife's bed. But Rochester then uses the wildly passionate night as evidence of Antoinette's hysteria, as reason to classify her insane: 'She'll ... laugh and coax and flatter', he tells himself, '(a mad girl. She'll not care who she's loving). She'll moan and cry and give herself as no sane woman would – or could. Or could' [WSS, p. 106]. The depth of Antoinette's desire and her ability to give herself over to sexual passion terrify Rochester to the point that he must convince himself she is simply insatiable, which, when translated into the masculine grammar of the female body, is called 'insane'. In her essay 'The Guilty One', Catherine Clément examines in great detail the relation between hysteria, sexuality, and sorcery. She discusses Freud's own awareness of the ways his patients replicated the behavior that damned women for witches in the sixteenth century. By examining the assumptions and questions of Freud, [and the French anthropologists Marcel] Mauss [1872–1950], and [Claude] Lévi-Strauss [1908–], she suggests, as Lévi-Strauss suggested, that the sorceress, the hysteric, and the woman artist might all be linked by a 'desire for disorder or rather for counterorder',[11] some sort of balance against prevailing and confining orthodoxy. The powerful sexuality of both the sorceress and the hysteric must be roped and tied into a category: witchcraft or insanity. The *Malleus Maleficarum* [*The Witch Hammer* (1486)] declares that 'all witchcraft comes from carnal lust, which in women is insatiable'.[12] The syllogism operating here is, 'No normal woman experiences intense sexual desire/This woman experiences intense sexual desire/This woman is not normal'.

In *Wide Sargasso Sea*, Rochester believes that he has been bewitched into a passion he cannot understand, and he attempts to reassert his self-control, paradoxically, by controlling his wife. He needs to confine the woman who makes him come out of himself so that he can again possess himself; fearing his own abandon, he must truss her up in a motionless, positionless place. As Clément writes, the 'feminine role, the role of sorceress, of hysteric, is ambiguous, antiestablishment and conservative at the same time. Antiestablishment because the symptoms – the attacks – revolt and shake up the public, the group, the men [but] *conservative* because every sorceress ends up being destroyed, and nothing is registered of her but mythical traces'.[13]

In Rhys's novel, Antoinette/Bertha's final gesture is to start the magnificent fire, the real consummation of her marriage to Rochester. She is absorbed into the moment of finality that he manages to survive, but her own life is what she has weighed as worth the price of the gesture. She sees the wall of fire as 'protecting [her]' [*WSS*, p. 123] and sees death as 'why [she] was brought here and what [she has] to do' [*WSS*, p. 124]. Death gives her life consequence. And – as happens to many heroines – once she is denied the possibility of love, death becomes her vocation. □

Though certainly refreshing in its difference from other accounts, Barreca's treatment of obeah in *Wide Sargasso Sea* is somewhat impressionistic and not always entirely convincing, not least in terms of its scholarship. In stating, in a strikingly cursory manner, that voodoo is 'known as obeah in Jamaica', Barreca implies that 'voodoo' and 'obeah' are simply two names for the same thing which are interchangeable with one another depending on context. This is misleading. As Richardson notes, the religions are quite distinct, both genealogically and in terms of the forms in which they characteristically find expression:

■ Obeah has been traced to Ashanti-Fanti origins (tribes of the Gold Coast or modern Ghana region) and is more purely concerned with magic or sorcery than voodoo, a more highly elaborated system of beliefs with origins in the Fon and Yoruba cultures (of the Dahomey or modern Benin region).[14] □

In this more nuanced light, Barreca's statement appears ill-informed. It also draws her into a perturbing alignment with the anonymous colonial author of *The Glittering Coronet of Isles* (the book Rochester reads in *Wide Sargasso Sea*), in which obeah and voodoo are similarly haphazardly conflated: 'Voodoo as it is called in Haiti – Obeah in some of the islands, another name in South America.' Indeed, the usage of 'voodoo' instead of 'obeah' throughout her discussion suggests that Barreca's is, ironically, one of those 'Eurocentric approaches' to African Caribbean culture which, according to Richardson, Rhys's novel 'effectively subverts'.

There are two further problems with Barreca's analysis. In proposing that voodoo (read obeah) provides a paradigm for theorizing the subversiveness of (white) women's writing, Barreca interestingly reverses the usual procedure by which the colonizer imposes a Western frame of reference upon the racially and culturally Other in order to domesticate it. As suggested in Chapter Three of this Guide, however, the analogical ground on which this reversal relies is open to question: to claim that 'Women writers are like voodoo [that is, obeah] practitioners' is to aggrandize the predicaments of the former at the expense of belittling those faced by the latter. In addition to this, it is doubtful whether *Wide Sargasso Sea* is particularly well served by an assimilation to a generalized notion of 'women's writing' as exclusively anti-patriarchal in its aims and concerns in the first place. As the entire burden of Rhys's novel makes clear, women writers do not always work together in a covert attempt to sabotage the patriarchal order of which their medium is itself a part. They sometimes also enter into conflicts with one another, finding it incumbent upon themselves – as Rhys does with respect to Brontë – to critique the colonial visions in which their seeming sisters are enmeshed. Far from conforming to Barreca's neat binary opposition between women's writing and patriarchal culture, *Wide Sargasso Sea* marks the point at which such a model begins to unravel. From this perspective, it is not surprising that Barreca should find herself capable of making only the most sparing of gestures towards the intertextual relation between Rhys's novel and *Jane Eyre*.

As its last and longest selection, this chapter reprints in full Judie Newman's chapter on *Wide Sargasso Sea* from *The Ballistic Bard: Postcolonial Fictions* (1995). The importance of this illuminating and adventurous piece lies in the two shifts of critical emphasis which it brings about. The first of these proves to be immensely fruitful and occurs in relation to the material included earlier in this chapter. In a departure from the critics sampled so far, Newman's analysis of the African Caribbean dimensions of Rhys's novel is focused less on obeah itself (which she, like Barreca, occasionally confuses with voodoo), than on the figure of the zombie. Extrapolating from the extensive scientific researches of Wade Davis, Newman shows how the process of zombification not only operates as a powerful trope for colonial and sexual exploitation but also may even take place as a literal event in Rhys's novel. Has Antoinette's mother, Newman wonders, been mysteriously zombified, suffering, as she does, both a 'real' death and 'the one people know about' (*WSS*, p.81)? What of Antoinette herself, suddenly renamed by Rochester as Bertha? Does his white obeah disfigure her into a zombie, 'Her hair [hanging] uncombed and dull into [...] eyes which were inflamed and staring' (*WSS*, p.93)?

The second shift arises with regard to the intertextual perspective normally brought to bear upon *Wide Sargasso Sea*. For Newman, Rhys's novel not only engages in a revision of the canonical *Jane Eyre*, but is also clearly influenced by 'a rather less prestigious source',[15] in the shape of Val Lewton's 1943 film, *I Walked with a Zombie*.[16] In plotting this film's influence on *Wide Sargasso Sea*, Newman offers a slant on the novel that is unusual in drawing attention to Rhys's largely unexplored debt to popular culture. Paradoxically, however, her excursus on Lewton and Rhys functions only as a detour back towards the realms of high culture, of which *Jane Eyre* is a powerful literary expression. While arguing that Rhys takes the figure of the zombie from a low cultural source, Newman herself deploys it as a way of mapping the complex and more culturally elevated dialogue between *Wide Sargasso Sea* and *Jane Eyre*. It is this part of Newman's analysis that is arguably the most productive and certainly the most ingenious. Here the zombie assumes a third meaning, raising 'questions of Eurocentric literary domination and resistance'[17] that become particularly acute in Part Three of Rhys's text. As a novel written before *Wide Sargasso Sea*, *Jane Eyre* would appear always to have the upper hand in the struggle for 'dominant text status'.[18] Yet, as Newman points out, the narrative possibilities of Rhys's novel are not fully in Brontë's grip. By ending the novel at the moment prior to the death inflicted upon Antoinette in *Jane Eyre*, Rhys opens up the possibility – however slight – of an alternative conclusion to the story she has inherited. In this way, she gives Brontë the intertextual slip, as it were, just as Antoinette herself might perhaps be imagined by the reader as having finally escaped from Thornfield. As well as thus resisting the narrative framework imposed upon it by *Jane Eyre*, *Wide Sargasso Sea* 'reverses' the seemingly one-way 'current of determinism' which flows from Brontë's text. This is a process that Newman sees most strongly exemplified in the blindness suffered by Rochester at the end of *Jane Eyre*. For readers innocent of *Wide Sargasso Sea*, Rochester's blindness is simply a condition resulting from his involvement in the fire that destroys his ancestral home. Those who have read Rhys's text, however, might want to account for it differently. As Newman herself contends, it can be viewed, for example, as the fulfilment of 'a West Indian obeah woman's curse',[19] uttered by Christophine in response to Rochester's claim that he 'would give [his] eyes never to have seen [the Caribbean]': 'And that's the first damn word of truth you speak. You choose what you give, eh? Then you choose' (WSS, p. 104). These power struggles between Rhys and Brontë over the meanings of the narrative they share are summarized by Newman when she comments: 'If the reader has read Jane Eyre there is a ghost haunting Wide Sargasso Sea. If we read Wide Sargasso Sea first, it will "possess" and control any subsequent reading of Jane Eyre.'[20]

■ In his review of Wide Sargasso Sea, John Hearne described the novel as the account of a marginal community, run over and then abandoned by history in a country which had never been a polity, only a plantation. In consequence, despite her identity as white Creole, Hearne applauded Rhys, along with Wilson Harris, as belonging absolutely to the West Indies, as

> Guerrillas, not outsiders. Independent of official supply lines; but perhaps more committed in the gut to the desperate campaign we are waging for identity than many who wear the issued uniforms, and who receive battle orders from the certified commanders-in-chief: whether these commanders be foreign readers; our own established politicians and administrators; the complacent, newly cultivated West Indian middle-class ... or the self-appointed high priests of mass culture.[21]

In this ringing denunciation, almost the only group to go unmentioned are women. Yet the need to question acculturated models is particularly acute for women writers whose double marginalisation brings into sharp focus the question: whose story is it? Adrienne Rich has emphasised the general need for women to lay claim to their own stories and to revise or 'revision' those of the past:

> Re-vision – the act of looking back, of seeing with fresh eyes, of entering an old text from a new critical direction – is for women more than a chapter in cultural history: it is an act of survival. Until we can understand the assumptions in which we are drenched we cannot know ourselves.[22]

Jean Rhys's Wide Sargasso Sea, a retelling of the story of Jane Eyre in order to supply the untold, silenced story of the first Mrs Rochester, therefore comes appropriately from both a female and a postcolonial pen. Few readers are unacquainted with the story of Jane Eyre, the orphan who finds true love with Mr Rochester, only to discover at the altar itself that he already has a wife – 'Bertha Antoinetta Mason' [JE, p. 304] – a madwoman incarcerated in his attic. Charlotte Brontë depicts

Rochester as a victim of his father and older brother (the system of patriarchy operating on a younger son) who marry him off to Bertha for her dowry in the full knowledge that madness runs in her family. For Jean Rhys the vital point was that Bertha was West Indian, a white Creole from Jamaica. Rhys had this to say of Bertha:

> The mad first wife in *Jane Eyre* has always interested me. I was convinced Charlotte Brontë must have had something against the West Indies and I was angry about it. Otherwise why did she take a West Indian for that horrible lunatic, for that really dreadful creature?[23]

Certainly Charlotte Brontë's portrayal of Bertha is designed to obliterate all sympathy for her. Bertha is described in the novel in terms which appeal to both racial and sexual prejudices. Her hereditary madness, which is supposedly accelerated by sexual excess, clearly reflects Victorian syphilophobia. (The nineteenth century had shifted the point of origin of syphilis to Africa). Brontë's Bertha has 'a discoloured face', 'a savage face' with 'fearful blackened inflation' of the features: 'the lips were swelled and dark' [*JE*, p. 297]. Successively described as a demon, a witch, a vampire, a beast, a hyena, and even an Indian Messalina,[24] Bertha unites in one person all the available pejorative stereotypes. Even worse, according to Rochester, she turns out to be five years older than him. In addition, Brontë's Rochester describes Jamaica as 'hell', its sounds and scenery those of the 'bottomless pit'. On one 'fiery West-Indian night' [*JE*, p. 324] Rochester even contemplates suicide, only to be saved by 'A wind fresh from Europe' [*JE*, p. 325]. When this [...] recalls him to England, he does not, of course, return empty-handed. Penny Boumelha has observed that in *Jane Eyre* all the money comes from colonial exploitation.[25] Jane Eyre herself gains her financial independence as a result of a legacy from an uncle in Madeira who is connected to the same firm which Mr Mason, Bertha's brother, represents in Jamaica. Jane shares out this loot, appropriately, between the church (her cousin Mary's husband), the military (her cousin Diana's husband) and the forces of cultural imperialism, in the shape of her cousin, St John, who [...] 'labours for his race' [*JE*, p. 476] as a missionary in India. With Bertha dead in a fire at Thornfield Hall, Jane and Rochester settle down to a happy married life on the proceeds of the Empire.

When Jean Rhys sets out to vindicate the 'madwoman' she emphasises her role as 'the legacy of imperialism concealed in the heart of every English gentleman's castle'.[26] Rechristening Bertha 'Antoinette', Rhys arranges the story in three parts, the first narrated by Antoinette, describing her childhood in Jamaica, the second largely narrated by

Rochester describing his honeymoon in Dominica, and the third narrated partly by Antoinette's jailer, Grace Poole, partly by Antoinette herself. The narrative method emphasises the fact that Antoinette loses control of her own story, once married to Rochester. [...] Rochester's now becomes the master narrative, and Antoinette is subject to the tales and inventions of others. It is only at the very end that she regains her voice and her ability to speak for herself. In Part One, which provides Antoinette with a history, Rhys cleverly reverses Brontë's tactics. Brontë makes Bertha and Jane opposites, the one an obstacle to the other's happiness, a dark subconscious *alter ego* of passion and anger. She makes it a war between women. Rhys, however, gives Antoinette a similar background to Jane Eyre: orphanhood, poverty, social humiliation, repressive religious schooling, lack of love. The only real difference between the two women is their cultural position, the one on the margins of Empire, the other at its centre. Throughout the novel, Antoinette's personal history is firmly politicised. As the hated offspring of a slaveowner in post-emancipation Jamaica, she is automatically detested by blacks and also by more prosperous whites, emancipation having reduced the family fortunes. Antoinette is also rejected by her mother, whose energies are focused on a younger brother. Imagistically Rhys emphasises the weakness of the mother–daughter bond as not only fatal to Antoinette's individual sense of self (a view which modern psychoanalysis confirms) but also as symbolic of the lack of sustenance and definition offered by the 'mother country' to its dependencies. *Wide Sargasso Sea*, a text which may be described as born from *Jane Eyre*, is deliberately situated before most of the events of *Jane Eyre* take place, in order to reconstitute itself as the 'mother text' or point of origin of the English novel. Rhys therefore links reproduction and textual production so that *Wide Sargasso Sea*, a 'post-dated prequel'[27] to *Jane Eyre*, becomes its necessary precursor. By commandeering *Jane Eyre* as her sequel, therefore, Rhys enjoins future readers to envisage Victorian Britain as dependent upon her colonies, just as Brontë's heroine depends upon a colonial inheritance to gain her own independence.

Antoinette's history also becomes representative of West Indian history in broader terms. In a society founded upon the buying and selling of human beings, Antoinette's marriage to Rochester is also envisaged as an economic transaction. Acquired for profit, given a more 'English' name, transported overseas, economically enslaved and then quite literally a captive with a keeper, treated as an animal and a degenerate, Antoinette experiences some, at least, of the evils of slavery in her own person. It is not surprising that she reacts, much as her father's ex-slaves did, by setting a torch to the Great House.

Rhys's Rochester – never named in the novel – is also a creature of his culture and history, his motivation reflecting both his engrained racial prejudice and the attitudes of his time to purity in women. In Part Two, on his honeymoon in Dominica, in a house which originally belonged to Antoinette's mother, Rochester clearly resents the female-identified world around him. *He* is dependent on Antoinette, here. Like Caliban in [William Shakespeare's] *The Tempest* [1611] she acquaints the newcomer with the flora and fauna of the island and interprets its customs to him. Like Prospero, Rochester's reaction is to resent her independent knowledge, accuse her of sexual guilt and to enslave her. Initially Rochester and Antoinette had enjoyed a honeymoon to their mutual satisfaction. Rochester, however, espouses proto-Victorian views on the proper forms of female sexuality. For him only a prostitute – or a madwoman – could take pleasure in sex. He comments that Antoinette would 'moan and cry and give herself as no sane woman would' [*WSS*, p. 106]. Once he learns that Antoinette's mother was insane he jumps at the chance to redefine his wife in conventional terms. Antoinette's failure to 'lie back and think of England' is well nigh fatal to her. After one last night of love, Rochester covers his wife's face with a sheet, as though she were dead, and retreats to the arms of her maid, a woman whom he can possess and dominate sexually without any complications – a paid woman. Henceforward Antoinette is essentially silenced. Rochester takes over her voice, and renames her (from Antoinette to Bertha, and even to Marionette). He finds himself drawing her as a stick-woman: 'a child's scribble, a dot for a head, a larger one for the body, a triangle for a skirt, slanting lines for arms and feet' [*WSS*, pp. 105–6]. As most readers would agree, Antoinette's identity has been erased by the politics of imperialism and of patriarchy. Only the skirt, the sexual marker, identifies her as a woman. Dehumanised, depersonalised, renamed, she is now a helpless puppet, a character under Rochester's control.

Or so it seems. If the story ended here, it would be difficult to quarrel with those critics who have argued that Rhys's novel is deterministic, that Antoinette cannot escape the fate which Brontë has prepared for her. In this connection the third part of the novel bears close examination, and will be fully comprehensible only in the light of an image which pervades *Wide Sargasso Sea* – that of the zombie. In *Wide Sargasso Sea* Rhys deliberately exacerbates the Gothic mode of her predecessor, supplying omens, premonitory dreams, references to zombies, obeah and poisonous potions, as part of the process of reclaiming the first wife for West Indian culture. Obeah, also known as voodoo, is the black religion of Jamaica, Dominica and other West Indian islands, a survival and development of West African religious beliefs, brought over by slaves. West African religion particularly venerates ancestors, who are believed to maintain a presence and an influence over their kinspeople's lives for many years after their deaths: they return as spirits, or living dead, to revisit their families. In the Caribbean context, the phrase 'living dead' has a rather different ring. Most of Rhys's readers will be familiar with the figure of the zombie from such horror films as *Night of the Living Dead* [1968], *I Walked with a Zombie, White Zombie* [1932] and so forth. A zombie may be defined as 'a body without character, without will',[28] generally as the result of sorcery, involving the raising of the dead. In *Wide Sargasso Sea* there can be little doubt that zombification occurs. Several different commentators have called attention to the number of references to obeah in the novel, to Rhys's own background knowledge (via her black nurse), and to a key incident in the plot: the use of a love-potion by Antoinette, bought from Christophine, the obeah woman, in an attempt to reclaim Rochester's affections.[29]

Now, why does Rhys introduce this material? If her aim is to revise Brontë's Bertha – described by Jane Eyre as the 'foul German spectre – the Vampyre' [*JE*, p. 297] – it is not much of an advance merely to substitute a zombie in her place. (Most readers would be just as unhappy meeting a zombie in the dark as a vampire). And if the aim is to refuse to provide the stereotypical image of the West Indies as tropical hell, the same objection arises. The popular image of voodoo, from horror film to James Bond, tends to involve sensational acts of cannibalism, human sacrifice and sexual orgies, a trend which was encouraged by the media during the American occupation of Haiti in order to legitimise the latter. So why employ this particular image? The answer, arguably, lies in the unique way in which the zombie, a figure with a special autobiographical significance for Rhys, unites issues of economic and sexual exploitation with questions of Eurocentric literary domination and resistance, problematising the nature of the 'real'.

In the classic folklore accounts, a zombie is created by the giving of a drug of some kind, which creates the appearance of death.[30] A common method is to sprinkle 'zombie poison' across the threshold where it is absorbed through the feet of the victim. The drug supposedly lowers the metabolic rate so that the victim seems dead, is cold, but can be restored to some sort of life by an antidote. The sorcerer digs up the body, administers a second potion (drugged rum is often cited) and gives the zombie a new name. From this point on, the zombie is the slave of the sorcerer, lacking all memory, willpower or thought, but capable of working night and day in the fields. The image suggests an obvious connection with the history of slavery. Frances Huxley, the anthropologist, speculates that 'the folklore surrounding [zombies] is partly a reminiscence of plantation days when the Negroes learned to endure forced labour ... by acting stupid and not allowing their resentment to show'.[31] In the myths the zombie can be recognised by staring eyes, lack of expression and a hoarse voice. Zombies will go on working forever, as long as they do not taste salt. One grain of salt, however, will restore the memory, and the zombie returns to the grave to 'die' all over again. Tales of zombies are particularly prevalent in Martinique, known as 'le pays des revenants' – the country of those who come back. Both Christophine and Antoinette's mother come from Martinique; Rhys originally entitled her novel 'Le Revenant'.

The zombie has a long pedigree in colonial fiction. The first West Indian novel was *Le Zombi du Grand Pérou* by Pierre Corneille Blessebois (1697).[32] Rhys, however, draws her zombie from a rather less prestigious source. Jane Eyre has walked with a zombie before. When the zombie enters Western discourse it is largely through the medium of popular film, which tends to focus on themes of economic or sexual exploitation. Zombies labour for masters in a sugar mill for example (*White Zombie*) or a mine (*Plague of the Zombies* [1966]). In *King of the Zombies* [1941] and *Revenge of the Zombies* [1943], zombies are enlisted to aid the Nazi cause, reflecting the idea that people may be turned by war into mindless killers.[33] And in some films – *White Zombie*, *Voodoo Man* [1944] and *Voodoo Woman* [1957] – the exploitation is implicitly sexual.

More specifically interesting, in the context of *Wide Sargasso Sea*, is *I Walked with a Zombie* (1943) described by its producer, Val Lewton, as '*Jane Eyre* in the tropics'.[34] In the film a white first wife (Jessica Holland) is supposedly turned into a zombie by her husband's mother, infuriated by her daughter-in-law's adultery with her brother-in-law. The plot: unchaste first wife, noble suffering husband and even more selfless Canadian nurse (the modern version of the governess who will become the second wife) is straightforwardly stolen from *Jane Eyre*. Two features of the film, however, are suggestive. First the director (Jacques Tourneur) goes to some lengths to emphasise the history of slavery as a curse both upon the fictional island of Saint Sebastian and the Holland family, who were entirely responsible for introducing it to the island. The economic exploitation continues in the film's present: menacing drums in the background turn out to be the rural factory hooter, summoning workers to the family sugar mill. Second, the introduction of a mother figure responsible for zombification has interesting connections with Rhys's own vexed relations with her mother, Antoinette's with her mother, and the relationship between mother- and daughter-texts. As her biography demonstrates [...] Jean Rhys felt herself 'zombified' by the mother country. Internal evidence strongly suggests that Rhys had seen *I Walked with a Zombie*. Quite minor incidents in the film are echoed in *Wide Sargasso Sea*. Holland, the Rochester figure, feels partly responsible for his wife's apparent madness, because when her adultery was discovered, he refused to allow her to leave him, insisting that he would keep her by force. Rochester similarly refuses to countenance separation from Antoinette. The islanders sing calypsos about the family scandal. Rochester fears featuring in *his* islanders' songs [*WSS*, p. 105]. The islanders suspect that Jessica is a zombie and attempt to take her by force. It is suggested that, for her safety, she should be removed to Saint Thomas. In *Wide Sargasso Sea* Antoinette's brother, Pierre, lies in a similar trance to Jessica's and is at similar risk. His mother insists that the family depart on the grounds, otherwise unmotivated, that 'It is not safe for Pierre' [*WSS*, p. 17]. When the blacks fire the house they begin with Pierre's bed. Though he dies shortly afterwards, Antoinette comments that 'He died before that' [*WSS*, p. 25]. In the film there is a tower with stone steps, up which Jessica climbs by night in her trance. Antoinette repeatedly dreams of climbing stone steps. Most importantly, the initiator of the obeah curse is white (the mother-in-law) acting to prevent the break-up of her family. Things go badly wrong, however, with Jessica eventually stabbed by her lover who then kills himself. The nurse also resorts to obeah, on one occasion taking her patient to visit the voodoo priest, though without success. In *Wide Sargasso Sea* Rhys places particular emphasis on the fact that white people meddling with obeah is dangerous. Christophine argues that 'that is not for *béké*. Bad, bad trouble come when *béké* meddle with that' [*WSS*, p. 71].

Just how much Antoinette does meddle with obeah becomes obvious in one crucial scene. On their last night of love, Rochester questions Antoinette about her mother. The dialogue is worth quoting in full:

'Is your mother alive?'
'No, she is dead, she died.'
'When?'
'Not long ago.'
'Then why did you tell me that she died when you were a child?'
'Because they told me to say so and because it is true. She did die when I was a child. There are always two deaths, the real one and the one people know about.' [*WSS*, p. 81]

When Rochester enters Antoinette's room he notices 'the white powder strewn on the floor' ostensibly against cockroaches. As he drinks from the glass she offers him, he tells her to forget the past: 'We are letting ghosts trouble us.' Antoinette replies, 'Christophine knows about ghosts too, but that is not what she calls them' [*WSS*, p. 87].

Rochester's voice alters, and he succumbs to her charms. When he awakens it is as an almost-dead man. 'I woke in the dark after dreaming that I was buried alive, and when I was awake the feeling of suffocation persisted. Something was lying across my mouth; hair ... . I was cold too, deathly cold' [WSS, pp. 87–8]. He is also almost incapable of thought or action: 'I thought, I have been poisoned. But it was a dull thought, like a child spelling out the letters of a word which he cannot read, and which if he could would have no meaning or context' [WSS, p. 88]. Rochester appears to have narrowly escaped zombification. The scene apparently incriminates Antoinette and makes Rochester, however imperfect, a victim of female witchcraft.

Antoinette, however, sees things rather differently. Earlier Rochester has insisted on calling her 'Bertha': 'on this of all nights, you must be Bertha' [WSS, p. 87]. When next he sees her she has indeed become 'Bertha': 'Her hair hung uncombed and dull into her eyes which were inflamed and staring'. Her voice is hoarse. For Antoinette, Rochester is guilty of obeah: 'Bertha is not my name. You are trying to make me into someone else, calling me by another name. I know, that's obeah too' [WSS, p. 94]. Rochester has already scripted Antoinette into the role of sex-mad Caribbean lunatic – his puppet, a character under his control. Such is his cultural conditioning that when he receives the letter denouncing her, he feels no surprise. It is as if he had been expecting it. It is rather as if he already knew the plot which Antoinette's life must now imitate. As a typical nineteenth-century Englishman, Rochester's view of his wife is entirely the product of paradigmatic plots promulgated by his culture, which expects anywhere outside England to be a place of evil and madness. In addition, Rochester's voodoo is also sexual. When Brontë's Jane Eyre is serenaded by Rochester, inviting her to die with him, her response is both characteristically forthright and obtuse: 'I had no intention of dying with him – he might depend on that' [JE, p. 286]. Antoinette, however, is in a state of complete erotic surrender. She whispers to Rochester: 'If I could die. Now, when I am happy. Would you do that? You wouldn't have to kill me. Say die and I will die.' Rochester's response is decidedly less romantic. '"Die then! Die!" I watched her die many times. In my way, not in hers' [WSS, p. 57]. Rochester understands death as the French understand the phrase la petite mort: as sexual orgasm. Unlike Jane Eyre, Antoinette is sexually bewitched. Rhys makes the point, forcefully, that it is sexuality which enslaves the woman and destroys her independence. Antoinette has become Rochester's sexual zombie before she attempts to turn the tables on him. There is, then, a form of double zombification at work here, in which both Rochester and Antoinette feature as victim and aggressor, possessor and possessed. The image underlines the dual dependence of coloniser and colonised

– and it also has implications for questions of literary domination and independence.

In literary terms, Jean Rhys may also be said to have suffered a double death. In the 1940s she had disappeared from view and was presumed dead. Francis Wyndham even referred to her publicly as 'the late Jean Rhys'.[35] In 1948 she saw an advertisement in the *New Statesman* placed by Selma Vaz Dias who had adapted Rhys's *Good Morning, Midnight* for radio and needed to find Rhys to obtain permission to perform it. The BBC had told her that Rhys was dead. Rhys commented that it made her feel like a ghost: 'I feel rather tactless at being alive!'.[36] Even worse, when she did make contact with the BBC one of her neighbours claimed that Rhys was 'an imposter [sic] "impersonating a dead writer called Jean Rhys"'.[37] When Selma met her she expressed surprise that Rhys was so quiet and well behaved. She had expected a raving and not too clean maniac with straws in gruesome, unwashed hair.[38] (This was an unsurprising reaction, given that Rhys was continually arrested for being drunk and disorderly. She had appeared in court eight times in two years). To cut a long story short, England had already 'zombified' Jean Rhys, who came back from the dead only when 'dug up' by another writer who wanted to use her work. What better revenge then, on Rhys's part, than to dig up Charlotte Brontë, to make *her* novel serve Rhys's purposes?

Rhys's work frequently displays her unease with the power of the book. In 'Temps Perdi' a character reflects:

Now I am almost as wary of books as I am of people. They are also capable of hurting you, pushing you into the limbo of the forgotten. They can tell lies – and vulgar trivial lies – and when they are so many saying the same thing, they can shout you down and make you doubt, not only your memory, but your senses.[39]

Helen Tiffin has argued persuasively that Eurocentric writing may be seen as a kind of obeah, as magically powerful, creating the sense in the Caribbean reader of being deadened, enslaved to other people's words, one's reality removed by Eurocentric definitions.[40] Rhys clearly undercuts the power of Western books in *Wide Sargasso Sea*: the books in Rochester's dressing room are being steadily eaten away by the West Indian climate. Yet while undercutting the power of Eurocentric fiction, Rhys was also, of course, writing a novel herself, taking over another woman's book – in a sense writing with Brontë's ghost at her elbow, a ghost powerless to intervene, but susceptible to economic exploitation. Rhys's unease is tangible. In her letters she progressively denies the connection to her literary ancestor; she claims that Brontë's story was based on reality; that there were many Antoinettes; and even that the tale came from a different novel. [...] Rhys was clearly uneasily aware that, in outgunning Charlotte Brontë, she risked becoming a slaver in her turn. It is a problem which recurs when dealing with intertextuality: its relation to intellectual property is a vexed one. Where does parody, intertextuality or play-giarism end, and the reader exclaim, 'It's a steal'? That Rhys was aware of this danger of exploiting Brontë is suggested in her repeated attempts to distance herself from *Jane Eyre*, both in her letters and within the novel itself. When she introduced the figure of the zombie into her text, she knew that what she was doing was to make issues of creative control central to her novel. If the figure of the zombie highlights issues of economic and sexual possession, it is no less relevant to the need to possess one's own imaginative reality.

Within the text of *Wide Sargasso Sea* the connection to *Jane Eyre* is purposefully oblique. 'Antoinette Cosway' does not immediately suggest 'Bertha Mason'; Rochester is never so named. Only the name Mason provides a clue, until the appearance of Grace Poole in Part Three. In addition, the time is out of joint. *Jane Eyre* is set in the early nineteenth century: Jane is given a newly published copy of [Sir Walter Scott's] *Marmion* (1808) near the end of the novel.[41] *Wide Sargasso Sea*, however, begins with Emancipation in 1833. The one date in the novel, 1839, is sewn on to a sampler by Antoinette in her seventeenth year. Of course, for Rhys's purposes the time scheme has to be 'wrong'. In terms of events, the action of *Jane Eyre* follows that of *Wide Sargasso Sea*, just as Jane follows Bertha. But in terms of influence, *Jane Eyre* precedes *Wide Sargasso Sea* and 'haunts' it for many readers, so the dates place *Wide Sargasso Sea* after the 1808 of *Jane Eyre*. The change also allows the novel to begin at the moment when slavery has ostensibly ended. In the West Indies, however, a period of 'apprenticeship' was envisaged, during which slaves were only gradually given full freedom. They were neither quite free nor quite enslaved, rather like the zombie's position between life and death.

Rhys's oblique handling of the relationship to her literary ancestor, therefore, creates a productive sense of liminality in the reading experience, redefining Gothic and problematising notions of possession in the process. Even the most informed reader is independent of Charlotte Brontë at first. But slowly, in the process of reading, we become haunted by another text – *Jane Eyre* – a kind of ghost inside the words, an echo, at times indistinct, at others very definite. As the two novels battle for dominant text status, for a position as master narrative, it is not going too far to argue that intertextuality becomes a form of zombification.[42] The reader has a sense of illegitimately crossing the boundaries between texts, an uneasy awareness of something already familiar returning to consciousness: a process which fulfils Freud's classic definition of the uncanny.[43] *Wide Sargasso Sea* becomes a vast echo chamber, a text criss-crossed by repetitions, hauntings, mirror-ings, plot-parallels and reenactments, as Antoinette reenacts her mother's fate, as Rochester acts out the role which his culture has pre-pared for him, and as both move towards the action of *Jane Eyre*.

One scene in particular focuses on these issues of possession, narrative control and domination: Rochester's interview with Christophine [*WSS*, pp.98–9]. When Christophine speaks to Rochester he does not immediately respond. Instead the text gives the reader a response in parentheses, reproduced in italics. The first two utterances are clearly Rochester's own thoughts. Then suddenly, 'every word she said was echoed, echoed loudly in my head' [*WSS*, p.98]. The final parenthetical utterance, however, is not Rochester's: '(*I lay awake all night long after they were asleep, and as soon as it was light I got up and dressed and saddled Preston. And I came to you. Oh Christophine. O Pheena, Pheena, help me*)' [*WSS*, p.99]. The voice is that of Antoinette, on one of only two occasions in Part Two where it interrupts Rochester's narrative; the other occasion is her visit to Christophine to seek the love-potion, an episode which could not logically be narrated by Rochester. What is happening here? Is Rochester becoming subordinate to Christophine, and to Antoinette, his mind able only to echo their words. Mary Lou Emery reads the scene persuasively in these terms.[44] On the other hand, the echoes are not quite identical to their source (as in the larger literary echoing which it models). In some cases they express Rochester's inner determination to abandon Antoinette:

'So that you can leave her alone.'
(Leave her alone)
'Not telling her why.'
(Why?)
'No more love, eh?'
(No more love) [*WSS*, pp.98–9]

During their last night of love, Rochester had attempted to force Antoinette to cry and to speak, but she had resisted. Now Rochester thinks/echoes '(*Force her to cry and to speak*)' [*WSS*, p.99] and her voice is heard. Has he finally succeeded in controlling her voice? When the voice speaks, however, it speaks to Pheena. The scene deliberately confronts the central questions raised by the novel. Is Antoinette merely an echo? Or is she independent? Can she speak for herself? Or only when enclosed, bracketed, by Brontë? Is the patriarchal Englishman calling the shots? Or is he simply echoing the dominant culture? Is the story coming to the reader from the male or the female, the imperialist or the imperialised? Rochester wins the duel with Christophine by threatening her with the 'Letter of the Law' [*WSS*,

p. 11]: police action. He reads her a letter from the local police chief, making the point that one word from him will be enough to gaol her. His words can become realities, deeds. At the close of the interview, however, the reader sees the same possibility in Christophine's hands. Rochester, exasperated, cries out, 'I would give my eyes never to have seen this abominable place.' Christophine laughs, 'And that's the first damn word of truth you speak' [WSS, p. 104]. The reader may remember that Jane Eyre sees Rochester blinded at its close. In allowing Christophine to pronounce the curse on Rochester, Rhys reverses the current of determinism.[45] What she does is to make the action of Jane Eyre the result of a West Indian obeah woman's curse. It is poetic justice for Rochester. He had insisted on the reality of England, and of English words. Now his words are echoed in the curse and made into a reality: he does give his eyes.

The scene also raises questions which can be extended to the novel itself. Who zombifies whom? Is Rhys dependent on Brontë? Or Brontë on the Empire? Does Rhys exploit Brontë? Or can the current of economic exploitation flow only towards England? Rochester believes that Antoinette has attempted to bewitch him by illicit means. Yet he has transformed her into a nameless automaton, entirely under his control. How actual is zombification? Is it merely a suggestive image, to be read in metaphoric terms? Western readers tend to recoil from any other reading: after all, unlike European ghosts, zombies are not 'real' to the Eurocentric reader, though they may be to African or Caribbean readers. Who controls the reality of the story, the imperial master narrative or the West Indian folk myth? Which woman is 'real' and which a ghost? If the reader has read Jane Eyre there is a ghost haunting Wide Sargasso Sea. If we read Wide Sargasso Sea first, it will 'possess' and control any subsequent reading of Jane Eyre.

It is in the light of these concerns that the final part of the novel makes sense. The ending of Wide Sargasso Sea, the burning of Thornfield Hall, has aroused considerable critical debate. For some readers, the idea that Antoinette is tied to a destiny created by Charlotte Brontë makes the whole novel an exercise in cultural determinism. Antoinette may have been revised from malevolent vampire to innocent victim, but she is a passive victim just the same. It is worth noting, however, that Rhys ends her novel before Antoinette's death. As readers, we may choose to 'finish her off' in Brontë's terms – or not. We know that her death lies just beyond the ending, but we are at liberty to ignore that knowledge; our imaginations are not the slaves of Charlotte Brontë. After all, Rhys was perfectly free to rewrite Jane Eyre in any way she pleased, as a more recent rewriting suggests. Robbie Kidd's The Quiet Stranger (1991) centres on black revolutionary women, with Jane Eyre as a witch and adventuress.[46]

In her dreams Antoinette sees herself fleeing to the battlements, and looking down to see *not* the stones of the yard, but the pool at Coulibri, her childhood home, which was burned by ex-slaves. In the pool she sees not her own reflection but the face of her black friend Tia, beckoning: 'I called "Tia!" and jumped and woke' [WSS, p.124]. On the simplest level, therefore, Antoinette's final action aligns her with a female and West Indian world and with a revolt against slavery. The 'suicidal' quality of the ending, potentially masochistic in European terms, is quite altered from the perspective of West Indian culture. In the first place the ending represents an awakening from a state of zombiehood. When last seen in Dominica, Antoinette had become 'only a ghost. A ghost in the grey daylight' [WSS, p.110]. Now, however, the text moves back to Antoinette's voice. The italics of quotation are reserved for Grace Poole. Antoinette's memory is also returning, thanks to illicit swigs of Grace Poole's alcohol, after which she feels that 'I could remember more and think again. I was not so cold' [WSS, p.116]. The process of recall is assisted by a visit from Richard Mason, whom she bites. In blood and fire Antoinette finds the antidote to her benumbed state. Up to this point *she* has been identified as the ghost of Thornfield. In her dream, however, the ghost is a separate entity:

> it seemed to me that someone was following me, someone was chasing me, laughing. Sometimes I looked to the right or to the left but I never looked behind me for I did not want to see that ghost of a woman who they say haunts this place. [WSS, p.122]

It is almost as if Jane Eyre were speaking, not the madwoman. Finally Antoinette encounters the 'ghost': 'It was then that I saw her – the ghost. The woman with streaming hair. She was surrounded by a gilt frame, but I knew her' [WSS, p.123]. The reader has two possibilities here. Either the frame is that of a mirror and the ghost is Antoinette, now so lacking in substance as to be unreal, ghostly. Or it may be the frame of a picture. In Brontë's novel, Jane Eyre paints a picture of a woman with streaming hair [JE, p.131]. In short, is this a mirror echoing Antoinette, or is it an independent, though familiar, work of art? The same duplicity reigns over the ending as a whole. It is a dream but a dream of a familiar book. It gives the reader precisely the feeling experienced by the victim of colonialism of real life being enclosed inside somebody else's fiction. At the close, however, it is *Jane Eyre* which has become the dream, from which Rhys's heroine can wake up and move forward into the future. The ending also revises the 'hellish' overtones of the West Indies. When Antoinette stands on the battlements she experiences a flood of memories as she looks at the sky: 'It was red and all my life was in it. I saw the grandfather clock and Aunt Cora's patchwork, all colours, I saw the orchids and the stephanotis and the jasmine and the tree of life in flames.' The final reference is to pre-Columbian myth.[47] The Arawak people, predecessors of the Caribs in Dominica, have a myth of the tree of the world, which reaches to heaven across the ages, a tree of life, bearing food and sustenance. In time of war, when the Arawaks took refuge in its branches, the tree was fired by the Caribs. The fire drove the Arawaks up and up into space, until they burned and were converted into sparks which flew up into heaven to become the stars. At the end of the novel Antoinette tells us that 'The wind caught my hair and it streamed out like wings. It might bear me up, I thought' [WSS, p. 123]. Imagistically then, Antoinette's dream-death is both a retaliation and a reentry into a lost paradise, a lost West Indian point of origin. In Christian myth fire and hellfire go together. Antoinette, however, takes flight into the heaven of a different culture. □

As well as offering an array of trenchant insights into the role of the zombie in *Wide Sargasso Sea*, Newman's reading is notable for its method, which places the novel in dialogue with twentieth-century and early Victorian texts (*I Walked With a Zombie* and *Jane Eyre*) alike. Such a double frame of reference also characterizes the material included in the final chapter of this Guide. In contrast to Newman, however, the next set of critical analyses is less concerned with questions of influence and inter-textuality than with the novel's negotiation of its historical contexts, whether they be the post-imperial England in which it was written or the post-emancipation Caribbean, in which it is principally set.

CHAPTER FIVE

'Not Even Much Record': The Place of History

■ [...] I'm wonderin' how dem gwine stan'
Colonizin' in reverse. ☐

Louise Bennett

■ It is important that Jean Rhys's fiction use as a point of departure [the] crucial postslavery period in the Caribbean. She grasps that her own locational identity as a Creole woman is a function of, and can be made intelligible only in terms of, this period, which was both a beginning and an end. It is this time and space that she elucidates with unswerving persistence in her work. ☐

Veronica Marie Gregg

■ The white man in tropical America was out of his habitat. Constant association with an inferior subject race blunted his moral fibre and he suffered marked demoralization. His transitory residence and the continued importation of Africans debased life. Miscegenation, so contrary to Anglo-Saxon nature, resulted in the rapid rise of a race of human hybrids. Planter society was based upon whites and blacks, removed to unfamiliar scenes, and their unhappy offspring. The saddest pages of imperial history relate the heartrending attempts to effect adjustment between these discordant elements. ☐

Lowell Joseph Ragatz[1]

As much of the material surveyed by this Guide so far shows, the status of *Wide Sargasso Sea* as a counter-text to Brontë's *Jane Eyre* has elicited a good deal of critical attention. In this chapter, however, the emphasis falls on the work of three critics, writing between the early and late 1990s, who have explicitly sought, albeit in different ways, to shift the focus from questions of literary history to those of literature and history, moving from the intertextual to the contextual. In the chapter's first extract, Maggie Humm situates *Wide Sargasso Sea* firmly within the context of the 1950s and 1960s, the period during which Rhys, living in England, was painstakingly engaged in writing and rewriting her novel in an effort to bring it to completion. For Peter Hulme and Laura E. Ciolkowski, who contribute the second and third extracts respectively, the central point of critical reference, by contrast, is the 1830s and 1840s, the period in which the novel's action is set. This is the immediate post-emancipation era that constitutes what Gregg calls 'the obsessive beginning in Rhys's writing on the West Indies'.[2]

Humm's reading of *Wide Sargasso Sea* originally appeared in *Border Traffic: Strategies of Contemporary Women Writers* (1991) and draws on socio-historical and psycho-biographical perspectives alike. In the short opening extract which follows, Humm divides her argument into two stages, beginning by noting that the moment in which Rhys writes *Wide Sargasso Sea* is also a moment of public and personal crisis. The public crisis takes the form of the rapid dissolution of British imperial power following the end of the Second World War and the concomitant immigration into England of peoples from formerly colonized nations. This process of 'Colonizin' in reverse', to cite this chapter's first epigraph, gives rise, in turn, to a 'truly "popular" language of race and nation', grounded in a violent 'taxonomy of the Black body' as the purveyor of 'sexual contagion and disease'. The personal crisis, on the other hand, results from the various serious illnesses which both Rhys and her husband suffered throughout the time of *Wide Sargasso Sea*'s composition. In a highly original insight, Humm argues that the place where the two crises intersect is the hospital. Here the 'elderly and alcoholic'[3] Rhys finds herself directly exposed to the effects of Bennett's reverse colonization in the shape of the care she receives at the hands of the newly arrived 'Black mother/nurse'.[4] While Rhys's letters and interviews reveal a certain ambivalence or even hostility towards this figure, Humm goes on to show, in the second stage of her argument, that such a response is significantly at odds with the far more positive way in which the figure is portrayed in *Wide Sargasso Sea*. By transforming the black mother/nurse who occupies her historical and psychic spaces into the fictional Christophine, Rhys is able, Humm suggests, to resolve the internal conflicts which this presence otherwise stimulates. At the same time, and perhaps more importantly, Rhys fashions, in Christophine, an image of the black female subject that runs counter to the racist discourses at work within the moment of her novel's production.

■ Rhys wrote *Wide Sargasso Sea* in an epistemological crisis specific to the early 1960s, a crisis occasioned by the break up of the British Empire and the need in Britain for fresh thinking about the Black subject, specifically the Black female subject. 'Race' is a concept used to classify and its reference point is always physical appearance. In the 1960s race was spoken in a new public voice, forced into speech by the Nottingham and Notting Hill riots against Black immigrants in 1958. The Conservative Party discussed the possibility of using 'Keep Britain White' as an electoral slogan as early as 1955. The 1962 Commonwealth Immigration Act 'legalised' English racism and the 1964 Smethwick election returned a white racist MP, Peter Griffiths. A fresh vocabulary of the enemy within, of white men and of the sexual contagion and disease of Blacks was named as such by Enoch Powell in his famous 'Rivers of Blood' speech [1968]. In other words, the period during which Rhys was writing *Wide Sargasso Sea* was a period in which a truly 'popular' language of race and nation flowered in Britain. Notions of Black sub-citizenship and Black people as objects of social reform were already current in the post-war period, drawn from debates about Indian independence, but the path travelled by racism in the late 1950s and early 1960s was strewn with a taxonomy of the Black body and specifically of gender. The Eugenics Society in 1959 argued that miscegenation was impossible to unmix and much racist writing was striking for the way in which images of race were gendered.

Equally the vibrancy of Christophine, Antoinette's nurse, and the strange excitement of their interdependence also have a relation to the elderly and alcoholic Rhys's dependence on, desire for, or distaste of Black nurses in the many nursing homes and hospitals she attended while writing *Wide Sargasso Sea*. Jean Rhys was intensively rewriting the manuscript from the 1950s until its publication in 1966. During these years her husband, Max, was often in hospital and Jean herself was hospitalised in Exe Vale Hospital and Surrey Hills Clinic for several months, and continuously had medication for a heart condition. These were also the years when Britain's hospitals were radically transformed by the recruitment of West Indian nurses.

From 1944, the National Health Service and the Ministry of Labour, working in consultation with the Colonial Office, set up a recruiting system with offices in Jamaica and Trinidad. It is notable that subsequent restrictions [on] immigration were not applied to unskilled ancillary labour where West Indian women were concentrated. Nursing was the main occupation for Black women and in addition 78 per cent of ancillary workers and 84 per cent of domestic workers were also from overseas. In 1964 Jean Rhys was 74 years old and Max was 80. In 1964 Jamaican women were seen as providing one *crucial* source of cheap labour to enable the National Health Service to meet the demands of Britain's changing demography. It was migrant, Caribbean women who catered for the ever increasing numbers of geriatric men and women in nursing homes and hospitals throughout Britain.

In *The Paris Review* Rhys dramatises her psychic separation from the first Black nurturer: 'at the start I hated my nurse. A horrid woman. It was she who told me awful stories of zombies and sucriants, the vampires'.[5] The early stereotype reveals something of Rhys's desire for, but initial defence against, her relations with older Black women. By *Voyage in the Dark*, Rhys could use directly the names of the significant Black women she knew as a child. In later encounters with Black nurses Rhys more adequately addresses the demands of her dependence and desire. At first, with Max in hospital, she felt 'Oh Lord! *If only they'd let us alone*. ... the nurses aren't very nice'[6] [and] 'The matron and most of the nurses are dreadful he says and they are *beastly*. I saw how they treated him when I was there.'[7] But, by the time of her own hospitalisation in St Mary Abbotts, Rhys was too weak to 'separate' from care. Although the following two months in geriatric wards made her 'not mad about the welfare state' her letters also reveal Rhys's deep need to more accurately signify the Black woman in her fiction: 'I've made the obeah woman, *the nurse*, too articulate. I thought of cutting it a bit ... . [But] there's no reason why one particular negro shouldn't be articulate enough'.[8]

The hospital is the place of Rhys's desire for a Black mother/nurse. Homi Bhabha hints at the symmetry of darkness with a maternal imaginary. Darkness, he suggests, signifies a desire to return to the fullness of the mother.[9] In Rhys's text this is visible in the extent to which the Caribbean woman of the 1840s is flooded with maternal images. 'When I was safely home I sat close to the old wall at the end of the garden ... . Christophine found me there when it was nearly dark, and I was so stiff she had to help me to get up. She said nothing, but next morning Tia was in the kitchen' [*WSS*, p. 9]. Later Christophine takes care of every physical detail of Antoinette's existence:

'I wake her up to sit in the sun, bathe in the cool river. Even if she dropping with sleep. I make good strong soup. I give her milk if I have it, fruit I pick from my own trees. If she don't want to eat I say, "Eat it up for my sake, *doudou*." ... I let her have rum'. [*WSS*, pp. 99–100]

The scenes are nodes of allusions to the nursing required by a geriatric alcoholic. David Plante describes a similar moment with appalling clarity: 'She [Jean] fell in the bathroom last night, getting up to pee. It was a struggle, I had to roll her on to a blanket and drag her back to bed'.[10] *Wide Sargasso Sea*'s emotional strength derives in part from the impression it gives of the total loving care of a Black to a Creole woman.

The equation patient = child, which creates the fictive term 'childlike' often accorded to the characteristics and identities of patients by most medical thought, provides another metaphorical space in which Rhys might see the Black nurse as 'mother'. [...] It is the imaginative engagement with Black women, through her childhood, in her adult illness and in reading about the Caribbean, which enables Rhys to develop a complex expression of race and sex. Black 'Other', in Rhys's writing, is not the colonial's Other but characters like Tia who is Antoinette's alter ego and Christophine who evokes the maternal. Rhys places the psychodynamics of mother/daughter relations in historicised narratives. □

Considered in terms of its general outlines, Humm's argument is suggestive, particularly in the speculations on the potential of fictional writing to rework the historical and psychic materials on which it draws. It is far less persuasive, however, in the more detailed claims it makes. It is certainly fair to say that Christophine's 'vibrancy' is one aspect of *Wide Sargasso Sea* that sets it apart from the dominant 'images of race' in circulation during the period in which the novel was written. Yet Humm's blunt assertion that the 'Black "Other", in Rhys's writing, is not the colonial's Other' is surely questionable. In locating the 'emotional strength' of *Wide Sargasso Sea* in 'the total loving care' imparted by 'a Black to a Creole woman', Humm seems entirely to miss the irony of her own statement. The image of black female subjectivity which she wishes to celebrate is itself a colonial stereotype, perpetuating the myth of the mammy critiqued by Maria Olaussen in Chapter Three of this Guide.

This chapter's second, and much longer, extract is taken from Hulme's 'The Locked Heart: The Creole Family Romance of *Wide Sargasso Sea*'. This essay was originally included in *Colonial Discourse/Postcolonial Theory* (1994), a wide-ranging collection edited by Francis Barker, Hulme himself and Margaret Iversen, and it provides a fascinating and highly distinctive account of the complex interplay between fiction and history in Rhys's novel. Like the volume of which it is a part, Hulme's essay is broadly concerned with an assessment of the benefits and problems entailed in the use of the term 'postcolonial'. In Hulme's view, the term is especially effective for pedagogical purposes, 'mark[ing] out a terrain on which [university] courses can be constructed in a way that both makes sense to students and puts on to the agenda questions of history, politics and canonicity'. As Hulme goes on to note, *Wide Sargasso Sea* is a text which enjoys a prominent status on such courses – including his own – and is invariably paired with *Jane Eyre* as a postcolonial response to 'the imperialist canon' in which Brontë's novel is so signally located. Yet even as Hulme sees a definite value in the use of 'postcolonial' as 'a teaching tool',[11] he argues that the term is not without its dangers. The most pressing of these stems, he suggests, from the term's tendency towards the general and the homogeneous. To speak of such a thing as the 'post-colonial' – or indeed the 'Third World' – is, in Hulme's estimation, to 'run the risk of imposing a single and simple (and usually metropolitan) label on an extraordinary variety of national and other traditions'.[12]

In order to counteract this potential flattening out of cultural differences, Hulme advocates the practice of a 'properly historical'[13] criticism, of which his own reading of *Wide Sargasso Sea* is a powerful instance. Ironically, however, Hulme's work takes its cue from Freudian psychoanalysis – a discipline which postcolonial critics often dismiss as both troublingly ahistorical and Eurocentric. In particular, Hulme utilizes the concept of the 'family romance', which Freud introduced into psychoanalysis in 1908 to refer to an aspect of prepubescent fantasy in which origins are reimagined. 'At about [this] period', Freud writes, 'the child's imagination becomes engaged in the task of getting free from the parents of whom he now has a low opinion and of replacing them by others, who, as a rule, are of higher social standing'.[14] For Hulme, something analogous to these genealogical ruses and revisions is operative in *Wide Sargasso Sea*, even as it is not a parent but a grandparent figure, in the shape of Edward Lockhart, from whom Rhys strives to distance herself. In the following extract, Hulme looks beyond or beneath the novel's rewriting of *Jane Eyre* to uncover its labyrinthine links with Rhys's family history, while simultaneously excavating the relationships between the latter and 'the larger history of the English colony of Dominica',[15] Rhys's place of birth. Hulme's localized analysis focuses specifically on the moment in Part One of the novel when Coulibri is burned down by the corps of ex-slaves. This event is assumed by Rhys's critics – as by Rhys herself – to be based on the actual destruction of the Lockharts' Dominican estate house during the 1844 census riots or so-called 'guerre nègre' ('negro war'), 'one of the salient incidents in nineteenth-century West Indian history'.[16] Yet as Hulme's own minute archival research demonstrates, such an event did not in fact take place, just as Lockhart's role in the riots was less that of the victim than the perpetrator of violence. Rhys's text, like the equally fictitious transgenerational memory on which it draws, thus performs a 'work of occlusion':[17] it at once compensates for and conveniently seals off parts of a plantocratic family history that might otherwise be difficult to acknowledge.

While Hulme's overarching concern is to affirm 'The local and the particular' and 'even [...] the familial'[18] as valid objects of postcolonial analysis, his essay closes with the dialectical recognition that 'the critical movement has finally to be outwards, towards the larger picture of which the locality forms only a part'. This larger movement reconnects Rhys's work to Brontë's: despite the temporal and geographical differences between them, the two novels are linked not only in intertextual terms but also by virtue of the fact that *Jane Eyre*, as Hulme briefly notes, is implicated – just as much as *Wide Sargasso Sea* itself – in 'matters of West Indian slavery'.[19]

■ One case to be argued in defence of the term ['postcolonial'] would centre on its usefulness as a teaching tool [...]. The term simplifies (as does every *single* term), but it does not, carefully used, do violence to the texts it designates. However, serious problems do arise when the term is pressed into service as an *analytical* tool [...]: in particular, the historical relationship supposedly suggested between 'colonial' and 'postcolonial' remains consistently undefined. *Wide Sargasso Sea* is a case in point: a novel published in 1966, at a time when the general decolonisation of the British Empire was well under way but before Dominica, the island of Jean Rhys's birth, had gained independence; a novel written by, in West Indian terms, a member of the white colonial élite, yet somebody who always defined herself in opposition to the norms of metropolitan 'Englishness'; a novel which deals with issues of race and slavery, yet is fundamentally sympathetic to the planter class ruined by Emancipation.

In a teaching context, *Wide Sargasso Sea* almost always appears alongside *Jane Eyre*, the postcolonial 'vindication' read after and against one of the novels which forms the imperialist canon. This is how I teach the book, too, and there is no doubt of its effective presence along with other revisionary couples: [Daniel Defoe's] *Robinson Crusoe* [1719] and [J.M. Coetzee's] *Foe* [1986], *The Tempest* and [George Lamming's] *Water with Berries* [1971]. None the less, if this pedagogical opposition between the 'colonial' and the 'postcolonial' is allowed to become too fixed, too orthodox a way of organising research projects on books like *Wide Sargasso Sea*, then the critical enterprise risks becoming located at such a high level of generality ('postcoloniality') that the particular conditions that produced particular books can remain ignored, indeed even unavailable. [...]

What follows makes no pretence of being a full historical reading of *Wide Sargasso Sea* [...]. This [...] is a sketch of a project now under way to study how the 'materials' that went into the writing of *Wide Sargasso Sea* might be reconstituted so as to throw light on to the dense particularity of that novel. That these materials are 'historical', in the full sense of that word, rather than a merely anecdotal and familial adjunct to a 'proper' colonial history, is part of the point I want to make. *Wide Sargasso Sea* is a postcolonial novel, if that term is used carefully enough; it is counter-discursive, if the dominant discourse is taken as a kind of received Englishness, but attention to its local circumstances suggests that it also needs reading as a reworking of the materials from *Jane Eyre* inflected by the received traditions of a planter 'family history'. In other words, literary production is viewed here less as a matter of individual creativity than as a trans-generational formation from 'event' to 'family memory' to 'literary text'.

On the first page of *Wide Sargasso Sea* Antoinette recalls hearing her mother talking to Mr Luttrell, her only friend, and saying 'Of course they have their own misfortunes. Still waiting for this compensation the English promised when the Emancipation Act was passed. Some will wait for a long time' [*WSS*, p. 5]. One of the families that waited in vain for compensation after the 1833 Emancipation Act was the Lockharts, Jean Rhys's mother's family. Rhys's great-grandfather had bought Geneva, one of the largest plantations on Dominica at the beginning of the nineteenth century. Geneva never recovered after losing its slave labour force, and was in genteel decay by the time of Rhys's childhood at the turn of the century.

Wide Sargasso Sea, as a writing out of that family history, a kind of extended autobiography or Creole family romance, is offered as in some sense a 'compensation' for the ruin of that family at the time of Emancipation, a compensation, though, which also serves to occlude the actual relationship between that family history and the larger history of the English colony of Dominica. This [essay] tries to compre-hend something of that work of occlusion.

Rhys may have started writing *Wide Sargasso Sea* as early as the late 1930s, soon after her return trip to Dominica in 1936. An early version may have been destroyed.[20] That return to the Caribbean in 1936 certainly seems to have initiated, or at any rate intensified, the collec-tion of West Indian material and memories which Rhys later refers to as 'Creole'. The final stage in the writing of *Wide Sargasso Sea* began in 1957, although it took nine more years for her to complete the book. In 1958 she wrote:

> For some time I've been getting down all I remembered about the West Indies as the West Indies used to be. (Also all I was told, which is more important). I called this 'Creole' but it had no shape or plan – it wasn't a book at all and I didn't try to force it.
> Then when I was in London last year it 'clicked in my head' that I had material for the story of Mr Rochester's first wife. The real story – as it might have been.[21]

By far the longest and most interesting of Rhys's letters about the com-position of *Wide Sargasso Sea* was written in April 1964 to Francis Wyndham, explaining how she had overcome the blockage which had prevented her completing the novel. It is an unusually long and full let-ter, which contains a poem called 'Obeah Night': 'Only when I wrote this poem – then it clicked – and all was there and always had been.'[22]

The poem is signed by Edward Rochester or Raworth (she was still toying with the explicitness of the connection with *Jane Eyre*), as '*Written in Spring* 1842' – and therefore in England. The poem is awkward and not always easy to construe, but focuses on the night of passionate and violent love between Rochester and Antoinette following her administration of the 'love-potion' supplied by Christophine:

How can I forget you Antoinette
    When the spring is here?
Where did you hide yourself

After that shameless, shameful night?
And why come back? Hating and hated?
Was it Love, Fear, Hoping?
Or (as always) Pain?
(*Did* you come back I wonder
Did I ever see you again?)

No. I'll lock that door
Forget it. –
The motto was 'Locked Hearts I open
    I have the heavy key'
Written in black letters
Under a Royal Palm Tree
On a slave owner's gravestone
'Look! And look again, hypocrite' he says
    'Before *you* judge *me'*

I'm no damn slave owner
I have no slave
Didn't she (forgiven) betray me
Once more – and then again
Unrepentant – laughing?
I can soon show her
    Who hates the best
Always she answers me
    I will hate last.[23]

'History' is here in ways which take some untangling. Rochester seems to suggest that he will (symbolically) lock his door against Antoinette's return, before remembering her family motto written on the patriarch's gravestone. ('Corda serrata pando', 'locked hearts I open', was the motto of Rhys's mother's family, the Lockharts [...]). She will have ways of opening his heart again if she so desires. But

Rochester moves quickly to an imagined address he hears from the gravestone, which seems to defend the slave-owning families against the kinds of criticism that Mason and Rochester both voice in the novel. Rochester chooses to make the connection with his wife, suggesting that she is no 'slave' since she has betrayed him more than once. Two 'clicks in the head' connect *Jane Eyre* with the personal memories and oral histories. This is what makes possible the next stage of the composition. If one factor were especially important, it might well be the coincidence of names: Edward was the name of Rhys's grandfather, a significant figure in her family story, as well as the name of Rochester, Brontë's hero in *Jane Eyre*.

My particular interest here, however, is in the significance of the *changes* which Rhys made to the chronology, topography and family relationships given by *Jane Eyre* once the decision had been taken to work with that narrative material. The crucial point about the chronological changes can best be gauged by quoting a letter Rhys wrote in 1962 when she sent the first two parts of *Wide Sargasso Sea* to her editor:

> The typed (and heavily corrected) part is the most important – it's the story of an old West Indian house burned down by the negroes who hate the ex-slave owning family living there. The time 1839, the white Creole girl aged about 14 is the 'I'.[24]

It was very unusual for Rhys to be that precise about dates. *Jane Eyre* is unspecific about its dates, although internal evidence would seem to set the West Indian episodes before 1820: they certainly take place before the watershed of Emancipation in 1833. So, for all the extraordinarily close connections and parallels that exist between *Jane Eyre* and *Wide Sargasso Sea*, Rhys has adapted the chronology in order to bring it in line with her own family history: 1825 is, for example, the approximate birth-date of Rhys's great aunt Cora, one of the models for Antoinette (though the name Cora is transferred to Antoinette's aunt, who corresponds to Jean's great-aunt Jane). The dramatic events in her family history to which she wanted to relate *Jane Eyre* are post-Emancipation, so the time-scale is adjusted accordingly.

The topographical transpositions in *Wide Sargasso Sea* work in the same direction. That the first part of the story should take place in Jamaica is given by *Jane Eyre*. Rhys had never been in Jamaica: the Cosway plantation, which becomes the property of the Masons, is based upon the Lockhart plantation of Geneva, though in *Wide Sargasso Sea* given the name of Coulibri, the next estate along the south coast of Dominica. Mention of Spanish Town, then capital of Jamaica, is also given by *Jane Eyre*, but there are no attempts to 'transfer' the Dominican references that pervade the early part of *Wide Sargasso Sea*.

The honeymoon island, home of Antoinette's mother, is also attended by Dominican references, although the island itself remains unnamed in the novel: the couple arrive at Massacre (a village just north of Roseau), there are persistent references to the Caribs, who are found only on Dominica; and Antoinette's house is clearly based on Rhys's father's estate, Amelia, though called in the novel Granbois, like Coulibri the name of a Dominican estate. More circumstantially, the *surrounding* topography relates to Dominica which has, for example, plenty of traffic with Martinique, unlike Jamaica. When Rochester writes to the Spanish Town magistrate, Mr Fraser, he gets a reply 'in a few days' [*WSS*, p. 91], which would be good going from Roseau, but inconceivable from Jamaica.

Let me use this example of the topographical references to try to clarify the argument. A fully 'autobiographical' reading – of the kind not being suggested here – would take all this as evidence that the 'Jamaica' of *Wide Sargasso Sea* is *really* Dominica. An aesthetic reading would say that it did not matter, that the 'Jamaica' of both novels exists in the parallel world of art, so that it makes no difference what topographical features are attached to it. What I am suggesting is that proper attention to the production of *Wide Sargasso Sea* would investigate the intertwining of 'Jamaica' and 'Dominica' in the novel, the Dominican materials produced from memory and family history appearing under some of the toponyms [place-names] provided by *Jane Eyre*.

In the West Indian family relationships the changes again involve alterations that inflect the materials closer to the Lockhart family history. In *Jane Eyre* the Mason family of Jamaica consists of husband and wife and three children, including Bertha. The black population of Jamaica is not directly mentioned, though arguably 'present' in some of the descriptions given by Jane of Bertha's 'thick and dark hair' and 'discoloured face' [*JE*, p. 297]. In addition, Brontë's use of the term 'Creole' – as in Rochester's 'Her mother, the Creole, was both a mad woman and a drunkard!' [*JE*, p. 306] – carries at least a hint of 'tainted' blood. What 'suits' Rochester, he says, must be the 'antipodes of the Creole', whom he now – as he tells Jane the story of his marriage – associates with 'the loathings of incongruous unions' [*JE*, p. 328], a phrase that echoes the Book of Ezra's warning about the dangers of taking 'strange wives' [Ezra x: 2]. Rhys makes several changes to this story. The basic structure of two parents and three children remains, but this new family is a combination of two earlier family units, with the result that Antoinette (Bertha from *Jane Eyre*) is not a Mason by blood, Richard, her brother from *Jane Eyre* becoming her stepbrother, and her father in *Jane Eyre* becoming her stepfather in *Wide Sargasso Sea*. The dead father, Cosway, Antoinette's mother's first husband, is therefore introduced into *Wide Sargasso Sea*, and with him another set of at least possible relatives, Daniel and Alexander Cosway, presumably half-brothers to Antoinette – though she and others later challenge the relationship – and Alexander's son Sandi, a kind of half-nephew whom Antoinette calls cousin, and with whom she is presumed to have a (cross-generational) affair. The lack of clarity about these relationships is deliberate: Brontë's category of 'Creole' is here being opened up and confronted. At one moment in *Wide Sargasso Sea* Rochester thinks that Antoinette looks like the servant-girl Amélie: 'Perhaps they are related, I thought. It's possible, it's even probable in this damned place' [*WSS*, p.81]. The 'reality' or otherwise of these family relationships remains unexplored in the text.

The significance of these shifts in the familial relationships is multiple. In one way they obviously connect with the change in the dating of the story, the Cosways becoming the old planter family destroyed by Emancipation, the Masons representing new capital from England, scornful of slavery but ignorant of the West Indies; a division entirely absent from *Jane Eyre*. As a result, Antoinette becomes a much more marginal figure even within her own society, a victim of historical forces rather than of inherited lunacy. The racial and cultural dimensions, ideologically dense in *Jane Eyre*, are unpacked in *Wide Sargasso Sea*. The white English 'norm' is still present, represented by Mason as well as Rochester, but the Creole otherness to that norm is no longer the undifferentiated realm of the alien tropics – lunacy, sexuality, excess, so memorably articulated in the story that Rochester tells to Jane Eyre [*JE*, pp.323–5]. Instead 'Creole' is broken down into black, white and coloured, and further subdivided with Annette and Christophine coming from Martinique and being therefore alien to the 'English' Creole of 'Jamaica'. Some interesting discussions of the novel have indeed turned on the character of Christophine, the black French Creole. My suggestion is that the really troubling figures 'in the margins' of *Wide Sargasso Sea* are the coloured Cosways, Daniel and Alexander.

'Old' Cosway, Antoinette's father, has clear parallels with the old Lockhart whose portrait still hung in the dining-room at Rhys's family home. Like Cosway, old Lockhart's official family resulted from his second marriage. The founding father has his memorial in *Wide Sargasso Sea*, described in bitter tones by the illegitimate and coloured son Daniel: 'My father old Cosway, with his white marble tablet in the English church at Spanish Town for all to see. It have a crest on it and a motto in Latin and words in big black letters' [*WSS*, p.77]. The 'old' Lockhart (James Potter Lockhart d. 1837) was commemorated with just such a marble plaque until the hurricane of 1979 destroyed the Anglican church in Dominica.

Daniel's bitter words about the man he claims as father provide a troubling chorus to Rochester's doubts about the Creole family relationships. Something of the highly mediated anxiety with which the offspring of these kinds of unofficial liaisons is invested can be gauged from the exchange between Rochester and Antoinette when they arrive for their honeymoon at Massacre, where Daniel Cosway lives. '[W]ho was massacred here?', Rochester asks, 'Slaves?' 'Oh no', Antoinette replies, 'Not slaves. Something must have happened a long time ago. Nobody remembers now' [WSS, p. 39]. Antoinette, like Rhys, would have known very well that the 'massacre' here was the killing in 1674 of Indian Warner, the half-Carib son of one of the foremost English colonists in the West Indies, Sir Thomas Warner. Indian Warner and his Carib allies were killed by his half-brother, Philip, the legitimate son of Sir Thomas.

These matters of race are negotiated by the novel in ways which take some unpacking. The dramatic events in the novel are those that deal with questions of race through confrontation, especially when the estate house, Coulibri, is burned down by black rioters, an event usually taken by Rhys herself, and by commentators on the novel, to be based on an incident from Rhys's family history, the burning down of her grandfather's estate house in the years after Emancipation. As Rhys writes in her autobiography, with reference to Edward Lockhart: 'It was during my grandfather's life, sometime in the 1830s, that the first estate house was burnt down by the freed negroes after the Emancipation Act was passed. He was, apparently, a mild man who didn't like the situation at all'.[25]

What interests me about this incident, and why it can become an emblem of the fraught relationship between literature and history, is that, because of Wide Sargasso Sea, this burning down of the estate house has passed into the history of Dominica as a fact. The argument has to be careful here because Wide Sargasso Sea is a fiction which makes no necessary historical claims itself: rather, readers and critics of the novel have wanted, too readily, to take Rhys's own remarks at face value and to install Wide Sargasso Sea as an 'authentic' and 'historical' response to the 'inauthentic' and 'fictional' version of West Indian Creole life offered by Jane Eyre. What tends to be lost sight of in this view is the way in which Wide Sargasso Sea itself offers a certain kind of negotiation of its nineteenth-century materials, a 'vindication' in Rhys's own word, or perhaps better the 'compensation' referred to on the opening page of the novel as so slow in coming to the Dominican estate owners. In fact, one could say that the family history reworked in Wide Sargasso Sea already itself offers a negotiation of that material; so the work of production has at least two distinct stages to it.

The events to which the novel 'refers' were the 1844 census riots in which a series of disturbances ensued after the rumour took hold that the census was a prelude to the reintroduction of slavery. Threats were made to whites, a few stones were thrown, a few houses ransacked – but none burned down; as a result, the militia was called out, several protestors were killed and one had his head cut off and displayed on a pike to discourage others. Three hundred people were arrested, four were charged with capital offences, and one, Jean Philip Motard, executed after a trial in which the accused was given no defence. He was convicted of attempted murder for throwing a stone at a white planter; the planter received a graze on his forehead. These incidents brought the simmering personal and political tensions on the island to a boil. The Colonial Office pressed its local officials for clarification; the Anti-Slavery Society became involved and demanded an inquiry. As a result of this furore the intermittent rioting of these three days in June 1844 became known as the 'guerre nègre' and is recalled as one of the salient incidents in nineteenth-century West Indian history.

Fire has symbolic power, as both *Jane Eyre* and *Wide Sargasso Sea* demonstrate, but there was no fire at Geneva: Mitcham House was stripped of its furnishings and some damage may have been done to its fabric, but none of the reports, either those sent to the Colonial Office or those kept in the local Minute Books, mention that the house was burned down. Statements of the value of property destroyed in the rioting, drawn up by William Elissonde of Stowe, Henry Bellot of St Patrick and Jane Maxwell Lockhart of Geneva, were forwarded to London by the local administrator, Laidlaw. The Lockharts' list referred to furniture at Mitcham House: tables, chairs, glass-ware, pianos, books, pictures, and a jewel-case, to a total value of £202 19s 5d. It is inconceivable that a fire could have occurred and not been mentioned.

So the Lockhart family memory produces a fire that – as far as can be told from written evidence – did not happen, but which becomes the key scene in a work of fiction, and is then reported by critics as an historical incident in nineteenth-century Dominica.[26] The 'memory' of something that did not happen is usually a screen-memory to occlude what did. It is clear from the documentation that Geneva Estate played an important part in the disturbances. Charles Leathem, its attorney, was, in turn, a proponent of violent response and a defender of the rights of the imprisoned peasantry (and in the course of this defence called Theodore Lockhart, probably the coloured son of James Potter Lockhart, as witness). It was on the road to Grand Bay (where the Geneva plantation was situated) that the incident occurred which led to the execution of Motard and, indeed, unusually, the execution was carried out at the scene of the crime, the better to impress its lesson upon the peasantry in the south of the island. The involvement of two Lockhart brothers was also substantial. William Brade Lockhart, Jean

Rhys's great-uncle, does not appear at all within the family memories, but the initial Census Proclamation was issued in his name, and he played a significant role in the judicial procedures as Motard's executioner, claiming expenses for taking the tools of his trade by boat to Point Michel, the scene of the crime.

Another brother, Edward, Rhys's 'mild' grandfather, was the subject of an investigation that went as far as the Colonial Office in London. Reports on the disturbances were dispatched by FitzRoy, Governor of the Leeward Islands, to Lord Stanley, the Colonial Secretary, in London. On 1 July 1844 FitzRoy's despatch enclosed the results of two particular investigations undertaken by Laidlaw, the acting Administrator and himself a prominent planter. The attorney for the Geneva estate, Charles Leathem, 'has been guilty of most wanton and outrageous acts of cruelty'.[27] He had apparently apprehended two people who were both pinioned when he stabbed one in the groin with a bayonet and struck the other a violent blow on the head with a musket. Laidlaw reported to FitzRoy that proceedings would be instituted against this man by the Attorney-general. The other incident, referred to by FitzRoy as 'the matter of Mr —', he had to explain to Stanley because it referred to something not previously mentioned in the correspondence: a complaint made directly to FitzRoy by the labourers at Geneva that one of the census commissioners had 'wantonly broken into several of their cottages on finding them deserted by their owners'.[28] Laidlaw's comment on this case had been brief: he had had the charge investigated 'and [was] happy to be able to acquit that young gentleman of any wilful intention of injuring them in the slightest degree'.[29] The 'young gentleman' was Edward Lockhart.

FitzRoy, under pressure from Stanley, was forced to pursue the matter of Edward Lockhart's behaviour. The two Justices of the Peace charged by Laidlaw to investigate the matter seem only to have collected an affidavit from Henry Hardcastle, schoolmaster of the Protestant school at Geneva (and therefore presumably an employee of the Lockhart family), who had been appointed enumerator for the census by Lockhart and who accompanied him on his rounds on 3 June. According to Hardcastle, Lockhart had merely rapped on three doors and windows with a small stick to see if people were home. Unfortunately the houses were so badly made that the doors and windows had fallen off. This may have convinced the JPs and Laidlaw, but it did not cut any ice with FitzRoy. He acquitted Lockhart 'of the charge of intentional violence on this occasion; but [could not] acquit him of having acted with very great indiscretion … [requesting Laidlaw to] caution Mr Edward Lockhart to act with greater consideration on any future occasion'.[30] Stanley's response focuses on the behaviour of some of the commissioners 'and especially of Mr Lockhart' as 'highly indiscreet'.[31]

In the petition drawn up by many of the people imprisoned after the disturbances and supported by Leathem and by Charles George Falconer, the prominent radical politician, Lockhart's wanton forcing of the doors and windows 'of our little dwellings' is particularly mentioned. Most of the three hundred persons seized were guilty only 'of having fled in terror when they saw armed men coming towards their houses'.[32] A 'mild man' Edward Lockhart may have been; but not many British citizens in the West Indies received a personal rebuke from Lord Stanley for their role in breaking down the houses of the people whose census details they were supposed to be collecting: corda serrata pando, indeed. [...]

Jean Philip Motard was executed for throwing a stone at the head of a white planter called Bremner. The following year (1845) Bremner's son married Cora Lockhart, daughter of the 'old' Lockhart who, as the original for Cosway, stands as father to Antoinette in *Wide Sargasso Sea*. During the burning of Coulibri in the novel, Antoinette's erstwhile black friend Tia throws a stone at her, cutting her head open. The compensations at work here, both discursive and psychological, are extremely complex, but they all work towards displacing the grotesque injustices of colonial violence with the story of an innocent childhood dream of friendship shattered by the realities of a racially-divided society. [...] The death of Jean Philip Motard, savagely and illegally executed in 1844, was hardly noticed at the time, so he could not exactly be said to have been 'forgotten'; but if a novel like *Wide Sargasso Sea* is going to be deprived of its 'locality' by the institution of Anglo-American literary criticism and made to replace and obscure a whole history of anti-colonial struggle in the smaller islands of the West Indies, then the effort of remembrance is necessary – for the better understanding both of colonial history and, ultimately, of *Wide Sargasso Sea* itself. [...]

The local and the particular, even, I have suggested, the familial, should be validated as appropriate and necessary areas for postcolonial research: after all, if one of the strategies of postcolonial discourse is the homogenisation of cultural differences, then counter-strategies must include the affirmation of those differences, the insistence that the local and the particular do matter.

But once the local has been fixed, once the materials out of which a text has been made have been located and studied, the critical movement has finally to be outwards, towards the larger picture of which the locality forms only a part, for too easy a contrast between *Jane Eyre* and *Wide Sargasso Sea* would risk missing that Charlotte Brontë and Jean Rhys do finally belong to the same world. Readings that focus on the counter-discursive strategies of *Wide Sargasso Sea* vis-à-vis *Jane Eyre*, though often carried out with impeccably radical motives, have tended to set the categories of 'colonial' and 'postcolonial' in stone, failing to see the multiple ways in which *Jane Eyre* is, in its production of its materials, already negotiating matters of West Indian slavery, even if the figure of Bertha is the only obvious textual residue of this negotiation. This is not to collapse differences but to argue for the need to understand the complex trafficking that exists between texts (and their authors) in the world, even ones that seem to invite consideration in terms of oppositions. It involves, for example, seeing the importance of the vast critical enterprise – starting in the case of *Wuthering Heights* with Charlotte Brontë herself – which produced the novels of the Brontës as works of genius unconnected with the conditions of their production and sheered from the materials which went into the making of them, materials already shot through with colonial colours. The 'Atlantic world' is a useful concept here, long a staple of slave-trade studies, recently given a cultural twist in Paul Gilroy's notion of a 'black Atlantic',[33] and intriguingly already present in the deeply meditated title of Jean Rhys's novel, which names that which slows down (and therefore makes more palpable) the channels of communication which criss-cross the Atlantic: 'I thought of "Sargasso Sea" or "Wide Sargasso Sea" but nobody knew what I meant.'[34] □

Brilliant as it is, Hulme's reading of *Wide Sargasso Sea* is not beyond question. In defining the novel as 'fundamentally sympathetic to the planter class', Hulme makes a claim which is ultimately exaggerated and predicated upon its own 'work of occlusion'.[35] This is manifested in the relative lack of attention that he gives to the formal complexity of Rhys's text, with its multiple first-person narratives competing against one another for authority in a way that deliberately impedes the reader's desire to adjudicate between them. While Antoinette's own narrative voice might articulate Rhys's plantocratic sympathies, it is contradicted by that of Daniel Cosway/Boyd, which explicitly denounces Antoinette's family as 'Wicked and detestable slave-owners since generations' (*WSS*, p. 59), with neither voice quite able to speak for the text as a whole.

The sense of Hulme's bid for critical mastery over the Modernist polyphony and shifting political allegiances of *Wide Sargasso Sea* is compounded by his promotion of Coulibri's destruction as the 'key scene' with which the novel's historical secrets may be unlocked. In using such a turn of phrase, Hulme becomes strangely doubled with the colonizing Lockhart himself, whose family motto is woven into Rhys's 'Obeah Night' poem: 'Locked Hearts I open / I have the heavy key'. The duplication of colonial and critical masteries is further underlined by the rhetorical aggression of Hulme's vocabulary, with its striking references to how 'Brontë's category of "Creole" is opened up' and 'broken down' by Rhys's text. At the risk of forcing the issue, it might be said that Hulme's essay bears the covert imprint of the brutal history that is its subject.

The final extract in this chapter is taken from Ciolkowski's 'Navigating the *Wide Sargasso Sea*: Colonial History, English Fiction, and British Empire', an article first published in *Twentieth Century Literature* in 1997. Like Hulme's essay, this article offers a reading of *Wide Sargasso Sea* that is fully responsive to the novel's historical dimensions, while at the same time being noticeably broader in its scope. For Ciolkowski, the most salient feature of Rhys's text consists in its status as an interrogation of the discourses by which white Creole and English identities are produced during the early nineteenth-century period both before and after Emancipation. In adopting such a perspective, she effectively brings the critical debate full circle, returning to concerns first adumbrated by Wally Look Lai and discussed in Chapter One of this Guide. As might be expected from a critic writing almost thirty years after Look Lai, Ciolkowski's treatment of these concerns is not only much more sophisticated but also quite distinct from that of her predecessor. Perhaps the major difference between their approaches is the much greater emphasis that Ciolkowski places on the role of sexual desire in Rhys's novel, particularly as it is played out in the form of miscegenation, the 'monstrous coupling'[36] of white and black bodies. Indeed, in her view, it is sexual desire that proves to be the determining factor in the production, maintenance and undoing of racial difference in *Wide Sargasso Sea*. As a white Creole woman, Antoinette comes to be constructed in terms of the 'self-indulgence and sexual appetite' that distinguish her from 'the proper Englishwoman'.[37] Rochester, on the other hand, lays claim to an authentic Englishness by distancing himself from the libidinal excesses of the slave-owners, most obviously embodied in Antoinette's father, old Cosway. Yet as Ciolkowski points out, Rochester 'repeats the sexual vices of the very plantocrats whom he claims to despise'.[38] His own identity turns out, ironically, to be as spurious as the one he confects for Antoinette, as *Wide Sargasso Sea* 'puts Englishness itself into crisis'.[39]

■ Part One of *Wide Sargasso Sea* is rocked by the disorienting textual motion between the colonial identification and disidentification with England. Rhys's text repeatedly calls attention to this intense ambivalence, lingering over the confusion of the Creole woman who is caught between the increasingly separate moral and economic logics of England and the West Indian colonies. By 1830, there was virtually a national consensus in England regarding the immorality of slavery. The abolitionist movement in England was steeped in the rhetorics of Christian fellowship, human rights, and moral law that not only aided in excluding the slaveholder from the community of respectable English men and women but also clearly invested him with the moral and sexual indecencies attached to the hateful system he espoused. Antoinette's plantocrat father, for example, is more than simply a slaveholder. He is also a promiscuous rake and a drunkard, producing 'half-caste' bastards almost as quickly as he produces profits and then consuming those profits with equal haste. On the second marriage of Antoinette's mother, the subject of conversation settles on old Cosway and his untimely death:

> Emancipation troubles killed old Cosway? Nonsense – the estate was going downhill for years before that. He drank himself to death. Many's the time when – well! And all those women! She never did anything to stop him – she encouraged him. Presents and smiles for the bastards every Christmas. [*WSS*, p. 13]

Missionaries, abolitionists, and, by midcentury, common English people of all sorts dwelled on the excesses of plantation society. So much so, in fact, that the West Indian plantation owner and, by association, all the members of his family were convenient symbols of evil and immorality by the time Charlotte Brontë chose to write about the moral recuperation of one such tainted personage in *Jane Eyre*.[40]

Rhys's Antoinette Cosway must navigate her way through these treacherous landscapes of Creole and English identity. In short, even before Rochester arrives on the scene to initiate the increasingly violent battle between his narration and hers, his vision and hers, his historical memory of the vices of preemancipation times and her cultivated forgetting, the struggle over meaning that underlies Antoinette's tortured queries about herself and her place in the world is already under way. Rochester observes:

> She was undecided, uncertain about facts – any fact. When I asked her if the snakes we sometimes saw were poisonous, she said, 'Not those. The *fer de lance* of course, but there are none here,' and added, 'but how can *they* be sure? Do you think *they* know?' Then, '*Our* snakes are not poisonous. Of course not.' [*WSS*, p. 54; emphases added]

Forced to shuttle between the multiple knowledges circulating within the text, Antoinette here dramatizes the ontological and epistemological tensions that are endlessly played out on both the visual landscapes and psychic spaces of *Wide Sargasso Sea*. The Creole uncertainty that is revealed so startlingly here and elsewhere in Rochester's narration (if simply because it is precisely this uncertainty that alternatively attracts and repels him), is the object of Rochester's intense concern. Over the course of Rhys's text, Rochester labors to make English sense out of this colonial confusion. He is determined to resolve Antoinette's ambivalence first into the singular tones of English womanhood, and second, once his failure to cast Antoinette as the chaste mother of English sons is totally clear, into the equally singular tones of a savage Otherness.

By endeavoring to incorporate Antoinette into nothing short of an English civilizing narrative whose racial logics and insidious global trajectory are so elegantly mystified by Charlotte Brontë in *Jane Eyre*, Rhys's Edward Rochester maps out the process by which English men and women are made. *Wide Sargasso Sea* takes on the issue of how difference – the difference between English and Creole, white and black, man and woman – organizes what we know and how we know it. It further traces the ways in which such a politics of knowledge is enmeshed in a social logic that exceeds the local limits of a single nation, race, or historical era. Rochester's reinvention of Antoinette as the 'red-eyed wild-haired stranger who was my wife' [*WSS*, p. 95] attaches the local interests of an English domestic economy that is dependent on the stigmatization of female self-indulgence and sexual appetite to the global interests of an English empire that is dependent on the very same elements of female bodily management for the successful reproduction of power. Unlike the Creole mad girl who 'thirsts for *anyone* – not for me ... She'll loosen her black hair, and laugh and coax and flatter (a mad girl. She'll not care who she's loving)' [*WSS*, p. 106], the proper Englishwoman ostensibly restricts all sexual activity to the domain of the patriarchal family and thereby regulates the genetic makeup of the English imperial race. The Englishwoman who must bear the sons responsible for expanding and defending the English empire consequently must also police the biological boundaries of Englishness. And because the healthy nation that embraces the values of the patriarchal family in order to reproduce itself also criminalizes the behaviors of overproductive subjects, the unchaste Creole woman must be the object of sustained legislative attention and state control. In his narrative, Rochester sets out the proper relationship between English Self and ethnic Other by establishing and defending the moral and physical differences that are enlisted as the signifiers of English national identity. Like Bertha Mason, the 'intemperate and unchaste' [*JE*, p. 323] West Indian lunatic of Brontë's novel, Antoinette is deemed unsuited for English domestic bliss not because of any psychological disorder from which she might be suffering but because of the appetites and excesses she so liberally exhibits.[41] The food, drink, and money that Antoinette distributes to her insatiable band of Creole relatives recall the equally careless distribution of sexual favors that Rochester believes Antoinette to be handing out in such abundance behind his back:

As for the money which she handed out so carelessly, not counting it, not knowing how much she gave, or the unfamiliar faces that appeared then disappeared, though never without a large meal eaten and a shot of rum I discovered – sisters, cousins, aunts and uncles – if she asked no questions how could I? [*WSS*, p. 55]

The story of imperial motherhood, of which the holy union of Jane and the reformed Rochester in *Jane Eyre* is one familiar variation, is explicitly recast in *Wide Sargasso Sea* as a tale of the battle over imperial control. Rhys's text follows the itinerary of the English imperialist's struggles to remake the colonial plantation, with all its excesses, into a shining example of the English patriarchal home. Rochester must put his imperial house in order, as it were, by countering the brazen challenge that is posed by the Creole woman who threatens to carry reproduction outside the domain of the English patriarchal family. If, as Rosemary George has argued, the triumph of the Englishwoman in the colonies was to 'replicate the empire on a domestic scale',[42] then the greatest threat posed by this Englishwoman's depraved West Indian counterpart was to reproduce the excesses of the colony in the empire. In the West Indies, as the expansive collection of Cosway children, wives, and bastards testifies, concubinage, miscegenation, rape, and bigamy were common. According to Barbara Bush, 'In the West Indies, sexual relationships between black and coloured women and white men were widespread, commonplace and generally accepted by the plantocracy to be an integral part of the social structure of the islands'.[43] And not all slave women remained illegitimate mistresses of white masters. Some actually married white plantation owners and, if the law allowed it, were able to legitimize their children, ironically bastardizing the English 'race' still further in the eyes of the English community at home. When Rochester compares his wife to the 'half-caste' [*WSS*, p. 39] servant girl, Amélie – 'For a moment she looked very much like Amélie. Perhaps they are related, I thought. It's possible, it's even probable in this damned place' [*WSS*, p. 81] – he puts his English horror of such couplings clearly on display.

The specter of racial mixing – miscegenation – that haunts the West Indian plantation and stubbornly adheres to all of its inhabitants reemerges with a vengeance in *Wide Sargasso Sea* as the obsessive signifier of colonial difference. The putrid colors of the Creole 'half-caste' join the already unnatural extremes of the text's West Indian landscape ('Everything is too much, I felt as I rode wearily after her. Too much blue, too much purple, too much green' [*WSS*, p. 42]) to illustrate a monstrous violation of limits. Antoinette describes one such 'half-caste' this way:

The boy was about fourteen and tall and big for his age, he had a white skin, a dull ugly white covered with freckles, his mouth was a negro's mouth and he had small eyes, like bits of green glass. He had the eyes of a dead fish. Worst, most horrible of all, his hair was crinkled, a negro's hair, but bright red, and his eyebrows and eyelashes were red. [*WSS*, pp. 26–7]

The hybrid body – half Negro, half white – simply cannot contain the copious signs of its racial and sexual degeneracy. White skin, Negro mouth, the colors of a white man and the textures of his debased Negro counterpart, are carelessly sewn together here into the corporeal pattern of the Creole grotesque. And the signs of such 'unnatural' subjects are everywhere: the 'yellow sweating face' [*WSS*, p. 79] of the bastard son who calls himself 'Daniel Cosway', the sexual appetite of Antoinette's 'colored' cousin, Sandi, who allegedly lusts after Antoinette and so returns to complete the incestuous circle of colonial degeneracy ('Sandi often came to see me when that man was away' [*WSS*, p. 120], Antoinette reveals).

The carnival cast of misfits and sexual deviants that wander through Rhys's text as the physical advertisements of the 'accursed system' of slavery and its aftermath finally advertises the threat of contamination that the slave economy necessarily carries along with it. The exotic excess Rochester records in his narrative promises to spill over into and infect the innocence of the English body. Rochester must, therefore, not only enter into the struggle to fix the common-sense logics of Englishness on the terrain of an utterly maddening colonial intransigence ('"England," said Christophine ... . "You think there is such a place? ... I know what I see with my eyes and I never see it"' [*WSS*, p. 70]). He must also attempt to manage the danger to English cultural identity that is introduced by a degenerate past. Rochester's understanding of himself as an English subject becomes, in Stuart Hall's formulation of cultural identity, 'a question of producing in the future an account of the past, that is to say it is always about narrative, the stories which cultures tell themselves about who they are and where they came from'.[44] In the early nineteenth century, stories of English identity commonly focused on the high moral standards (specifically the opposition to slavery) and religious mission adopted by the English. In fact, British imperial power was understood in no uncertain terms to be the moral right of a morally righteous English people. When David Livingstone traveled to Africa in the 1850s, 'opening up' the African continent for the multinational scramble soon to follow, it was both as a British imperialist and as a Christian missionary. Never doubting for a moment either the moral content or the imperialist necessity of his African venture, Livingstone enthusiastically acted out his belief in the virtuous partnership of 'commerce and Christianity'. As Tim Jeal has put it, Livingstone 'seemed to his successors to have provided the moral basis for massive imperial expansion'.[45]

Yet, the moral basis of the English colonial pursuit in the early nineteenth-century universe of *Wide Sargasso Sea* proves to be not so easy to sustain for Rhys's Edward Rochester. Beset by doubts about himself and the English values in which a figure like David Livingstone would come to place his faith, Rochester wrestles with his recognition of the emptiness of the English moral and ethical claims he makes and with the ways in which these claims are profoundly compromised by the abominable history of slavery in the West Indies. The troublesome traces of historical memory are everywhere and nowhere in Rhys's text. As Coral Ann Howells has argued, there is in *Wide Sargasso Sea* 'always the menace of history',[46] embedded as it is in the disavowed past of a village called Massacre ("'And who was massacred here? Slaves?' 'Oh no.' She sounded shocked. 'Not slaves. Something must have happened a long time ago. Nobody remembers now'" [*WSS*, p. 39] or in the language of a hypocritical churchyard epitaph ("'Pious,' they write up. 'Beloved by all'. Not a word about the people he buy and sell like cattle'" [*WSS*, p. 77]). This churchyard tale of indecency, etched so clearly into the gravestone of Antoinette's father but left deliberately unread by so many of the plantation men and women who mourn his passing, is also repeated on the marble memorial tablets decorating the walls of the church in which Rochester and Antoinette are married. Unlike old Cosway's colonial mourners, however, Rochester does not leave the terrible tale recounted in this inscription unread. Rather, he constructs a damning interpretation that neatly recasts the story of plantocrat indecency as a modern variation on the theme of female disease and bodily contamination. Rochester fixates on the transmission through marriage of a diseased historical legacy in which he convinces himself he is unimplicated, in spite of England's ongoing economic involvement in the colonies. Instead, he imagines himself to be the unsuspecting victim of a highly infectious female carrier of disease – an impression that by midcentury was, perhaps, best illustrated by Victorian images of beautiful yet syphilitic women and by the reams of medical exposés of the polluted bodies of outwardly seductive prostitutes. Rochester ultimately becomes convinced that his healthy body is defiled at the very moment that he takes the ice-cold hand of his lovely West Indian wife in his:

> I remember little of the actual ceremony. Marble memorial tablets on the walls commemorating the virtues of the last generation of

planters. All benevolent. All slave-owners. All resting in peace. When we came out of the church I took her hand. It was cold as ice in the hot sun. [*WSS*, p. 47]

Antoinette's 'bad blood' ostensibly contaminates Rochester's body; her diseased bodily fluids purportedly infect Rochester in much the same way as the obeah draught that Antoinette surreptitiously administers to Rochester in order to compel him to love her. After unknowingly drinking the poisonous mixture, Rochester recalls:

> I was too giddy to stand and fell backwards on to the bed, looking at the blanket which was of a peculiar shade of yellow. After looking at it for some time I was able to go over to the window and vomit. It seemed like hours before this stopped. I would lean up against the wall and wipe my face, then the retching and sickness would start again. When it was over I lay on the bed too weak to move. [*WSS*, p. 88]

Rochester physically expels that which both literally and symbolically contaminates him. At the center of his endeavor to fix the difference between an 'English' core and an 'ethnic' periphery and to organize the epistemological frameworks through which peripheral subjects can be classified, managed, and perhaps even mastered, there is, for Rochester, the imperative to eliminate the threat of contamination posed by an immoral and indecent past – a threat that is embodied for him by Antoinette.

The text's insistent figuration of a legacy of indecency as female 'bad blood' transcodes the problem of England's colonial history into a problem of bodily violation. It further reveals some of the more intimate connections between the local economy of meaning [to] which Brontë's English novel endeavors to restrict itself and the global economies of imperial power within which it nevertheless also moves. The British West Indian colonies that provided the English ladies and gentlemen across the ocean with the sugar for their afternoon tea were, for example, routinely cast by abolitionists in the late eighteenth century as a site of a moral pollution whose despicable foreign products must not infiltrate the local English body at any cost. The abolitionist William Fox proclaimed: 'The laws of our country may indeed prohibit us the sugar cane, unless we receive it through the medium of slavery. They may hold it to our lips, steeped in the blood of our fellow creatures; but They cannot compel us to accept the loathsome portion'.[47] The very integrity of Englishness is, here, contingent on the protection of the English body from the foreign matter that threatens it. Charlotte Sussman explains: 'abolitionists imagined a domestic body in constant danger from a poisonous world; in order to make their moral point they mobilized fears of bodily pollution'.[48] While the 'loathsome portion' that Rochester ingests in *Wide Sargasso Sea* is bitter rather than sweet like the slave-grown sugar William Fox abhors, it nevertheless recalls this potentially morally poisonous relationship between Britain and its colonies (Rochester thinks to himself, 'I have been poisoned' [*WSS*, p. 88]) and reenacts the global struggle over identity that is persistently played out by England and the West Indian colonies on the body. If Rochester's identity is left uncertain by the English laws of primogeniture that provide the younger son with nothing to inherit but his name, at least his physical body and the English tastes and aversions that shape it continue to remind him of his cultural heritage and the colonial power to which it is linked. Alternatively attracted to and repelled by the sights and smells of the West Indies, Rochester learns over the course of Rhys's text to discipline his body like an Englishman; he learns to define himself by the English tastes that, like the love for tea and crumpets and the late eighteenth-century abolitionist's repugnance for slave-grown sugar, help to secure the identity to which he feels at times so tenuously entitled. Following the British abolitionist subject's physical aversion to the West Indian plantocrats and the morally dubious products they market, Rochester's intense physical disgust for Daniel or his literal expulsion of the obeah draught given to him by Antoinette maps out the limits of the English body; it marks him as an English subject whose body ever vigilantly polices the moral and physical differences celebrated by abolitionists like Fox.

Rochester lays claim to 'Englishness' with increasing confidence over the course of Rhys's text. Yet, his defense of its integrity and the ways in which he must continually monitor its borders reveal the perilously open and unfinished terrain of colonial difference. Rochester's physical disgust for Daniel, therefore, marks more than just the difference between an English Self and a colonial Other. It also marks the place at which the notion of Englishness itself can be said to unravel insofar as Rochester's physical disgust discloses a point of identification and disidentification between the Englishman and the colonial 'half-caste'. The scene of Rochester's meeting with Daniel in a small, hot room shadowed only by the framed biblical text, 'Vengeance is Mine' [*WSS*, p. 77], exposes both Rochester's horrified rejection and his spirited embrace of the signs of otherness he confronts. If Daniel repeats the truth about Rochester's acute feelings of disgust when he observes, 'A tall fine English gentleman like you, you don't want to touch a little yellow rat like me eh?' [*WSS*, p. 80], he also reveals the lie of Rochester's 'pure' English difference by exposing the similarities between the 'fine English gentleman' and the 'little yellow rat' he loathes. The gentleman and the rat of *Wide Sargasso Sea* may appear to occupy the opposite poles in a spectrum of segregated colonial bodies but they ironically share the same fixations and dream the same dreams. Daniel and Rochester each see themselves as disinherited sons who must struggle for wealth, power, and the ever elusive patronymic, the name of the father that Cosway has refused to Daniel and that Jean Rhys has refused to Edward Rochester. In spite of the distance Rochester urgently wants to sustain between them, Daniel and Rochester share a resentment for the father, a hunger for legitimacy, and a fascination with the savage propagation of untruths. They also hate Antoinette – with a passion. Daniel tells Rochester:

> 'They fool you well about that girl. She look you straight in the eye and talk sweet talk – and it's lies she tell you. Lies. Her mother was so. They say she worse than her mother, and she hardly more than a child. Must be you deaf you don't hear people laughing when you marry her. Don't waste your anger on me, sir. It's not I fool you, it's I wish to open your eyes.' [*WSS*, p.80]

When Rochester mistakenly recalls Daniel's suggestive parting sentiments of love for Antoinette as a grotesque expression of Daniel's deviant sexuality and incestuous desire, he merely speaks the unspeakable truth of his own questionable claim to English morality and sexual purity. But Rochester's meeting with Daniel not only reveals the tenuousness of Rochester's differentiation of himself and the colonial subjects he despises; it also succeeds in calling into question the very integrity of the English culture and identity that the disenfranchised Rochester and Daniel so urgently desire.

Englishness emerges in *Wide Sargasso Sea* as an empty fiction that is as seductive and dangerous as any of the other tales of identity that circulate in and around the text. Like the gilt rather than golden bourgeois artifacts proudly displayed in Daniel's imitation English sitting room, and like Granbois, the shabby home that 'looked like an imitation of an English summer house' [*WSS*, p.43], the morally upright English gentleman and the superior religious and ethical principles with which he is ostensibly invested mask the utter emptiness of the 'authentic' English model to which they refer. The English gentleman of Rhys's text is himself no more than a pretender. Predictably, Rochester replicates the vices of the yellow, sweating figure of Daniel and repeats the sexual vices of the very plantocrats whom he claims to despise. Antoinette accuses Rochester: 'You abused the planters and made up stories about them, but you do the same thing. You send the girl away quicker, and with no money or less money, and that's all the difference' [*WSS*, p.94]. And like the slavemaster who assigns to his slaves 'new and often ridiculous names'[49] in an attempt to separate them from their exotic cultures and dangerously alien social structures, Rochester renames Antoinette 'Bertha', blasphemously baptising her the madwoman of Charlotte Brontë's Victorian attic.

Wide Sargasso Sea is saturated with 'bad copies' that are dangerous not because they are themselves somehow inauthentic but because they undermine the very possibility of authenticity. Rhys shares with other twentieth-century writers of postcolonial fiction an intense suspicion of authenticity and the cultural identities such authenticity necessarily underwrites. If Antoinette and Christophine are uncertain as to whether England really exists, Rhys is uncertain as to whether Englishness itself is real. [...] Describing some of her experiences as a child, Rhys records in a journal entry:

My relations with 'real' little English boys and girls (real ones) were peculiar ... .

I nearly always disliked them. I soon discovered the peculiarly smug attitude which made them quite sure that I was in some way inferior. My accent! Did I have a bath every morning or did I have it in the evening. Very important. I'm glad to remember that I slapped one little English girl good and hard once. I also soon realised another thing. If I said I was *English* they at once contradicted me – or implied a contradiction – No a colonial – you're not English – inferior being. My mother says colonials aren't ladies and gentlemen, etc., etc.

If on the other hand I'd say exasperated, 'All right then I'm not English as a matter of fact I'm not a bit. I'd much rather be French or Spanish. They'd get even more amazed at that. I was [a] traitor. You're British they'd say ... . Neither one thing nor the other. Heads you win tails I lose – And I never liked their voices any better than they liked mine.[50]

Rhys's rhetorically awkward emphasis on 'the real' in this passage succeeds in casting doubt on both the English identity she is forced to reject and the alternative national identities to which, as a 'British' subject, she is finally prohibited from laying claim. A colonial who is trapped within the logic of a nation-state that enforces her British status while insisting that she can never really be English, Rhys exposes national identity itself as an imperial fiction that is always subject to confusion. As long as Englishness is so unreliable that even the quotation marks, parentheses, and italics of Rhys's journal entry cannot pin it down, 'colonial identity' too must remain in doubt. Rhys's work is traitorous, therefore, not merely because it threatens to reposition the colonial within the imperialist narratives of the nineteenth and twentieth centuries. It is traitorous because it betrays the basic trust in the logic of the nation-state and in the authenticity of those subjects whom the nation-state endorses.

In short, *Wide Sargasso Sea* resists English imperial common sense, mapping out instead the multiple battles over what gets to count as the way things are. That Rhys plays out these battles on the terrain of the English novel, situating her text both beside and against Charlotte Brontë's nineteenth-century canonical narrative of English womanhood, is no surprise; rather, such explicitly intertextual struggles have helped critical readers of Rhys's fiction to place Rhys within a postcolonial literary tradition that is specifically interested in rewriting the fictions of English empire. [...] In *Wide Sargasso Sea*, Rhys writes back not only to Charlotte Brontë but also to the imperial logics and commonsense structures in which Brontë's text is produced and consumed. Her inquiry into the history of certain kinds of social difference and the processes by which English and colonial subjects are differentiated consequently unsettles both the emergent liberal-feminist narrative of *Jane Eyre* and the larger colonialist enterprise in which it is so heavily invested.

Wide Sargasso Sea lends itself exceedingly well to the many inspired readings of postcolonial opposition and political resistance. [...] Yet, Rhys's text also frustrates literary critical attempts to cast Antoinette as the Other whose native resistance single-handedly challenges the shape of English hegemonic vision. In spite of Rhys's celebrated promise to give Brontë's silent madwoman a chance to tell her story [...] Antoinette persists in replicating many of the basic elements of the English imperial narratives she scorns. In *Wide Sargasso Sea*, Antoinette follows in the path of the Englishman who routinely elides the differences among the native populations over whom he rules. For example, when she looks out on a crowd of islanders, Antoinette carefully surveys the collection of black people standing before her but is unable to distinguish anyone: 'They all looked the same, it was the same face repeated over and over, eyes gleaming, mouth half open to shout' [*WSS*, p.22]. Despite Rochester's conviction that Antoinette's 'dark alien eyes' [*WSS*, p.40] ensure that she is neither a European nor an Englishwoman, Antoinette's failure of vision here brands her such a woman just as surely as Rochester's inability to distinguish between Creole bodies ('Thin or fat they all looked alike' [*WSS*, p.47]) brands him an Englishman. And if the Englishman is repulsed by the spectacle of racial mixing that is to be found virtually everywhere on the islands, Antoinette is similarly horrified. The scene she witnesses between her mother and a black servant incites in her a response that could just as easily have come from her estranged English husband:

I dismounted and ran quickly on to the veranda where I could look into the room. I remember the dress she was wearing – an evening dress cut very low, and she was barefooted. There was a fat black man with a glass of rum in his hand ... . I saw the man lift her up out of the chair and kiss her. I saw his mouth fasten on hers and she went all soft and limp in his arms and he laughed ... . Christophine was waiting for me when I came back crying. 'What you want to go up there for?' she said, and I said, 'You shut up devil, damned black devil from Hell.' [*WSS*, pp. 85–6]

The black mouth fastened on Antoinette's mother threatens to swallow up whole the racial and class differences that purport to organize bodies in space. Anticipating Rochester's English imperialist reinvention of Antoinette as 'Bertha Mason', Antoinette endeavors to reassert order by shoring up the difference between herself and the others who surround her. In other words, if Christophine is a 'damned black devil from Hell', then perhaps the difference that was momentarily put in doubt by the monstrous coupling Antoinette witnesses is still safe. Antoinette's racial disgust and her inability to tell the difference between the individual black bodies that everywhere confront her further reveal some of the ways in which Antoinette's epistemological universe and Rochester's can be said to correspond. Rhys's text troubles the operations of a postcolonial feminism that unconditionally aligns itself with the rejuvenated figure of Brontë's West Indian madwoman because it discloses the complicated relationship between Antoinette's complicity with and her resistance to the English imperial project.

The relationship between complicity and resistance in *Wide Sargasso Sea* calls attention to the highly mystified ways in which the feminist critique of empire also routinely reproduces the empire's most basic philosophical principles and cultural assumptions. Like Antoinette, who replicates English imperialist structures of vision in her own racist disgust and in the desire it partially masks; and like Rhys, who expresses in her letters and interviews an envy and hatred for black men that sit awkwardly beside her celebrated literary refusals of English patriarchy and her critique of the moral discourse of imperialism,[51] feminist critiques of English empire have largely been formulated through the reigning (imperialist) modes of making sense. English feminists at the turn of the nineteenth century, for example, openly contested the notion that the female object of the English civilizing gaze is inherently diseased, morally corrupt, and sexually degenerate (and therefore in need of rigorous surveillance and sexual management) even as they actively endorsed the principles of English racial purity and moral superiority that underwrote the very civilizing gaze they questioned. According to Antoinette Burton:

> Most [late nineteenth-century English] feminists believed in the superiority of the Anglo-Saxon race, frequently citing possession of empire as evidence of a superiority that was not just racial, but religious and cultural as well ... . A strong sense of female superiority combined readily with other assumptions of imperial supremacy to make British feminists conceive of 'The Anglo-Saxon Woman' as the savior of her race, not to mention as the highest female type.[52]

Twentieth-century feminist critics of empire are the inheritors of this acutely contradictory program. Contemporary feminist critique necessarily follows in the tradition Burton describes by replicating the tangle of antiimperialist politics, spirited challenges to patriarchal structures, and a fundamentally racist investment in something called 'English civilization'. The borderland in which *Wide Sargasso Sea* is set consequently not only anticipates but also replays the uneven and contestatory relations of Western feminism as it moves from the twentieth into the twenty-first century. Unlike the stagnant seaweed in the waters between England and the West Indies for which Christopher Columbus first named the Sargasso Sea, Jean Rhys's *Wide Sargasso Sea* is all about struggle. *Wide Sargasso Sea* does not simply replicate English imperial common sense but rather maps out the myriad disputes over what gets to count as the ways things are. In short, feminist inquiry must, like Rhys's text, concern itself with the struggle over borders; it must, finally, resist seduction by futuristic visions of a pluralist peace that is really only the stagnation of Columbus's Sargasso Sea. □

Ciolkowski's closing assertion that *Wide Sargasso Sea* 'is all about struggle' might well be applied to the vibrant critical history that Rhys's novel has engendered since its original appearance in 1966. As this Guide demonstrates, Rhys's text has precipitated a range of responses that are often implicitly (and sometimes explicitly) at odds with one another. Perhaps the only certainty is that the critical debate will continue to develop, as new readers set out to chart the meanings of this haunting text and interpretation duly shifts with the interpreter.

NOTES

INTRODUCTION

1 The epigraph to this chapter is
taken from Jean Rhys, *Letters,
1931–1966*, ed. Francis Wyndham
and Diana Melly (Harmondsworth:
Penguin, 1985), p. 50.
2 The others were Leslie Tilden
Smith and Max Hamer. Rhys
divorced Lenglet in 1933, marrying
Tilden Smith in the following year.
Tilden Smith died in 1945, with
Rhys marrying Hamer in 1947.
Hamer himself died in March 1966,
seven months before *Wide Sargasso
Sea* was published.
3 Coral Ann Howells, 'Jean Rhys
(1890–1979)', in *The Gender of
Modernism: A Critical Anthology*, ed.
Bonnie Kime Scott (Bloomington
and Indianapolis: Indiana University
Press, 1990), p. 373.
4 This phrase appears on the dust-
jacket to *The Left Bank and Other
Stories*, as noted by Francis
Wyndham in his 'Introduction' to
Jean Rhys, *Wide Sargasso Sea*
(Harmondsworth: Penguin, 1968),
p. 5.
5 V. S. Naipaul, 'Without a Dog's
Chance', *New York Review of Books*,
18 May 1972, p. 29.
6 Vaz Dias proffers this information
in an article on Rhys entitled 'In
Quest of a Missing Author', which
was featured in the *Radio Times* of 3
May 1957. The article was written
as a trailer to Vaz Dias's adaptation
of *Good Morning, Midnight*, broadcast
on the BBC's Third Programme one
week later. See Carole Angier, *Jean
Rhys* (Harmondsworth: Penguin,

1992), p. 472.
7 Rhys (1985), p. 148.
8 On this point see Howells (1990),
p. 373 and Angier (1992), p. 223.
9 Rhys (1985), p. 213.
10 Rhys (1985), p. 296.
11 Helen Carr, *Jean Rhys* (Plymouth:
Northcote House, 1996), p. xii.

CHAPTER ONE

1 The epigraph to this chapter is
taken from Jean D'Costa, 'Jean
Rhys 1890–1979', in *Fifty Caribbean
Writers*, ed. Daryl Cumber Dance
(New York: Greenwood Press,
1986), p. 390.
2 Elaine Savory, *Jean Rhys*
(Cambridge: Cambridge University
Press, 1998), p. 196.
3 Hunter Davies, 'Rip Van Rhys',
Sunday Times, 6 November 1966,
p. 13.
4 Neville Braybrooke, 'Shadow and
Substance', *Spectator*, 28 October
1966, p. 560.
5 Colin MacInnes, 'Nightmare in
Paradise', *Observer*, 30 October
1966, p. 28.
6 Ford Madox Ford, cited in
Wyndham (1968), p. 5.
7 Angier (1992), p. 578.
8 Wyndham (1968), p. 9.
9 Carr (1996), p. 6.
10 Carr (1996), p. 6.
11 Savory (1998), p. 268, n. 18.
12 Wally Look Lai, 'The Road to
Thornfield Hall: An Analysis of Jean
Rhys' *Wide Sargasso Sea*', in *New
Beacon Reviews: Collection One*, ed.
John La Rose (London: New Beacon
Books, 1968), p. 38.
13 Look Lai (1968), p. 38.
14 Look Lai (1968), p. 39.
15 Rhys did in fact once return to
the Caribbean – albeit briefly – in

1936. The details of her visit are documented in Peter Hulme and Neil L. Whitehead, eds., *Wild Majesty: Encounters with Caribs from Columbus to the Present Day* (Clarendon Press: Oxford, 1992), p. 299.

16 Look Lai (1968), p. 45.

17 Kenneth Ramchand, 'Terrified Consciousness', *Journal of Commonwealth Literature*, 7 (1969), p. 8.

18 Ramchand (1969), p. 9.

19 Frantz Fanon, *The Wretched of the Earth*, trans. Constance Farrington, Preface by Jean-Paul Sartre (Harmondsworth: Penguin, 1967), p. 27 (emphasis added).

20 Ramchand (1969), p. 11.

21 Edward Kamau Brathwaite, *Contradictory Omens: Cultural Diversity and Integration in the Caribbean* (Kingston, Jamaica: Savacou Publications, 1974), p. 33.

22 Brathwaite (1974), p. 34.

23 Brathwaite (1974), p. 38.

24 Brathwaite (1974), p. 34.

25 Brathwaite (1974), p. 35.

26 Savory (1998), p. 206.

27 See Elgin W. Mellown, 'Character and Themes in the Novels of Jean Rhys', *Contemporary Literature*, 13 (1972), pp. 458–75.

28 Look Lai (1968), p. 52.

29 See Helen Tiffin, 'Post-Colonial Literatures and Counter-Discourse', *Kunapipi*, 9:1 (1987), p. 22: '*canonical counter-discourse ... is [a strategy]* in which a post-colonial writer takes up the assumptions of a British canonical text, subverting the text for post-colonial purposes'.

CHAPTER TWO

1 The epigraph to this chapter is taken from Elizabeth Vreeland, 'Jean Rhys: The Art of Fiction LXIV'

(interview with Jean Rhys), *Paris Review*, 76 (1979), p. 235.

2 Rhys (1985), p. 157.

3 Rhys (1985), p. 262.

4 The question of the intertextual dialogue between Rhys and Brontë has continued to stimulate critical and theoretical debate throughout the 1990s. See, in particular, Romita Choudhury, '"Is There a Ghost, a Zombi There?" Postcolonial Intertextuality and Jean Rhys's *Wide Sargasso Sea*', *Textual Practice*, 10 (1996), pp. 315–27; Rose Kamel, '"Before I Was Set Free": The Creole Wife in *Jane Eyre* and *Wide Sargasso Sea*', *Journal of Narrative Technique*, 25:1 (1995), pp. 1–22; Caroline Rody, 'Burning Down the House: The Revisionary Paradigm of Jean Rhys's *Wide Sargasso Sea*', in *Famous Last Words: Changes in Gender and Narrative Closure*, ed. and intro. Alison Booth (Charlottesville: University Press of Virginia, 1993), pp. 300–25; and R. McClure Smith, '"I Don't Dream About It Any More": The Textual Unconscious in Jean Rhys's *Wide Sargasso Sea*', *Journal of Narrative Technique*, 26:2 (1996), pp. 113–36.

5 Dennis Porter, 'Of Heroines and Victims: Jean Rhys and *Jane Eyre*', *Massachusetts Review*, 17 (1976), p. 540.

6 Porter (1976), p. 541.

7 Porter (1976), p. 542.

8 Porter (1976), p. 543.

9 Porter (1976), p. 542.

10 Porter (1976), p. 542.

11 Gayatri Chakravorty Spivak, 'Three Women's Texts and a Critique of Imperialism', *Critical Inquiry*, 12 (1985), p. 252.

12 Porter (1976), p. 545.

13 Porter (1976), p. 540.

14 Dell Hymes, ed., Preface to *Pidginization and Creolization of Languages*, (London: Cambridge University Press, 1971), p. 5.

15 Elizabeth R. Baer, 'The Sisterhood of Jane Eyre and Antoinette Cosway', in *The Voyage In: Fictions of Female Development*, ed. Elizabeth Abel, Marianne Hirsch and Elizabeth Langland (Hanover and London: University Press of New England, 1983), p. 133.

16 Baer (1983), p. 136.

17 Baer (1983), p. 133.

18 Baer (1983), p. 137.

19 Baer (1983), p. 146.

20 Nancy K. Miller, 'Emphasis Added: Plots and Plausibilities in Women's Fiction', *PMLA*, 96 (1981), p. 44.

21 Adrienne Rich, *On Lies, Secrets, and Silence: Selected Prose, 1966–1978* (New York: Norton, 1979), pp. 89–106.

22 This term is borrowed from Judith Fetterley, *The Resisting Reader: A Feminist Approach to American Fiction* (Bloomington and London: Indiana University Press, 1978).

23 Penny Boumelha, *Charlotte Brontë* (Hemel Hempstead: Harvester, 1990), p. 60.

24 Robert J. C. Young, *Colonial Desire: Hybridity in Theory, Culture and Race* (London and New York: Routledge, 1995), p. 163.

25 Spivak (1985), p. 243.

26 Spivak (1985), p. 248.

27 Rhys (1985), p. 156.

28 Spivak (1985), p. 252.

29 Spivak (1985), p. 259.

30 Thomas F. Staley, *Jean Rhys: A Critical Study* (London: Macmillan, 1979), pp. 108–16.

31 Benita Parry, 'Problems in Current Theories of Colonial Discourse', *Oxford Literary Review*, 9:1–2 (1987), p. 38.

32 Gayatri Chakravorty Spivak, 'Imperialism and Sexual Difference', *Oxford Literary Review*, 8:1–2 (1986), p. 226.

33 Spivak (1986), p. 238.

CHAPTER THREE

1 The epigraph to this chapter is taken from the unpublished manuscript of Jean Rhys's *Black Exercise Book*. The passage is cited in Coral Ann Howells, *Jean Rhys* (Hemel Hempstead: Harvester, 1991), p. 21.

2 Maggie Humm, *Border Traffic: Strategies of Contemporary Women Writers* (Manchester and New York: Manchester University Press, 1991), p. 62.

3 Helen Tiffin, 'Mirror and Mask: Colonial Motifs in the Novels of Jean Rhys', *World Literature Written in English*, 17 (1978), p. 328.

4 Tiffin (1978), p. 329.

5 Jean Rhys, *Voyage in the Dark* (Harmondsworth: Penguin, 1969), p. 19.

6 bell hooks, *Ain't I a Woman: Black Women and Feminism* (London: Pluto Press, 1982), p. 126. For a subtle elaboration of hooks's argument, see Karen Sánchez-Eppler, 'Bodily Bonds: The Intersecting Rhetorics of Feminism and Abolition', in *The New American Studies: Essays from Representations*, ed. Philip Fisher (Berkeley and Oxford: University of California Press, 1991), pp. 228–59.

7 Lee Erwin, '"Like in a Looking-Glass": History and Narrative in *Wide Sargasso Sea*', *Novel*, 22 (1989), p. 143.

8 Erwin (1989), p. 144.

9 Erwin (1989), p. 143.

10 Erwin (1989), p. 154.

11 Erwin (1989), p. 145.

12 Erwin (1989), p. 147.

13 Elizabeth Nunez-Harrell, 'The Paradoxes of Belonging: The White West Indian Woman in Fiction', *Modern Fiction Studies*, 31 (1985), pp. 281–93.

14 Gayatri Chakravorty Spivak, 'The Production of Colonial Discourse: A Marxist-Feminist Reading' (course presented as part of the Conference on Marxism and the Interpretation of Culture, University of Illinois at Urbana-Champaign, 1983).

15 John Davy, *The West Indies, Before and Since Slave Emancipation* (London: Frank Cass, 1971), p. 74.

16 Sander L. Gilman, 'Black Bodies, White Bodies: Toward an Iconography of Female Sexuality in Late Nineteenth-Century Art, Medicine, and Literature', in *Race, Writing, and Difference*, ed. Henry Louis Gates, Jr. (Chicago and London: University of Chicago Press, 1986), p. 256.

17 Spivak (1985), p. 252.

18 Wyndham (1968), p. 11.

19 Gilman (1986), p. 250.

20 Gordon K. Lewis, *Main Currents in Caribbean Thought: The Historical Evolution of Caribbean Society in its Ideological Aspects, 1492–1900* (Baltimore and London: The Johns Hopkins University Press, 1983), p. 66.

21 For detailed readings of *Jane Eyre* along these lines see, in particular, Susan Meyer, *Imperialism at Home: Race and Victorian Women's Fiction* (Ithaca and London: Cornell University Press, 1996), pp. 60–95;

and Carl Plasa, *Textual Politics from Slavery to Postcolonialism: Race and Identification* (Basingstoke and London: Macmillan, 2000), pp. 60–81.

22 Maria Olaussen, 'Jean Rhys's Construction of Blackness as Escape from White Femininity in *Wide Sargasso Sea*', *Ariel*, 24:2 (1993), p. 69.

23 Olaussen (1993), p. 68.

24 Homi K. Bhabha, *The Location of Culture* (London and New York: Routledge, 1994), p. 123.

25 Olaussen (1993), p. 81.

26 Mary Lou Emery, *Jean Rhys at 'World's End': Novels of Colonial and Sexual Exile* (Austin: University of Texas Press, 1990), p. 19.

27 Hazel V. Carby, *Reconstructing Womanhood: The Emergence of the Afro-American Woman Novelist* (Oxford: Oxford University Press, 1987), p. 23.

28 Carby (1987), p. 27.

29 Barbara Christian, *Black Feminist Criticism: Perspectives on Black Women Writers* (New York: Pergamon Press, 1985), p. 2.

30 Christian (1985), p. 5.

31 Herbert S. Klein, *African Slavery in Latin America and the Caribbean* (Oxford: Oxford University Press, 1986), p. 170.

32 Klein (1986), p. 172.

33 Hortense J. Spillers, 'Mama's Baby, Papa's Maybe: An American Grammar Book', *Diacritics*, 17:2 (1987), p. 74.

34 Elaine Showalter, *The Female Malady: Women, Madness, and English Culture, 1830–1980* (London: Virago Press, 1987), p. 55.

35 Emery (1990), p. 40.

36 Virginia Hamilton, *Stories Around the World* (London: Hodder and Stoughton, 1990), p. 102.

CHAPTER FOUR

1 The epigraph to this chapter is taken from Rhys (1985), p. 216. The rather obscure term, 'dots', is of mid-nineteenth-century currency and refers to 'A woman's marriage portion, of which the annual income alone is under her husband's control' (OED).

2 Markman Ellis, *The History of Gothic Fiction* (Edinburgh: Edinburgh University Press, 2000), p. 210.

3 Teresa F. O'Connor, *Jean Rhys: The West Indian Novels* (New York and London: New York University Press, 1986), p. 210.

4 Edward Kamau Brathwaite, *The Development of Creole Society in Jamaica, 1770–1820* (Oxford: Clarendon Press, 1971), p. 162.

5 Brathwaite (1971), p. 162.

6 Brathwaite (1971), pp. 255–6.

7 In situating *Wide Sargasso Sea* in relation to the writings of the early Romantic period, Richardson departs from the critical norm which fixes the intertextual horizon of Rhys's novel at *Jane Eyre*. The Rhys/Brontë link is also productively broken by Sue Thomas in her discussion of *Wide Sargasso Sea* as a partial reworking of William Shakespeare's *Othello* (1604). See Sue Thomas, *The Worlding of Jean Rhys* (Westport, CT and London: Greenwood Press, 1999), pp. 171–8.

8 Alan Richardson, 'Romantic Voodoo: Obeah and British Culture, 1797–1807', *Studies in Romanticism*, 32 (1993), p. 5.

9 Maya Deren, *Divine Horsemen: The Living Gods of Haiti* (New York: McPherson, 1953), p. 6.

10 See Sandra M. Gilbert and Susan Gubar, *The Madwoman in the Attic: The Woman Writer and the Nineteenth-Century Literary Imagination* (New Haven and London: Yale University Press, 1979).

11 Catherine Clément, 'The Guilty One', in Hélène Cixous and Catherine Clément, *The Newly Born Woman*, trans. Betsy Wing, intro. Sandra M. Gilbert (Manchester: Manchester University Press, 1986), p. 30.

12 Heinrich Kramer and Jacob Sprenger, 'The Malleus Maleficarum', in *Witchcraft in Europe, 1100–1700: A Documentary History*, ed. Alan C. Kors and Edward Peters (Philadelphia: University of Pennsylvania Press, 1972), p. 127.

13 Clément (1986), p. 5.

14 Richardson (1993), p. 5.

15 Judie Newman, *The Ballistic Bard: Postcolonial Fictions* (London: Edward Arnold, 1995), p. 18.

16 For a less detailed but none the less valuable consideration of the influence of Lewton's film on Rhys's novel, see Edna Aizenberg, '"I Walked with a Zombie": The Pleasures and Perils of Postcolonial Hybridity', *World Literature Today*, 73 (1999), pp. 461–6. The link between Rhys and Lewton is also briefly noted by Ellis (2000), p. 236.

17 Newman (1995), p. 17.

18 Newman (1995), p. 22.

19 Newman (1995), p. 23.

20 Newman (1995), p. 24. Newman's sense of the capacity of Rhys's novel to transform its Brontëan original is echoed by Aizenberg: 'So potent is Rhys's postcolonial rewriting of Bertha Mason', she suggests, 'that she has, à la Borges, "created" her precursor. [...] Rhys's *Wide Sargasso Sea* has had an enormous impact on

subsequent readings and productions of *Jane Eyre*, inevitably in the direction of greater focus on the colonial Afro-Caribbean dimension and greater positive Africanization of Antoinette. Rhys has achieved the height of postcolonial pleasure, if you will, emptying the master text and filling it with an audacious revisionist content' (Aizenberg [1999], p. 464). See also Thomas (1999), p. 167.

21 John Hearne, 'The Wide Sargasso Sea: A West Indian Reflection', *Cornhill Magazine*, 1080 (1974), p. 323.

22 Rich (1979), p. 35.

23 Cited in Hannah Carter, 'Fated to be Sad', *Guardian*, 8 August 1968, p. 5.

24 Messalina was married to the Roman emperor Claudius and was notorious for her profligacy.

25 Penny Boumelha, '"And What Do the Women Do?" Jane Eyre, Jamaica, and the Gentleman's House', *Southern Review*, 21 (1988), pp. 111–22.

26 Boumelha (1988), p. 112.

27 Baer (1983), p. 132.

28 Wade Davis, *The Ethnobiology of the Haitian Zombie* (Chapel Hill: University of North Carolina Press, 1988), p. 31.

29 [*Newman's Note:*] Among those who have commented on the role of obeah in the works of Jean Rhys, Thomas Loe, 'Patterns of the Zombie in Jean Rhys's *Wide Sargasso Sea*', *World Literature Written in English*, 31 (1991), pp. 34–42, concentrates on the zombie as a significant allusive base and central metaphor energising and unifying the text, and relates it to West Indian belief systems and social control mechanisms. See also Anthony E. Luengo, 'Wide Sargasso Sea and the Gothic Mode', *World Literature Written in English*, 15 (1976), pp. 229–45; Elaine Campbell, 'Reflections of Obeah in Jean Rhys's Fiction', *Kunapipi*, 4:2 (1982), pp. 42–50; Françoise Defromont, 'Mémoires Hantées: De *Jane Eyre* à *Wide Sargasso Sea*', *Cahiers Victoriens et Edouardiens*, 27 (1988), pp. 149–57; Mona Fayad, 'Unquiet Ghosts: The Struggle for Representation in Rhys's *Wide Sargasso Sea*', *Modern Fiction Studies*, 34 (1988), pp. 437–52. Perhaps because of the concern with establishing Rhys's authenticity as a West Indian writer, the influence of film, and of Rhys's own experience of being presumed dead, do not form part of their arguments.

30 See Davis (1988) and C. H. Dewisme, *Les Zombis ou le Secret des Morts-Vivants* (Paris: Grasset, 1957).

31 Cited in Gene Wright, *Horror-Shows: The A- to Z- of Horror in Film, TV, Radio and Theatre* (London: David and Charles, 1986), p. 227.

32 Pierre Corneille Blessebois, *Le Zombi du Grand Pérou* (Paris: Editions Civilisations Nouvelles, 1970). See Jack Corzani, 'West Indian Mythology and its Literary Illustrations', *Research in African Literatures*, 25 (1994), pp. 131–9.

33 [*Newman's Note:*] See Ellen Draper, 'Zombie Women When the Gaze is Male', *Wide Angle*, 10:3 (1988), pp. 52–62 (discussing early zombie films as exploring the camera's domination of women); Alan Frank, *The Horror Film Handbook* (London: Batsford, 1982); Barry Keith Grant, ed., *Planks of Reason: Essays on the Horror Film* (London

and Metuchen: Scarecrow Press, 1984); Peter Haining, ed., *Stories of the Walking Dead* (London: Severn House, 1986).

34 Cited in Leslie Halliwell, *The Dead That Walk* (London: Paladin, 1988).

35 Angier (1992), p.471.

36 Angier (1992), p.449.

37 Angier (1992), p.450.

38 Angier (1992), p.451.

39 Jean Rhys, 'Temps Perdi', in *Tales of the Wide Caribbean*, ed. Kenneth Ramchand (London: Heinemann, 1985), p.145.

40 Helen Tiffin, 'Transformative Imageries', in *From Commonwealth to Post-Colonial*, ed. Anna Rutherford (Sydney: Dangaroo Press, 1992), p.434.

41 [*Newman's Note:*] Veronica Marie Gregg, 'Ideology and Autobiography in the Jean Rhys *Oeuvre*', in Rutherford (1992), p.415. Peter Hulme argues that Jean Rhys adapts the chronology to fit her own family history (the Lockharts). See Peter Hulme, 'The Locked Heart: The Creole Family Romance of *Wide Sargasso Sea*', in *Colonial Discourse/Postcolonial Theory*, ed. Francis Barker, Peter Hulme and Margaret Iversen (Manchester and New York: Manchester University Press, 1994), pp.72–88.

42 [*Newman's Note:*] Howells (1991), p.114, discusses the relationship between *Jane Eyre* and *Wide Sargasso Sea* as a Gothic one.

43 [*Newman's Note:*] Freud defines the uncanny as that class of the frightening which leads back to what is known of old and long familiar. See Sigmund Freud, 'The Uncanny', in *Art and Literature*, Pelican Freud Library, vol. 14, trans. James Strachey, ed. Albert Dickson (Harmondsworth: Penguin, 1985), pp.339–76.

44 Emery (1990), pp.35–62.

45 Todd K. Bender, 'Jean Rhys and the Genius of Impressionism', *Studies in the Literary Imagination*, 11:2 (1978), pp.43–55.

46 Robbie Kidd, *The Quiet Stranger* (Edinburgh: Mainstream, 1991).

47 Wilson Harris, 'Carnival of Psyche: Jean Rhys's *Wide Sargasso Sea*', *Kunapipi*, 2:2 (1980), pp.142–50.

CHAPTER FIVE

1 The epigraphs to this chapter are taken, respectively, from Louise Bennett, 'Colonisation in Reverse', in *Post-Colonial Literatures in English*, ed. John Thieme (London: Edward Arnold, 1996), p.845; Veronica Marie Gregg, *Jean Rhys's Historical Imagination: Reading and Writing the Creole* (Chapel Hill and London: University of North Carolina Press, 1995), pp.23–4; and Lowell Joseph Ragatz, *The Fall of the Planter Class in the British Caribbean, 1763–1833: A Study in Social and Economic History* (New York: Century, 1928), p.5.

2 Gregg (1995), p.8.

3 Humm (1991), p.87.

4 Humm (1991), p.89.

5 Vreeland (1979), p.230.

6 Rhys (1985), p.222.

7 Rhys (1985), p.223.

8 Rhys (1985), p.297 (emphasis added).

9 Bhabha (1994), p.82.

10 David Plante, *Difficult Women: A Memoir of Three* (London: Gollancz, 1983), p.52.

11 Hulme (1994), p.72.

12 Hulme (1994), p.73.

13 Hulme (1994), p.73.

14 Sigmund Freud, 'Family Romances', in *On Sexuality*, Pelican Freud Library, vol. 7, trans. James Strachey, ed. Angela Richards (Harmondsworth: Penguin, 1977), pp.222–3.

15 Hulme (1994), p.76.

16 Hulme (1994), p.81.

17 Hulme (1994), p.76.

18 Hulme (1994), p.84.

19 Hulme (1994), p.85.

20 Angier (1992), p.223.

21 Rhys (1985), p.153.

22 Rhys (1985), p.262.

23 Rhys (1985), pp.265–6.

24 Rhys (1985), p.214.

25 Jean Rhys, *Smile Please: An Unfinished Autobiography* (Harmondsworth: Penguin, 1981), p.33.

26 [*Hulme's Note:*] According to Louis James, 'Geneva estate was looted and burned' (Louis James, *Jean Rhys* [London: Longman, 1978], p.47), an event Teresa F. O'Connor speaks of as 'recast in *Wide Sargasso Sea*' (O'Connor [1986], p.20). The estate house at Geneva was burned down in 1932 during a period of unrest in which the incumbent Lockhart was very unpopular. This happened just four years before Jean Rhys returned to the island for a brief visit, and stories about the incident may have been transposed to the older family stories about the post-emancipation riots.

27 'Copies or Extracts of Correspondence Relative to the Late Disturbances Among the Negroes in the Island of Dominica', *Accounts and Papers*, (3), 34 (House of Commons, 1844), p.247.

28 House of Commons (1844), p.246.

29 House of Commons (1844), p.247.

30 'Copies or Extracts of Correspondence Relative to the Late Disturbances Among the Negroes in the Island of Dominica', *Accounts and Papers*, (4), 31 (House of Commons, 1845), p.104.

31 House of Commons (1845), p.114.

32 House of Commons (1845), p.123.

33 See Paul Gilroy, *The Black Atlantic: Modernity and Double Consciousness* (London and New York: Verso, 1993).

34 Rhys (1985), p.154.

35 For a critique of Hulme's position see Carine M. Mardorossian, 'Double (De)colonization and the Feminist Criticism of *Wide Sargasso Sea*', *College Literature*, 26:2 (1999), pp.91–2.

36 Laura E. Ciolkowski, 'Navigating the *Wide Sargasso Sea*: Colonial History, English Fiction, and British Empire', *Twentieth Century Literature*, 43 (1997), p.352.

37 Ciolkowski (1997), p.343.

38 Ciolkowski (1997), p.349.

39 Ciolkowski (1997), p.339.

40 [*Ciolkowski's Note:*] Like Antoinette's father in *Wide Sargasso Sea*, Edward Rochester's 'gross, impure, depraved' (*JE*, p.323) lunatic wife in *Jane Eyre* attaches the excesses of temper (drink) to the excesses of sex (chastity). If Brontë's Rochester is made savage by his bond to such a wife, however, he is both literally and symbolically purified by the heavenly heroine, Jane Eyre. Joyce Zonana has read Jane Eyre's recuperative gesture as one, more specifically, of Westernization. Zonana

argues that Rochester 'is "Eastern" in his ways, and for Jane to be happy, he must be thoroughly Westernized'. Joyce Zonana, 'The Sultan and the Slave: Feminist Orientalism and the Structure of *Jane Eyre*', *Signs*, 18 (1993), p. 597. Such a reading is actually taken up in *Wide Sargasso Sea* insofar as Rhys is interested in the ways in which Rochester struggles to sever himself from the West Indian influence introduced by his unfortunate (and horrifying) matrimonial attachment.

41 [*Ciolkowksi's Note:*] Rochester's attempt to recount to Jane the story of his courtship and marriage to Bertha Mason and, finally, the horrifying tale of Bertha's precipitous decline reveal the preoccupation with sexual appetite that is taken up and embellished on by Rhys in *Wide Sargasso Sea*. Rochester's collection of petty evidence of his West Indian wife's madness – she is by Rochester's estimation guilty of the crimes of backward social skills, bad taste, a nasty temper, and a weak intellect – is juxtaposed with the clearly frightful sexual vices of which Bertha is both implicitly and explicitly accused. The litany of evidence introduced by Rochester powerfully (and predictably) culminates in the startling revelation of Bertha's unchastity.

42 Rosemary Marangoly George, 'Homes in the Empire, Empires in the Home', *Cultural Critique*, 26 (1993–4), p. 108.

43 Barbara Bush, *Slave Women in Caribbean Society, 1650–1838* (Bloomington and Indianapolis: Indiana University Press, 1990), p. 11.

44 Stuart Hall, 'Negotiating Caribbean Identities', *New Left Review*, 209 (1995), p. 5.

45 Tim Jeal, *Livingstone* (New York: Putnam's, 1973), p. 4.

46 Howells (1991), p. 117.

47 William Fox, cited in Charlotte Sussman, 'Women and the Politics of Sugar, 1792', *Representations*, 48 (1994), p. 51.

48 Sussman (1994), p. 50.

49 Bush (1990), p. 24.

50 Rhys, cited in O'Connor (1986), p. 19.

51 [*Ciolkowski's Note:*] In a conversation with David Plante, Rhys confesses: 'I hate. I hate [the blacks in Dominica]. We didn't treat them badly. We didn't. I hate them .... And yet, I was kissed once by a Nigerian, in a café in Paris, and I understood, a little. I understand why they are attractive. It goes very deep. They danced, danced in the sunlight, and how I envied them.' David Plante, 'Jean Rhys: A Remembrance', *Paris Review*, 76 (1979), p. 248. In *Smile Please*, Rhys expresses similar sentiments. She recounts: 'Side by side with my growing wariness of black people there was envy. I decided that they had a better time than we did; they laughed a lot though they seldom smiled. They were stronger than we were, they could walk a long way without getting tired. Carry heavy weights with ease' (Rhys [1981], p. 50).

52 Antoinette M. Burton, 'The White Woman's Burden: British Feminists and the Indian Woman, 1865–1915', *Women's Studies International Forum*, 13:4 (1990), p. 296.

SELECT BIBLIOGRAPHY

'A Fairy-Tale Neurotic', unsigned review of *Wide Sargasso Sea, Times Literary Supplement*, 17 November 1966, p. 1039.

Aizenberg, Edna, '"I Walked with a Zombie": The Pleasures and Perils of Postcolonial Hybridity', *World Literature Today*, 73 (1999), pp. 461–6.

Allen, Walter, 'Bertha the Doomed', *New York Times Book Review*, 18 June 1967, p. 5.

Angier, Carole, *Jean Rhys* (Harmondsworth: Penguin, 1992).

Baer, Elizabeth R., 'The Sisterhood of Jane Eyre and Antoinette Cosway', in *The Voyage In: Fictions of Female Development*, ed. Elizabeth Abel, Marianne Hirsch and Elizabeth Langland (Hanover and London: University Press of New England, 1983), pp. 131–48.

Barreca, Regina, 'Writing as Voodoo: Sorcery, Hysteria, and Art', in *Death and Representation*, ed. Sarah Webster Goodwin and Elisabeth Bronfen (Baltimore and London: The Johns Hopkins University Press, 1993), pp. 174–91.

Bender, Todd K., 'Jean Rhys and the Genius of Impressionism', *Studies in the Literary Imagination*, 11:2 (1978), pp. 43–55.

Brathwaite, Edward Kamau, *Contradictory Omens: Cultural Diversity and Integration in the Caribbean* (Kingston, Jamaica: Savacou Publications, 1974).

Braybrooke, Neville, 'Shadow and Substance', *Spectator*, 28 October 1966, pp. 560–1.

Brontë, Charlotte, *Jane Eyre*, ed. and intro. Margaret Smith (Oxford and New York: Oxford University Press, 1998).

Bruner, Charlotte H., 'A Caribbean Madness: Half Slave and Half Free', *Canadian Review of Comparative Literature*, 11 (1984), pp. 236–48.

Campbell, Elaine, 'Reflections of Obeah in Jean Rhys' Fiction', *Kunapipi*, 4:2 (1982), pp. 42–50.

Carr, Helen, *Jean Rhys* (Plymouth: Northcote House, 1996).

Carter, Hannah, 'Fated to be Sad', *Guardian*, 8 August 1968, p. 5.

Choudhury, Romita, '"Is There a Ghost, a Zombi There?" Postcolonial Intertextuality and Jean Rhys's *Wide Sargasso Sea*', *Textual Practice*, 10 (1996), pp. 315–27.

Ciolkowski, Laura E., 'Navigating the *Wide Sargasso Sea*: Colonial History, English Fiction, and British Empire', *Twentieth Century Literature*, 43 (1997), pp. 339–59.

Davidson, Arnold E., *Jean Rhys* (New York: Frederick Ungar, 1985).

Davies, Hunter, 'Rip Van Rhys', *Sunday Times*, 6 November 1966, p. 13.

D'Costa, Jean, 'Jean Rhys 1890–1979', in *Fifty Caribbean Writers*, ed. Daryl Cumber Dance (New York: Greenwood Press, 1986), pp. 390–404.

Ellis, Markman, *The History of Gothic Fiction* (Edinburgh: Edinburgh University Press, 2000).

Emery, Mary Lou, *Jean Rhys at 'World's End': Novels of Colonial and Sexual Exile* (Austin: University of Texas Press, 1990).

Erwin, Lee, '"Like in a Looking-Glass": History and Narrative in *Wide Sargasso Sea*', *Novel*, 22 (1989), pp. 143–58.

Fayad, Mona, 'Unquiet Ghosts: The Struggle for Representation in Rhys's *Wide Sargasso Sea*', *Modern Fiction Studies*, 34 (1988), pp. 437–52.

Ferguson, Moira, 'Sending the Younger Son Across the *Wide Sargasso Sea*: The New Colonizer Arrives', *Jean Rhys Review*, 6:1 (1993), pp. 2–16.

Forrester, Faizal, 'Who Stole the Soul in *Wide Sargasso Sea*?', *Journal of West Indian Literature*, 6:2 (1994), pp. 32–42.

Freud, Sigmund, 'Family Romances', in *On Sexuality*, Pelican Freud Library, vol. 7, trans. James Strachey, ed. Angela Richards (Harmondsworth: Penguin, 1977), pp. 217–25.

Frickey, Pierrette M., ed., *Critical Perspectives on Jean Rhys* (Washington, DC: Three Continents Press, 1990).

Friedman, Ellen G., 'Breaking the Master Narrative: Jean Rhys's *Wide Sargasso Sea*', in *Breaking the Sequence: Women's Experimental Fiction*, ed. Ellen G. Friedman and Miriam Fuchs (Princeton: Princeton University Press, 1989), pp. 117–28.

Gardiner, Judith Kegan, *Rhys, Stead, Lessing and the Politics of Empathy* (Bloomington and Indianapolis: Indiana University Press, 1989).

Gregg, Veronica Marie, *Jean Rhys's Historical Imagination: Reading and Writing the Creole* (Chapel Hill and London: University of North Carolina Press, 1995).

Harris, Wilson, 'Carnival of Psyche: Jean Rhys's *Wide Sargasso Sea*', *Kunapipi*, 2:2 (1980), pp. 142–50.

Harrison, Nancy R., *Jean Rhys and the Novel as Women's Text* (Chapel Hill and London: University of North Carolina Press, 1988).

Hearne, John, 'The Wide Sargasso Sea: A West Indian Reflection', *Cornhill Magazine*, 1080 (1974), pp. 323–33.

Hope, Francis, 'The First Mrs Rochester', *New Statesman*, 28 October 1966, pp. 638–9.

Howells, Coral Ann, *Jean Rhys* (Hemel Hempstead: Harvester, 1991).

Howells, Coral Ann, intro. and ed., 'Jean Rhys (1890–1979)', in *The Gender of Modernism: A Critical Anthology*, ed. Bonnie Kime Scott (Bloomington and Indianapolis: Indiana University Press, 1990), pp. 372–92.

Huggan, Graham, 'A Tale of Two Parrots: Walcott, Rhys, and the Uses of Colonial Mimicry', *Contemporary Literature*, 35 (1994), pp. 643–60.

Hulme, Peter, 'The Locked Heart: The Creole Family Romance of *Wide Sargasso Sea*', in *Colonial Discourse/Postcolonial Theory*, ed. Francis Barker, Peter Hulme and Margaret Iversen (Manchester and New York: Manchester University Press, 1994), pp. 72–88.

Humm, Maggie, *Border Traffic: Strategies of Contemporary Women Writers* (Manchester and New York: Manchester University Press, 1991).

James, Louis, *Jean Rhys* (London: Longman, 1978).

James, Selma, *The Ladies and the Mammies: Jane Austen & Jean Rhys* (Bristol: Falling Wall Press, 1983).

Johnson, Freya, 'The Male Gaze and the Struggle Against Patriarchy in *Jane Eyre* and *Wide Sargasso Sea*', *Jean Rhys Review*, 5:1–2 (1992), pp. 22–30.

Kamel, Rose, '"Before I Was Set Free": The Creole Wife in *Jane Eyre* and *Wide Sargasso Sea*', *Journal of Narrative Technique*, 25:1 (1995), pp. 1–22.

Kendrick, Robert, 'Edward Rochester and the Margins of Masculinity in *Jane Eyre* and *Wide Sargasso Sea*', *Papers on Language and Literature*, 30 (1994), pp. 235–56.

Kloepfer, Deborah Kelly, *The Unspeakable Mother: Forbidden Discourse in Jean Rhys and H. D.* (Ithaca and London: Cornell University Press, 1989).

Koenen, Anne, 'The Fantastic As Feminine Mode: *Wide Sargasso Sea*', *Jean Rhys Review*, 4:1 (1990), pp. 15–27.

Lawson, Lori, 'Mirror and Madness: A Lacanian Analysis of the Feminine Subject in *Wide Sargasso Sea*', *Jean Rhys Review*, 4:2 (1991), pp. 19–27.

Le Gallez, Paula, *The Rhys Woman* (New York: St Martin's Press, 1990).

Little, Judy, 'Signifying Nothing: A Shakespearean Deconstruction of Rhys's Rochester', *Jean Rhys Review*, 7:1–2 (1996), pp. 39–46.

Loe, Thomas, 'Patterns of the Zombie in Jean Rhys's *Wide Sargasso Sea*', *World Literature Written in English*, 31 (1991), pp. 34–42.

Look Lai, Wally, 'The Road to Thornfield Hall: An Analysis of Jean Rhys' *Wide Sargasso Sea*', in *New Beacon Reviews: Collection One*, ed. John La Rose (London: New Beacon Books, 1968), pp. 38–52.

Luengo, Anthony E., '*Wide Sargasso Sea* and the Gothic Mode', *World Literature Written in English*, 15 (1976), pp. 229–45.

MacInnes, Colin, 'Nightmare in Paradise', *Observer*, 30 October 1966, p. 28.

Mardorossian, Carine M., 'Double (De)colonization and the Feminist Criticism of *Wide Sargasso Sea*', *College Literature*, 26:2 (1999), pp. 79–95.

Mardorossian, Carine M., 'Shutting Up the Subaltern: Silences, Stereotypes, and Double-Entendre in Jean Rhys's *Wide Sargasso Sea*', *Callaloo*, 22 (1999), pp. 1071–90.

Maurel, Sylvie, *Jean Rhys* (Basingstoke and London: Macmillan, 1998).

Maxwell, Anne, 'The Debate on Current Theories of Colonial Discourse', *Kunapipi*, 13:3 (1991), 70–84.

Mellown, Elgin W., 'Character and Themes in the Novels of Jean Rhys', *Contemporary Literature*, 13 (1972), pp. 458–75.

Mezei, Kathy, '"And It Kept Its Secret": Narration, Memory and Madness in Jean Rhys' *Wide Sargasso Sea*', *Critique*, 28:4 (1987), pp. 195–209.

Naipaul, V. S., 'Without a Dog's Chance', *New York Review of Books*, 18 May 1972, pp. 29–31.

Nebeker, Helen, *Jean Rhys: Woman in Passage* (Montreal: Eden, 1981).

Neck-Yoder, Hilda van, 'Colonial Desires, Silence, and Metonymy: "All Things Considered" in *Wide Sargasso Sea*', *Texas Studies in Literature and Language*, 40 (1998), pp. 184–208.

Newman, Judie, *The Ballistic Bard: Postcolonial Fictions* (London: Edward Arnold, 1995), pp. 13–28.

Nunez-Harrell, Elizabeth, 'The Paradoxes of Belonging: The White West Indian Woman in Fiction', *Modern Fiction Studies*, 31 (1985), pp. 281–93.

Oates, Joyce Carol, 'Romance and Anti-Romance': From Brontë's *Jane Eyre* to Rhys's *Wide Sargasso Sea*', *Virginia Quarterly Review*, 61:1 (1985), pp. 44–58.

O'Connor, Teresa F., *Jean Rhys: The West Indian Novels* (New York and London: New York University Press, 1986).

Olaussen, Maria, 'Jean Rhys's Construction of Blackness as Escape from White Femininity in *Wide Sargasso Sea*', *Ariel*, 24:2 (1993), pp. 65–82.

Parry, Benita, 'Problems in Current Theories of Colonial Discourse', *Oxford Literary Review*, 9:1–2 (1987), pp. 27–58.

Plante, David, *Difficult Women: A Memoir of Three* (London: Gollancz, 1983).

Plasa, Carl, *Textual Politics from Slavery to Postcolonialism: Race and Identification* (Basingstoke and London: Macmillan, 2000), pp. 82–97.

Porter, Dennis, 'Of Heroines and Victims: Jean Rhys and *Jane Eyre*', *Massachusetts Review*, 17 (1976), pp. 540–52.

Ramchand, Kenneth, 'Terrified Consciousness', *Journal of Commonwealth Literature*, 7 (1969), pp. 8–19.

Rhys, Jean, *After Leaving Mr Mackenzie* (Harmondsworth: Penguin, 1971).

Rhys, Jean, *The Collected Short Stories* (New York: Norton, 1987).

Rhys, Jean, *Good Morning, Midnight* (Harmondsworth: Penguin, 1969).

Rhys, Jean, *The Left Bank and Other Stories*, Preface by Ford Madox Ford (London: Jonathan Cape, 1927).

Rhys, Jean, *Letters, 1931–1966*, ed. Francis Wyndham and Diana Melly (Harmondsworth: Penguin, 1985).

Rhys, Jean, *My Day: Three Pieces by Jean Rhys* (New York: Frank Hallman, 1975).

Rhys, Jean, *Quartet* (Harmondsworth: Penguin, 1973).

Rhys, Jean, *Sleep It Off Lady* (Harmondsworth: Penguin, 1979).

Rhys, Jean, *Smile Please: An Unfinished Autobiography* (Harmondsworth: Penguin, 1981).

Rhys, Jean, *Tales of the Wide Caribbean*, ed. Kenneth Ramchand (London and Kingston, Jamaica: Heinemann, 1985).

Rhys, Jean, *Tigers Are Better-Looking* (Harmondsworth: Penguin, 1972).

Rhys, Jean, *Voyage in the Dark* (Harmondsworth: Penguin, 1969).

Rhys, Jean, *Wide Sargasso Sea*, ed. and intro. Angela Smith (Harmondsworth: Penguin, 1997).

Richardson, Alan, 'Romantic Voodoo: Obeah and British Culture, 1797–1807', *Studies in Romanticism*, 32 (1993), pp. 3–28.

Rody, Caroline, 'Burning Down the House: The Revisionary Paradigm of Jean Rhys's *Wide Sargasso Sea*', in *Famous Last Words: Changes in Gender and Narrative Closure*, ed. and intro. Alison Booth (Charlottesville: University Press of Virginia, 1993), pp. 300–25.

Savory, Elaine, '"Another Poor Devil of a Human Being …": Jean Rhys and the Novel as Obeah', *Jean Rhys Review*, 7:1–2 (1996), pp. 26–38.

Savory, Elaine, *Jean Rhys* (Cambridge: Cambridge University Press, 1998).

Scharfman, Ronnie, 'Mirroring and Mothering in Simone Schwarz-Bart's *Pluie et Vent sur Télumée Miracle* and Jean Rhys' *Wide Sargasso Sea*', *Yale French Studies*, 62 (1981), pp.88–106.

Smith, R. McClure, '"I Don't Dream About It Any More": The Textual Unconscious in Jean Rhys's *Wide Sargasso Sea*', *Journal of Narrative Technique*, 26:2 (1996), pp.113–36.

Spivak, Gayatri Chakravorty, 'Three Women's Texts and a Critique of Imperialism', *Critical Inquiry*, 12 (1985), pp.243–61.

Staley, Thomas F., *Jean Rhys: A Critical Study* (London: Macmillan, 1979).

Thomas, Sue, *The Worlding of Jean Rhys* (Westport, CT and London: Greenwood Press, 1999).

Thorpe, Michael, '"The Other Side": *Wide Sargasso Sea* and *Jane Eyre*', *Ariel*, 8:3 (1977), pp.99–110.

Tiffin, Helen, 'Mirror and Mask: Colonial Motifs in the Novels of Jean Rhys', *World Literature Written in English*, 17 (1978), pp.328–41.

Tiffin, Helen, 'Post-Colonial Literatures and Counter-Discourse', *Kunapipi*, 9:1 (1987), pp.17–34.

Vaz Dias, Selma, 'In Quest of a Missing Author', *Radio Times*, 3 May 1957, p.25.

Vreeland, Elizabeth, 'Jean Rhys: The Art of Fiction LXIV', *Paris Review*, 76 (1979), pp.219–37.

Wickramagamage, Carmen, 'An/Other Side to Antoinette/Bertha: Reading "Race" into *Wide Sargasso Sea*', *Journal of Commonwealth Literature*, 35:1 (2000), pp.27–42.

Wilson, Lucy, '"Women Must Have Spunks": Jean Rhys's West Indian Outcasts', *Modern Fiction Studies*, 32 (1986), pp.439–48.

Wyndham, Francis, 'Introduction' to Jean Rhys, *Wide Sargasso Sea* (Harmondsworth: Penguin, 1968), pp.5–11.

ACKNOWLEDGEMENTS

The editor and publisher wish to thank the following for their permission to reprint copyright material: *New Statesman* (for material from 'The First Mrs Rochester'); *The Times Literary Supplement* (for material from 'A Fairy-Tale Neurotic'); *New York Times Book Review* (for material from 'Bertha the Doomed'); New Beacon Books (for material from 'The Road to Thornfield Hall: An Analysis of Jean Rhys' *Wide Sargasso Sea*' in *New Beacon Reviews: Collection One*); *Journal of Commonwealth Literature* (for material from 'Terrified Consciousness'); Savacou Publications (for material from *Contradictory Omens: Cultural Diversity and Integration in the Caribbean*); *Massachusetts Review* (for material from 'Of Heroines and Victims: Jean Rhys and *Jane Eyre*'); University Press of New England (for material from 'The Sisterhood of Jane Eyre and Antoinette Cosway' in *The Voyage In: Fictions of Female Development*); *Critical Inquiry* (for material from 'Three Women's Texts and a Critique of Imperialism'); *Oxford Literary Review* (for material from 'Problems in Current Theories of Colonial Discourse'); *World Literature Written in English* (for material from 'Mirror and Mask: Colonial Motifs in the Novels of Jean Rhys'); *Novel: A Forum on Fiction* (for material from '"Like in a Looking-Glass": History and Narrative in *Wide Sargasso Sea*'); *Ariel* (for material from 'Jean Rhys's Construction of Blackness as Escape from White Femininity in *Wide Sargasso Sea*'); New York University Press (for material from *Jean Rhys: The West Indian Novels*); *Studies in Romanticism* (for material from 'Romantic Voodoo: Obeah and British Culture, 1797–1807'); Johns Hopkins University Press (for material from 'Writing as Voodoo: Sorcery, Hysteria and Art' in *Death and Representation*); Edward Arnold (for material from *The Ballistic Bard: Postcolonial Fictions*); Manchester University Press (for material from *Border Traffic: Strategies of Contemporary Women Writers*, and 'The Locked Heart: The Creole Family Romance of *Wide Sargasso Sea*' in *Colonial Discourse/Postcolonial Theory*); and *Twentieth Century Literature* (for material from 'Navigating the *Wide Sargasso Sea*: Colonial History, English Fiction, and British Empire').

There are instances where we have been unable to trace or contact copyright holders before our printing deadline. If notified, the publisher will be pleased to acknowledge the use of copyright material.

Carl Plasa is a Senior Lecturer in English Literature at Cardiff University. He is the author of *Textual Politics from Slavery to Postcolonialism: Race and Identification* and editor of the Icon Readers' Guide to Toni Morrison's *Beloved*. He is currently writing a book on Charlotte Brontë.

INDEX

Abel, Elizabeth 48
abolition of slavery 128, 138–9, 144–5
  see also emancipation
Acton, William 91
Acts of Assembly 98
After Leaving Mr Mackenzie 8
Alexander (Cosway/Boyd) 132
Allrey, Phyllis Shand 28
  The Orchid House 28, 29, 30
alienation 31–2: see marginalization
Allen, Walter 9
  Caribbean 21
  heroines 21–2
  Wyndham 20–1, 22
Amélie
  Antoinette 132, 141
  Rochester 65–6, 81, 89–90, 110
  white cockroach song 65–6
American reviewers 14–15
Angier, Carole 17
Annette
  Antoinette 113, 148–9
  Christophine 85, 86
  madness 18
  Mason 29
  sexual relations 148–9
  zombified 106
Anti-Slavery Society 134
Antoinette
  Amélie 132, 141
  Annette 113, 148–9
  aphrodisiac 52, 55, 80, 100, 103, 111
  Christophine 66, 87, 122, 124
  contamination 43, 76, 78, 143–4,
    158 n40
  critics
    Baer 49–50, 52–4, 55–6
    Ciolkowski 140–1, 144, 147, 148–9
    Erwin 73, 74–5, 76, 78, 80, 82–3
    Look Lai 23, 27–8
    Newman 109, 113–15, 117–20
    Olaussen 84–6, 90, 91–2, 93–4
    Ramchand 30–3
    Spivak 57–8
    Tiffin 69–70
  dispossessed 18–19
  dreams 32, 49–51, 53–4, 58, 74–5,
    85–6, 93, 94

England 18, 84–5, 91–2
fire 52–3, 54, 104
identity 52, 71, 93–4
  national 72–4, 148–9
  racial 42, 66, 84, 85–6, 92
Jane 17, 56, 109
madness 25, 27–8, 30, 103–4
marginalized 27–8, 31–2, 132
marriage 18, 42, 51–2, 67, 109
narrative voice 12–13, 119
patriarchy 117–18
racial imagination 83
renamed 18, 22–3, 52, 57, 67, 93–4,
  101, 103, 108, 110, 114, 147
sexuality 85–6, 103–4, 140
sexual relations 23, 26, 33–4, 50, 76
as slave 69–70, 93–4
Thornfield Hall 18, 21, 25, 27, 104
as victim 16, 18, 22, 90
as zombie 52, 106
  see also Bertha
aphrodisiac
  Antoinette/Christophine 52, 55, 80,
    100, 103, 111
  Rochester 52, 81, 93, 103, 114, 144
Ariel 83–95

Baer, Elizabeth R. 39
  Antoinette 49–50, 52–4, 55–6
  dreams 49, 53–4
  feminist analysis 10
  Jane 48, 55–6
  narrative voices 51
  obeah 52
  patriarchy 48
  phallic imagery 50
  Rochester 48–9, 51
  sexual equality 55
  surface/submerged texts 48–9, 52
  zombie 52
The Ballistic Bard: Postcolonial Fictions
  (Newman) 105
Baptiste 79–80, 96
Barker, Francis 125
Barreca, Regina
  colonialism 105
  female sexuality 103–4
  obeah 11, 101–2, 105
  patriarchy 101
  voodoo 102–3, 104–5
  women's suffering 101–2
Bennett, Louise 121

Bertha
  critics
    Parry 62
    Porter 39
  humanity/bestiality 57, 62
  imprisoned 21, 25, 27, 84
  Jane Eyre 7, 44, 107–8
  madness 44, 47
  sexuality 91, 108, 140, 159 n41
  stereotypes 108
  see also Antoinette
bestiality/humanity 57, 62
Bhabha, Homi K. 56, 84
black female subject
  Britain 123
  critics
    Olaussen 83–4, 85, 89–90
    Parry 10
    Spivak 10
  family relations 88–9
  independence 89
  maternal 122–3
  nurses 122, 123–4
  sexuality 87–8
  stereotypes 11, 84, 87–8, 125
  see also Christophine; race
black feminist criticism 70–1, 83–4, 90–1
blackness 12
  see also race
Blessebois, Pierre Corneille 112
blindness 46, 72, 106–7, 118
blood 119
books, Caribbean climate 115
Border Traffic: Strategies of Contemporary
  Women Writers (Humm) 122
Boumelha, Penny 55–6, 108
Brathwaite, Edward Kamau
  historical account 34–5
  Look Lai 35–7
  metropole/plantation 36–7
  O'Connor 98
  race relations 10, 34–5, 37
  Ramchand 35–6
  religious conflict 97, 98
  Britain 122–3
  see also England
Bronfen, Elisabeth 101
Brontë, Charlotte
  Bertha/Jane 107–8, 109
  Creoles 38–9, 131, 132
  madness 65, 91
  plantocracy 139
  sex/class 45–6

  see also Jane Eyre
Burton, Antoinette 149–50, 159 n52
Bush, Barbara 141

candle imagery 18
Carby, Hazel 87–8
Caribbean
  black nurses 123–4
  census riots 126, 133–4
  climate/books 79, 115
  critics
    Allen 21
  cultural tradition 97
  decadence 19
  exuberance 16, 29–30, 69, 108, 141–2
  Gothic atmosphere 21, 40, 75
  guerre nègre 126, 134
  liminality 11
  menace 33
  race relations 10
  sexual relations 141
  stereotypes 99–100
  see also Creoles; plantocracy; white
    Creoles
Caribbean critics 10, 14–15, 24
Carr, Helen 22
census riots 126, 133–4
Christian, Barbara 88
Christophine
  Annette 85, 86
  Antoinette 66, 87, 122, 124
  aphrodisiac 52, 55, 80, 100, 103, 111
  critics
    black feminism 83–4
    Erwin 72, 78, 80–2
    Newman 106–7, 117–18
    O'Connor 99
    Olaussen 83–4, 86–8
    Parry 61–2, 63–4
    Spivak 57, 60–1, 63–4
  departure 81–2
  family relations 88–9
  independence 125
  language 39–40, 41, 60, 63
  narrative voice 12–13
  obeah 33, 63, 80–1, 94, 99, 102–3,
    113–14
  Rochester 63–4, 72, 97–8, 99, 106–7,
    117–18
  room 102
cinema, zombie films 106, 112–13
Ciolkowski, Laura E. 122
  Antoinette 140–1, 144, 147, 148–9

historical criticism 138
imperialism 141, 142–3, 149–50
Jane 141
miscegenation 141–2
patriarchy 145–6
plantocracy 139, 141
Rochester 143–6
sexuality 12, 138
struggle 150
white Creole/English identities 138,
    139–40, 146–8
class/sexuality 45–6, 73
Clément, Catherine 103–4
Coetzee, J.M. 127
Colonial Discourse/Postcolonial Theory
    (Barker, Hulme and Iversen) 125
colonialism 10, 14
    critics
        Barreca 105
        Fanon 28
        Ramchand 28–30
        Tiffin 67
    English/African sources 65
    gender relations 67
    identity 147–8
    Jane Eyre 38–9, 56, 108
    as metaphor 67
    morality 143
    postcolonialism 127, 137
    renaming 23
    sexuality 42–4, 75–6
    sexual relations 18, 41–2
    slavery 39, 41–2
    Thornfield Hall 40
    Wide Sargasso Sea 84
colour symbolism 68, 69
Commonwealth Immigration Act 123
conjure woman 88
contamination
    Antoinette 43, 76, 78, 143–4,
        158 n40
    Daniel 43, 76, 78
    Jane Eyre 131
Cora, Aunt 92, 130, 136
Cosway family 113–14, 131–2
    financial ruin 17–18, 21
    idiot son 18, 78
    sexuality 75–6
    wealth from slavery 76, 77, 78
    see also Annette; Antoinette; Daniel
        (Cosway/Boyd)
Cosway father
    bastards 89, 139

drunkenness 18
gravestone 80, 132–3, 143
Coulibri
    fire 31, 34, 37, 38, 54, 72, 73, 93, 94,
        126, 133, 136
    slaves 66
Creoles
    and blacks 62
    Brontë 38–9, 131, 132
    cultural traditions 20
    heiresses 32, 115–16
    language 39–40, 41–2
    marginalization 107
    metropole 36
    plantocracy 28
    uncertainty 139–40
    see also white Creoles
Critical Inquiry 56
cultural identity 61–2, 142

Daniel (Cosway/Boyd)
    appearance 142
    contamination 43, 76, 78
    Cosway family 89, 132, 137
    critics
        Erwin 76, 77–8, 80
    disinherited son 146
    father's grave 80, 132, 133
    language 41
    letter 43, 76, 79
    narrative voice 12
    Rochester 34, 77–8, 89, 90, 145–6
Davies, Hunter 15
Davis, Wade 105
D'Costa, Jean 14
death 114–15
    see also zombies
Death and Representation 101
decolonization 29
Defoe, Daniel 127
Deren, Maya 101
determinism, reversed 106, 118
Deutsch, André 8
difference 10
    see also otherness
Dominica 8, 126, 128, 131
double frame of reference 102, 120
dowry 32, 42
Drayton, Geoffrey
    Christopher 28, 29, 30
dreams
    Antoinette 32, 49–51, 53–4, 58, 74–5,
        85–6, 93, 94

critics
    Baer 49, 51–2, 53–4
    Erwin 74–5
    Olaussen 85–6, 93, 94
    Ramchand 32
    Spivak 58
    Jane Eyre 49
    sexual violation 86, 93
    Tia 35, 37

Edgeworth, Maria 99
Edwards, Bryan 96
Ellis, Markman 97
emancipation 17–18, 21, 26, 66, 116
    see also abolition of slavery; slavery
Emancipation Act 29–30, 72, 74, 116,
    128
Emery, Mary Lou 85, 92
Emtage, J. B.
    Brown Sugar 28
England
    Antoinette 91–2
    feminists/imperialism 150
    identity 138
    racism 123
    reviewers 14–15
Englishness 17, 145–6, 147
Erwin, Lee 70
    Amélie 81
    Antoinette 73, 74–5, 76, 78, 80, 82–3
    Baptiste 79–80
    Christophine 72, 78, 80–2
    class 73
    Cosway family 76, 77, 78
    Daniel 76, 77–8, 80
    dreams 74–5
    gender 75–6
    mirror imagery 73–4
    narrative voice 71, 75
    national identity 72
    patriarchy 71, 77, 80, 83
    racial identity 11, 66–7, 70, 72–3, 83
    Rochester 72, 76–83
Eurocentrism 106, 115
exploitation 44–5

Falconer, Charles George 136
family
    black female subject 88–9
    Jane Eyre 127–8
    Rhys 126
family romance 12, 126
Fanon, Frantz 28

Faulkner, William
    The Sound and the Fury 16
female subjectivity
    sexuality 91, 103–4, 110, 114
    stereotypes 87–8
    suffering 30, 101–2
feminist criticism 10, 11–12, 39, 48, 70–1
Fetterley, Judith 48, 56
fire
    Coulibri 31, 34, 37, 38, 54, 72, 73, 93,
        94, 126, 133, 136
    imagery 119–20
    Poole 52
    symbolic power 134
    Thornfield Hall 34, 37, 44, 58, 68–9,
        70, 72, 93, 104, 109, 118–19
    Tia 54, 69, 92, 94, 119, 136
    warmth 52–3
flying image 53, 94
Ford, Ford Madox 7–8, 15, 16, 20
form/content 16–17
Fox, William 144, 145
French criticism 44
Freud, Sigmund
    family romance 12, 126
    female sexuality 103–4
    uncanny 116, 157 n43
friendship 67–8, 73, 85, 124

gender relations 23, 67
George, Rosemary 141
Gilbert, Sandra M. 48, 56, 102
Gilroy, Paul 137
Goethe, W. von 45
Goldsmith, Oliver 47
Good Morning, Midnight 8
Goodwin, Sarah Webster 100–1
Gothic atmosphere 21, 40, 75, 78
Granbois 52, 75, 78, 131, 146
Gregg, Veronica Marie 121, 122
Griffiths, Peter 123
Gubar, Susan 48, 56, 102
guerre nègre 126, 134

Hall, Stuart 142
Hamer, Max 151 n2
Hamilton, Virginia 94
Harris, Wilson 60, 94, 107
Hearne, John 107
heroines
    Antoinette/Jane 55–6
    critics
        Allen 21–2

Look Lai 25–6
destiny 49–50
Jane Eyre 17, 45–6, 47–8
Rhys 18–19, 21–2, 25
suffering 30
Wide Sargasso Sea 21–2, 48, 55–6
Hirsch, Marianne 48
historical criticism 12, 122, 126, 127–8,
   138
hooks, bell 71
Hope, Francis 9–10
   New Statesman review 15–16
Howells, Coral Ann 143
Hulme, Peter
   family history 130–2
   Freudian psychoanalysis 126
   historical criticism 12, 122, 126, 127–8
   Jane Eyre 130
   letter to Wyndham 128–9
   Lockhart family 128, 129–30, 133,
      134–6, 137–8
   postcolonial criticism 125–6, 127
   vocabulary used 137–8
humanity/bestiality 57, 62
Humm, Maggie
   blackness 12
   immigration 122–4
   mother/daughter relations 125
   nurses 124–5
   racial identity 66
hybridity 11, 121, 141–2, 145–6

I Walked with a Zombie (Lewton film) 12,
   106, 112–13
identity
   Antoinette 52, 71, 93–4
   colonial 10, 14
   critics
      Spivak 61–2
   cultural 61–2, 142
   mirror imagery 73–4, 93–4
   national 72–4, 83, 147–9
   race 11, 31, 42, 66, 73–4, 84, 85–6, 92,
      138
   white Creoles 37, 121, 138, 139–40,
      146–8
immigration 122–3
imperialism 57, 108
   Britain 122–3
   critics
      Ciolkowski 141, 142–3, 149–50
      Newman 108–9
      English feminists 150

Jane Eyre 141
   missionary work 142–3
   motherhood 141
   resistance 149
   independence 89, 125
Innocenzia 38
intertextuality 116–17
Iversen, Margaret 125

James, Henry 19
Jane (*Jane Eyre*) 141, 159 n41
   and Antoinette 17, 55–6, 109
   and Bertha 107–8, 109
   critics
      Baer 48, 55–6
      Ciolkowski 141
      Newman 114
Jane Eyre 12, 15
   Bertha 21, 44
   colonialism 38–9, 56, 108
   contamination 131
   dreams 49
   family history 127–8
   heroine 17, 45–6, 47–8
   historical dating 116
   imperial control 141
   madness 65
   Mason family 131
   patriarchy 107–8
   Rhys on 9, 38, 108
   Rochester 141, 159 n41
   sexual equality 46–7
   sexuality 45–6
   slavery 126–7, 137
   transformation 55
   white Creole woman 10
   see also Thornfield Hall
Jeal, Tim 143
Journal of Commonwealth Literature 28

Kidd, Robbie 118
Klein, Herbert S. 89

Lacan, Jacques 76
Laidlaw, Dominican administrator 135–6
Lamming, George 127
Langland, Elizabeth 48
language, English/Creole 23, 39–40, 41,
   60, 63
Leatham, Charles 134, 135, 136
The Left Bank and Other Stories 8
   Ford's preface 8, 16, 20
Lenglet, Jean 7, 151 n2

Lévi-Strauss, Claude 103
Lewton, Val 12, 106, 112–13
Lilièvre, Père 79, 80
liminality 11
Livingstone, David 142–3
Lockhart, Edward 126, 133, 135–6
Lockhart, Theodore 134
Lockhart, William Brade 134–5
Lockhart family 128, 129–30, 133, 134, 137–8
Long, Edward 96
Look Lai, Wally 138
    Antoinette 23, 27–8
    Brathwaite on 35–7
    gender 23, 67
    heroines 25–6
    race relations 10, 34–5, 37
    rejection 25, 27–8
    Rochester 26–7
    West Indian critics 24–5

madness
    Annette 18
    Antoinette 25, 27, 28, 30, 103–4
    Bertha 47
    Brontë 65, 91
Malleus Maleficarum 104
mammy/whore stereotype 11, 88, 89–90
marginalization
    Antoinette 27–8, 31–2, 132
    Creoles 107
    critics
        Newman 107–8
    women's writing 107
marriage, Antoinette/Rochester 18, 42, 51–2, 67, 109
Martinique 60, 112, 132
Mason, Mr 29, 50, 86, 93
Mason, Richard 57, 119, 131
Mason family 77, 116, 131, 132
Massachusetts Review 39
Massacre village 131, 133
master/slave binary 65
Mauss, Marcel 103
menace 30, 33
metropole 36–7
Miller, Nancy K. 48, 49–50
mirror imagery
    Antoinette 53, 58, 119
    critics
        Spivak 58
        Tiffin 70
    ghost 53, 58

identity 73–4, 93–4
Tia 62, 68, 70, 73
miscegenation 121, 131, 138, 141–2, 149
missionary work 142–3
Modernism 7–8, 13, 16–17
morality 138–9, 143, 144–5
Motard, Jean Philip 134, 136
mother/daughter relations 109, 113, 124–5, 141, 149
My Day: Three Pieces by Jean Rhys 8

Naipaul, V.S. 8
Name-of-the-Father 76, 77, 80, 83
    see also patronymic
Narcissus 20, 57, 58
narrative, politics of 10–11
narrative voices
    Antoinette 12–13, 119
    Christophine 12–13
    critics
        Baer 51
        Erwin 71, 75
        Newman 109–10
    Daniel 12
    Modernism 13
    Poole 12, 109
    Rochester 12–13, 51–2
    Wide Sargasso Sea 12–13, 17–18, 40–1, 109, 117
national identity
    Antoinette 72–4, 148–9
    critics
        Spivak 72, 83
    Rhys 147–8
New Beacon Reviews 23
New Statesman review 15–17
New York Times Book Review 20
Newman, Judie
    Antoinette 109, 113–15, 117–20
    Christophine 106–7, 117–18
    Cosway family 113–14
    Creole heiresses 115–16
    cultural determinism 118
    double frame of reference 120
    fire imagery 119–20
    imperialism 108–9
    intertextuality 116–17
    Jane 114
    marginalization 107–8
    narrative voices 109–10
    obeah 106–7, 110–11
    postcolonial criticism 107–8

Rochester 106–7, 109–10, 113–15, 117–18
zombies 11–12, 105–6, 110–12, 118
Nunez-Harrell, Elizabeth 72
nurses, black 124–5

obeah 11
Christophine 33, 63, 80–1, 94, 99, 102–3, 113–14
colour of dress 68–9
critics
Baer 52
Barreca 11, 101–2, 105
Newman 106–7, 110–11
O'Connor 11, 97, 98
Richardson 11, 99–100, 104
Eurocentrism 115
resistance 11
Rochester 79–80, 96–7, 97, 103, 144
voodoo 97, 101, 104, 105
whites 98, 113
Obi; or, Three-Fingered Jack 99
O'Connor, Teresa F.
Brathwaite 98
Christophine 99
obeah 11, 97, 98
religious conflict 99
Rochester 97–9
Oedipal theme 59
Olaussen, Maria
Amélie 89–90
Antoinette 84–6, 90, 91–2, 93–4
black female subject 83–4, 85, 89–90
Christophine 83–4, 86–8
dreams 85–6, 93, 94
race 11, 66–7, 95
Rochester 89–90
sexuality 91–2, 95
stereotypes 88, 125
transformation through voyage 84–5
oppression
patriarchy 10, 39, 48
racial 87
slavery 71
otherness 125, 140, 145–6

The Paris Review 124
Parry, Benita 39
Bertha 62
black female subject 10
Christophine 61–2, 63–4
Spivak 61–2

patriarchy 76
Antoinette 117–18
critics
Baer 48
Barreca 101
Ciolkowski 145–6
Erwin 71, 77, 80, 83
Jane Eyre 107–8
oppression 10, 39, 48
renaming 23
Rochester 59–60, 108, 145
slavery 71, 85
subversion of 11
see also primogeniture
patronymic 60, 63, 146
see also Name-of-the-Father
phallic imagery 50
Plante, David 124, 159 n51
plantocracy 137, 139
Creoles 28
excesses 139
metropole 36–7
sexual relations 78, 141, 143, 146–7
Poole, Grace 18, 67, 116
alcohol 119
colours 68, 69
fire 52
knife attack 57
narrative voice 12, 109
suffering 19
popular culture 106, 111
see also cinema
Porter, Dennis 67
Bertha 39
colonialism 10, 39
language registers 39–40, 41–2
plurality of texts 44
postcolonialism 10
sexuality 10, 42–3, 45–8
style 39–40
postcolonialism 127, 137, 148
postcolonial criticism
critics
Hulme 125–6, 127
Newman 107–8
Porter 10
Spivak 56
slavery 70–1
Wide Sargasso Sea 107–8, 125–6
Pound, Ezra 16
Powell, Enoch 123
power 22, 39, 107, 134

prejudice 110, 123
primogeniture 32, 76–7, 108, 145, 146

Quartet 8

race 10
  black feminist criticism 90–1
  Caribbean 10
  conflict 14
  critics
    Brathwaite 10, 34–5, 37
    Olaussen 11, 66–7, 95
    Ramchand 10, 30–1
  identity 11, 31, 73–4, 138
    Antoinette 42, 66, 84, 85–6, 92
  language 23, 39–40, 41, 60, 63
  oppression 87
  other 140
  prejudice 110, 123
  Rhys 45, 65, 159 n51
  sexuality 95
  slavery 133
  stereotypes 11, 67–8, 83–4, 87–8,
    89–90, 124, 125
  Wide Sargasso Sea 37, 66
  see also black female subject; Creoles;
    Englishness; white Creoles
racial imagination 83
Ragatz, Lowell Joseph 121
Ramchand, Kenneth
  Antoinette 30–3
  Brathwaite on 35–6
  colonialism 28–30
  Creole heiresses 32–3
  decolonization 29
  Emancipation Act 29–30
  race 10, 30–1
  Rochester 33–4
  sexuality 33–4
  West Indian literature 28, 29–30
readers
  resistance 55, 56
  Victorian 15
rejection 25, 27–8, 68, 93
  see also marginalization
religious conflict 97, 98, 101–2
renaming
  Antoinette/Bertha 18, 22–3, 52, 57, 67,
    93–4, 101, 103, 108, 110, 114, 147
  colonialism 23
  patriarchy 23
  slavery 146–7

resistance
  imperialism 149
  obeah 11
  readers 55, 56
  temptation 54–5
revenancy 9, 112
'Le Revenant' 9, 112
revision of texts 107, 127
Rhys, Jean
  Caribbean background 7, 15–17, 21,
    72, 96, 107, 121, 126
  family history 126
  heroines 18–19, 21–2, 25
  illness 122, 124
  on *Jane Eyre* 9, 38, 108
  letter
    to Vaz Dias 56
    to Wyndham 9, 128–9
  Lockhart family 129–30
  national identity 147–8
  The Paris Review 124
  popular culture 106
  race 45, 65, 159 n51
  return to Dominica 128
  reviewers 14–15
  works
    After Leaving Mr Mackenzie 8
    Good Morning, Midnight 8
    The Left Bank and Other Stories 8,
      16, 20
    My Day: Three Pieces by Jean Rhys 8
    'Obeah Night' poem 128–9
    Quartet 8
    'Le Revenant' 9
    Sleep It Off Lady 8
    Smile Please: An Unfinished
      Autobiography 8
    'Temps Perdi' 115
    Tigers Are Better-Looking 8
    'Vienne' 7–8
    Voyage in the Dark 8, 124
    'Wedding in the Carib Quarter' 9
  zombie 112–13
  see also Wide Sargasso Sea
Rich, Adrienne 48, 54, 107
Richardson, Alan
  obeah 11, 99–100, 104
  voodoo 104
Rivers, St John 46, 48, 60
Rochester, Edward
  Amélie 65–6, 81, 89–90, 110
  aphrodisiac 52, 81, 93, 103, 114, 144

blinding 46, 72, 106–7, 118
Caribbean exuberance 16, 29–30, 69, 108, 141–2
Caribbean ruined house 96
Christophine 63–4, 72, 97–8, 99, 106–7, 117–18
critics
  Baer 48–9, 51
  Ciolkowski 143–6
  Erwin 72, 76–83
  Look Lai 26–7
  Newman 106–7, 109–10, 113–15, 117–18
  O'Connor 97–9
  Olaussen 89–90
  Ramchand 33–4
  Spivak 58–60, 76
Daniel 34, 77–8, 89, 90, 145–6
Englishness 17, 138, 140, 145–6
and Jane 141, 159 n41
letter to father 59, 78–9
marriage 18, 42, 51–2, 67, 109
narrative voice 12–13, 51–2
obeah 79–80, 96–7, 103, 144
'Obeah Night' poem 129
patriarchy 59–60, 108, 145
primogeniture 32, 77, 108, 145, 146
racial prejudice 110
sexual relations 23, 26, 33–4, 42–3, 50, 91
sexuality 12, 46, 48, 110
transformed in Caribbean 19, 84, 143–4
Victorian readers 15
wealth from slavery 76–7
Rochester, Mrs: see Antoinette; Bertha

Said, Edward W. 56
Sandi 132, 142
Savory, Elaine 14–15, 17, 23, 34, 35
sexuality 12
  Antoinette 85–6, 103–4, 140
  Bertha 91, 108, 140, 159 n41
  black feminist criticism 90–1
  black women 87–8
  Brontë 45–6
  class 45–6
  colonialism 42–4, 75–6
  Cosway family 75–6
  critics
    Ciolkowski 12, 138
    Olaussen 91–2, 95
    Porter 10, 42–3, 45–8

Ramchand 33–4
  female subject 91, 103–4, 110, 114
  Jane Eyre 45–6
  race 95
  Rochester 12, 46, 48, 110
  slavery 75–6
  voodoo 114
  witchcraft 104
sexual relations 37
  Annette 148–9
  Antoinette 23, 26, 33–4, 50, 76
  Caribbean 141
  colonialism 18, 41–2
  critics
    Baer 55
  Jane Eyre 46–7
  plantocracy 78, 141, 143, 146–7
  power 39
  Rochester 23, 26, 33–4, 42–3, 50, 91
sexual violation 86, 93
Shakespeare, William
  King Lear 30
  The Tempest 127
Shelley, Mary 56
Shepherd, William 99
Showalter, Elaine 91
slavery
  abolitionist movement 128, 138–9, 144–5
  black kinship systems 89
  colonialism 39, 41–2
  critics
    Caribbean 10
    Tiffin 69–70
  emancipation 17–18, 21, 26, 66, 116
  flying legend 94
  Jane Eyre 126–7, 137
  oppression 71
  patriarchy 71, 85
  postcolonial criticism 70–1
  race 133
  religious conflict 97, 98
  renaming 146–7
  sexuality 75–6
  wealth from 76–7
  see also Coulibri; plantocracy
Sleep It Off Lady 8
Smile Please: An Unfinished Autobiography 8
Smith, Leslie Tilden 151 n2
Spillers, Hortense J. 89
Spivak, Gayatri Chakravorty 39
  Antoinette 56, 57–8

black female subject 10
Christophine 57, 60–1, 63–4
cultural identity 61–2
dreams 58
language 40
mirror imagery 58
Narcissus 57, 58
national identity 72, 83
native voice 64
Parry 61–2
postcolonial criticism 10, 56
Rochester 58–60, 76
Stanley, Lord 136
Stein, Gertrude 16
stereotypes
Bertha 108
black female subject 11, 84, 87–8, 125
Caribbean 99–100
critics
Olaussen 88, 125
female subjectivity 87–8
race 11, 67–8, 83–4, 87–8, 89–90, 124, 125
Studies in Romanticism 99
suffering 19, 30, 101–2
sugar consumption 144
Sussman, Charlotte 144–5
syphilis 78, 108, 143

'Temps Perdi' 115
temptation/resistance 54–5
textual plurality 44, 49, 52
Thornfield Hall
Antoinette 18, 21, 25, 27, 104
colonialism 40
exploitation 44–5
fire 34, 37, 44, 58, 68–9, 70, 72, 93, 104, 109, 118–19
Tia
dreams 35, 37
fire 54, 69, 92, 94, 119, 136
friendship 67–8, 73, 85, 124
mirror images 62, 68, 70, 73
rejection 68, 93
stone-throwing 31, 58, 62, 68, 70, 73
Tiffin, Helen 66
Antoinette/slavery parallel 69–70
colonialism 67
colour symbolism 68
Eurocentric writing 115
mirror imagery 70
white Creoles 11
Tigers Are Better-Looking 8

The Times Literary Supplement 9, 17–20, 28
transformation 19, 55, 84–5, 143–4
translantic review (Ford) 7–8
Twentieth Century Literature 138

uncanny (Freud) 116, 157 n43

Vaz Diaz, Selma 8, 9, 56, 115, 151 n6
victim imagery 16, 18, 22, 90
'Vienne' 7–8
voodoo
obeah 97, 101, 104, 105
popular culture 111
sexuality 114
women's texts 101–2
The Voyage In: Fictions of Female Development (Abel, Hirsch and Langland) 48
Voyage in the Dark 8, 124

wealth from slavery 76–7
see also colonialism; plantocracy
'Wedding in the Carib Quarter' 9
West Indies 24–6, 28, 29–30, 35, 53
see also Caribbean
white Creoles
and blacks 62
critics
Brathwaite 37
cultural traditions 20
identity 37, 121, 138, 139–40, 146–8
Jane Eyre 10
obeah 98, 113
plantocracy 28
white cockroach 42, 65–6, 90
white nigger 42, 66, 73, 85, 86
whore/mammy stereotypes 11, 88, 89–90
Wide Sargasso Sea 7, 8, 9, 24–6
awards 8
colonialism 84
critical acclaim 9–10, 15, 24
economy of form 16
heroine 21–2, 48
historical dating 74, 116
naming 129–30
narrative voices 12–13, 17–18, 40–1, 109, 117
postcolonial criticism 107–8, 125–6
race 37, 66
sexual politics 37
witchcraft 104
women's writing 101–2, 107
World Literature Written in English 66–7

Wyndham, Francis
    Allen 20–1, 22
    inbreeding 78
    letters from Rhys 9, 128–9
    preface to *Wide Sargasso Sea* 20–1
    and Rhys 8, 115
younger sons 32, 59–60, 76
    see also primogeniture
zombie 11
    Annette 106

    Antoinette 52, 106
    critics
        Baer 52
        Newman 11–12, 105–6, 110–12, 118
    emancipated slaves 116
    films 12, 106, 112–13
    Rhys 112–13
    Rochester's reading on 52, 97
Zonana, Joyce 158–9 n40

Printed in the United States
84174LV00006B/7-9/A

9 781840 462685